CULTURAL
DNA

THE PSYCHOLOGY OF GLOBALIZATION

GURNEK BAINS

W0010648

WILEY

Published by John Wiley & Sons, Inc., Hoboken, New Jersey
Published simultaneously in Canada

For general information about our other products and services, please contact our Customer Care Department within the United States at (800) 762-2974, outside the United States at (317) 572-3993 or fax (317) 572-4002.

Wiley publishes in a variety of print and electronic formats and by print-on-demand. Some material included with standard print versions of this book may not be included in e-books or in print-on-demand. If this book refers to media such as a CD or DVD that is not included in the version you purchased, you may download this material at http://booksupport.wiley.com. For more information about Wiley products, visit www.wiley.com.

Library of Congress Cataloging-in-Publication Data:

Bains, Gurnek.
  Cultural DNA : the psychology of globalization / Gurnek Bains.
    pages cm
  Includes index.
    ISBN 978-1-118-92891-2 (hardback : alk. paper)   1. Cultural intelligence.
  2. Leadership—Psychological aspects.   3. Career development.   4. Culture and globalization.   I. Title.
  HM621.B343 2015
  303.48'2—dc23
                                                        2014044837

Printed in the United States of America
10 9 8 7 6 5 4 3 2 1

Contents

Acknowledgments

From the start this project has been a family affair. My wife Kylie has provided much support in generating ideas. Her Australian cultural DNA has also ensured that the project actually happened, rather than staying a piece of "Indian reflective enquiry". My two teenage children, Akal and Aman, have also helped. Akal's interest in economics and Aman's in psychology has meant that I have been able to give them significant sub-projects. In what we quickly discovered was a very ambitious undertaking.

I also want to thank everyone at YSC who has contributed and all of our global offices for their local insights. Our research department has also undertaken painstaking analysis of our database. I also want to thank, Evgeniya Petrova, who did much of the literature research and Rosemary Burke-Kennedy who helped bring the manuscript to fruition.

Gurnek Bains
London 2015

Introduction

We live in a world that is becoming flatter and flatter. Global business and trade, the ease of air travel, and the unending flow of information and communication are all combining to create a kind of homogenized, cultural soup into which we are all being inexorably pulled. Whether you are in Beijing, Dubai, or Reykjavík, the ubiquity of global brands and the extent of cultural fusion can make everything around you look and feel comfortingly familiar, if somewhat blandly uniform. Backpackers know this and go to great lengths, admittedly sometimes in a self-defeating, cattle-like manner, to discover corners of the world that our global culture has not yet infiltrated or homogenized.

However, one theme emerges with surprising regularity when you talk to people who have moved to a different culture and lived there for some time—this surface similarity is something of an illusion only held by the transient tourist or business traveler. "You don't realize just how different this place really is once you have been here some time," people who have deeper experience will often say. While things can appear familiar on the surface, over time a gradual realization sinks in that the deep psychological and cultural instincts of different societies really *are* different in profound, nonsuperficial ways. You find that while it might have been easy to engage the culture initially, you eventually hit a permafrost layer through which an outsider cannot penetrate. Over time, you often become aware of just what you *don't* know or can't comprehend. The initial surface familiarity can be deceptive; just because people in Shanghai wear Gucci or Missoni or carry Prada handbags, it doesn't mean that they are Italians at heart.

The same happens when people from different cultural backgrounds marry or form long-term relationships, as is increasingly the case in our globalized village of a world. Initial assumptions around the similarity of values are tested over time and it frequently begins to dawn on people that their partner's original culture is more ingrained in them than they might have assumed. Subtle differences in attitude and orientation begin to emerge once the fog of early infatuation and surface familiarity lifts. This is not to say that relationships across cultural barriers are doomed or problematic. I myself, being Indian and married to an Australian, know and appreciate the richness that is inevitably a part of cross-cultural relationships. However, both my wife and I have realized over time that I am more Indian than I might have thought in my deepest instincts and actually she is more Australian—despite the fact that both of us on the surface appear to be quintessential exponents of middle-class British mores and values.

The central argument of this book is that while there is much that is common between humans, there are also subtle but profound differences between the psychological instincts of different cultures. Furthermore, the ultimate causes of these differences frequently lie buried in the past—often in the very early period when that part of the world was being settled by the first human migrations. It is this echo from distant times that fundamentally affects each culture's psychological outlook. Like a distant drumbeat, this cultural DNA reverberates through the society, affecting the historical cycles it has experienced, its economic performance, political institutions, business ethos, and just about every other aspect of people's experience. People are not better than one another, or always *very* different, just sometimes so. As the world globalizes, it is likely that some of these differences will be ironed out. However, it is also likely that we will become more conscious, rather than less, of differences below the surface.

The Psychology of the Eurozone Crisis

The problems in the European Community around creating a single currency illustrate the tensions that arise when overoptimistic globalizing sentiments hit the wall of deeply ingrained psychological differences. When the Euro was introduced in 1999, many multinational businesses greeted the idea of a single currency across the consenting EC countries with enthusiasm. A significant number of multinationals essentially dismantled their European national operations in favor of regional structures. There was massive investment in the European project from outside. For example, in spite of the prominence given to emerging markets, more than half of the investment of U.S. multinationals abroad in the period 2002 to 2011 actually went to Europe.[1]

However, the initial optimism quickly faded as the problems in the Eurozone surfaced. It is rare nowadays to meet a CEO of a global company who does not see their European operations on, at best, a slow plateau of growth, or more often as a disaster zone, irrespective of their organizational strengths or the talent of their people in the region. None of these factors can override the problems caused by the huge divisions within the Eurozone economies. The European operations of multinationals came to be inundated with specialists from treasury, accounting, tax, legal affairs, and human resources—all tasked with the job of mitigating risk should the situation deteriorate even further.

Essentially what happened was that everyone got taken in by the heady catch-up growth of the southern European and Irish economies without discerning whether the momentum was sustainable or the euro project viable. People overlooked the relevance of deep-seated cultural factors to the issue of economic sustainability. The exact same thing is happening with respect to gauging the economic prospects of India, China, and other emerging market economies today. It is easy to get caught up with the high, catch-up growth figures in all these regions and not to see the cultural problems bubbling underneath the surface that will, over time, influence whether this performance is sustainable. Global CEOs need to become cultural experts, psychologists, and historians if they are to make the right long-term calls for their companies.

The importance of this is illustrated by looking more deeply into the Eurozone crisis. The drive to create a single economic entity with a common currency, free movement of people, and consistent rules is predicated on the unstated, but nevertheless strong, assumption that there is a high level of cultural similarity across the nations involved. In one sense this is true; but in another sense the cultural and psychological instincts of Greeks are not the same as those of Germans. This is not to pass judgment on either, but rather to say that beyond obvious and superficial differences—like Greeks being more persistent and ingenious in circumventing EC rules around smoking in public places—there lurked deeper differences in attitudes toward financial and economic matters that the creators of the common currency failed to recognize or were blithely optimistic about. It is now apparent that many of the problems arose from the very different attitudes toward economic management, payment of taxes, attitudes toward borrowing, and orientation to work that exist in the Eurozone and which threaten the whole project or at the least threaten to stymie growth in the region for some time.

Going a bit deeper, many of these attitudinal and behavioral differences arise from profound differences in some underlying values. In particular, as will be discussed later, southern European countries have at their core a more religious, relational, and in-the-moment set of values—versus the northern countries where more secular, individualistic, and long-term psychological instincts are more evident. Individualistic cultures require mechanisms other than religious authority or the sanction of one's community to regulate people's behavior, and hence place much greater emphasis on the rules set down by the state or other institutions. In the more relational cultures of southern Europe and Ireland, it is easier to trump rules imposed by more distant institutions; it is the obligations to one's immediate circle that count. Furthermore, if you live in a culture with a more short-term orientation, you are likely to take the plunge when economic opportunities created by, for example, money being available at low interest rates present themselves without thinking too hard about the long-term consequences. This is the case whether you are a government doling out pensions and benefits or an individual making a property investment. As a result, a different and more flexible attitude existed toward the interpretation of fiscal and financial rules—not only at national levels but also in the behavior of banks and at the level of individual financial decision making—in the southern versus northern Eurozone countries.

But where do these differences in underlying values themselves come from? We can go deeper still. Surprising as it may sound, from a cultural DNA point of view, the different psychological instincts in the southern European countries and Ireland versus northern Europe make sense when one looks at how modern humans settled Europe some 45,000 years ago. As will be demonstrated later, the original hunter-gatherer population of Europe came through two clearly differentiated routes—something that's had a powerful impact on the continent's psychological and cultural DNA.[2] One path was through the Middle East, into Anatolia, then into the Balkans and southern Europe. The other involved a more northerly route through the Caucuses and Western Russia into Eastern Europe, Poland, and Germany. It is likely that the two earliest modern human cultures recorded in Europe—the Aurignacian and Gravettian—mirror these two movements. The former is named after a village in southern France where relics relating to the culture were first found; it is believed to have first appeared in Europe—in Bulgaria—around 50,000 years ago, and gradually spread across the south of the continent and then along the Atlantic coast. The Gravettian culture, again named after a site in France, is believed to have entered later, perhaps 30,000 years ago. Core features of this culture include specialized weapons for mammoth hunting, the use of mammoth bones for house construction, and mechanisms for harnessing fire for heating and cooking—adaptations that all point to a more northerly origin.

Although subsequent severe ice age events scrambled the picture later on, many of the peoples in northern Europe are descended from the population that followed the second path, and those in southern Europe, to a greater extent, the first path. Furthermore, when expansion occurred from the ice age, refugees, those who moved north, coped for tens of thousands of years with a radically different ecological environment compared to that which they left behind in the south. Interestingly, there is also considerable evidence that a movement of people from Spain went along an Atlantic coastal route to repopulate Ireland and the west of Scotland. Today, there is still a clear genetic dividing line running through the UK that reflects this movement.[3] What is interesting is that many cultural traits, including Catholicism, map this pattern of entry and diffusion in Europe. Even in Scotland, Catholicism is more a pattern in the west of the country. Later still the south was the recipient of the first agriculturalists who came from the Middle East—the genetic signature of this migration also distinguishes southern and northern European populations.

The Eurozone crisis also follows this exact pattern, including Ireland's involvement. A sound argument can be made for the view that the pattern of migration and the different environmental challenges that humans faced in the south and along the Atlantic coast led to their psychological and cultural instincts evolving in a different way from those who had the challenge after the ice age of surviving in the ecological conditions of the north. The detail of all this will be unpacked later in the chapter on Europe. For now, however, the point is that while all this happened so long ago that the relevance to current events seems unlikely, or at best highly speculative, a good case can be made for the idea that the ultimate cause of the current tensions in the Eurozone is that the system ignored the deep-seated psychological and cultural differences between the countries that it encompassed.

Understanding the deeper reasons for these difficulties is not just an exercise in intellectual exploration—it also has implications for the future. Solving the crisis in a genuinely long-term manner will require surfacing and working on these cultural differences. This will require the northern countries questioning their instincts and adapting as much as the countries who are experiencing the problems. All round it will require empathy for ways of looking at the world that just seem alien from one's own perspective.

We Are Not All the Same and That Is Good

If you were to line up a European, an African, an Indian, an Arab, and someone from China and ask any adult in the world to pick out who has come from where, just about everybody would be likely to get it right. If you made each person's skin pigmentation and hair color the same, differences in the size of the forehead, the shape of the eyes, or the structure of the chin would give the game away. Even if you covered up everyone's faces, most people would make a reasonable stab purely on the basis of body type. In fact, those who know what to look for are able to distinguish regional origin with a high level of accuracy from skeletal features alone.

An astonishing fact about these physical differences is that they could only have evolved less than 70,000 years ago—a blink of an eye in terms of evolutionary timescales. This is because overwhelmingly, the DNA, fossil, and climatic evidence converges on 60,000 to 80,000 years ago as being the period in which a tiny group of modern humans made a crossing out of Africa to set up fragile roots in Asia. This group's offspring—perhaps no more than 100 to 200 people strong—then went on to populate the rest of the world. Members of this group bred only negligibly with prior species of humans in other regions. At the time of settling on the shores outside of Africa, all non-Africans must have looked the same and, in all probability, not much different from the African cousins that they had left behind. Most, but not all, of the physical differences that are apparent can be related to adaptations required to survive in the multifarious environments that modern humans encountered as they populated the world.

However, while discussing physical differences is uncontroversial—if only because it is self evidently obvious—the idea that people's underlying psychology might be different is more difficult for people to accept. Sure, we have no problem accepting small behavioral differences. It's clear that people from different parts of the world differ in manners, eat different things, wear different clothes, and like different sports. However, despite these relatively superficial differences, many informed and educated people fundamentally do want to believe that we are all the same deep down. Contrary thoughts are left to those who don't know any better. Suggesting such differences in polite company typically generates embarrassment. This is not just because people want to be politically correct; rightly we do not feel comfortable putting our friends or acquaintances into boxes.

The issue of differences between groups is therefore, to put it mildly, controversial. All too often, we can risk exaggerating differences between people and failing to recognize the fact that people everywhere have the same desires, fears, motivations, and challenges to overcome in life. In fact, when it comes to global business, it is not a bad idea to sometimes put aside notions of cultural differences and assume that everyone is pretty much the same. When looking at other cultures sometimes we exaggerate differences, and other times we oversimplify and assume uniformity where there is variety and differentiation. In fact, there are powerful reasons for why we engage in such stereotyping beyond the obvious need to feel good about ourselves in relation to others.

Our social world is complex and taxes our cognitive and emotional coping strategies. The human brain evolved predominantly in hunter–gatherer times when humans typically congregated in groups of between 50 and 100. Our brains are finely tuned instruments for navigating that early environment. The only problem is that, unless you happen to be a Kalahari Bushman or an Inuit, this finely tuned instrument is required to operate in environments that were never imagined back when it was constructed. Imagine turning up to sort out a problem on a piece of complicated IT software armed not with an operating manual but with a soldering iron, and you will begin to get the picture. One of the simplifying processes is to stereotype people and to relate to them as members of a group as opposed to having to understand every person we need to engage individually and from scratch. A danger in talking about psychological differences between people from different cultures is simply that it reinforces narrow and frequently false stereotypes about people. Hence, rightly, there is a reluctance to talk about difference.

This has not always been the case. In Victorian England and most of European society at the turn of the century, it was common for people to overtly and with confidence opine about the attributes of others. Favell Mortimer—a descendant of the family that founded Barclays Bank—wrote widely about other people. Two of her most popular books were *The Countries of Europe Described* and *Far Off: Asia and Australia Described*.[4] Mortimer presents, with breathtaking insensitivity and at times open contempt, her views on the nations of the world. The Spaniards are "not only idle they are very cruel;" the French "like things smart but are not very clean." When she talks of Italy, Mortimer cannot get over the number of murders committed in the country and how unsafe it feels. Further afield, if anything her observations grow even more rancorous. When she talks of Afghanistan, she observes "the men are terrible looking creatures—tall, large, dark and grim." The Burmese, she informs her readers, are "very deceitful and tell lies on every occasion." When she comes to Siam, she makes the judgment that "there would be very little trade in Bangkok if it were not for the Chinese."[5]

This is the sort of writing that gives observations on different people a bad name. The point of all this is that stereotypes, even strongly held ones, can all too often be wrong. One reason for this is that people frequently fail to account for contextual factors when interpreting others' behaviors and thus attribute tendencies to people that are more accurately ascribed to the situation that they inhabit. This effect is so powerful that it has a name in psychology: the fundamental attribution error. A second reason that stereotypes are frequently wrong is that they are often less about describing the world than justifying our position or actions within it. Mortimer's views make a good deal more sense when looked at through the lens of rationalizing British imperial activities.

Unconscious Bias

Few people nowadays would openly serve up the kind of fare that Mortimer offers her readers. However, as the whole field of unconscious bias in psychology has uncovered, even people who are openly and vehemently against anything that smacks of stereotyping often show evidence of intergroup bias when their behavior is examined more closely. A legion of studies have demonstrated that when one looks at people's actual behavior and decision making, or aspects of their reactions they cannot control, they do hold profound views about intergroup differences. If, for example, white people are shown on a computer screen positive and negative adjectives, each paired with a white or ethnic sounding name and asked to say whether the adjective is good or bad, they show much faster reaction times when the positive adjective is paired with a white sounding name or the negative ones with the ethnic sounding name. When the pairing violates people's internal stereotypes, by putting positive adjectives next to ethnic sounding names or negative ones next to white-sounding names, the brain takes time to orient itself to this unexpected reality.[6]

In fact, a range of research looking at things people cannot control, such as reaction times, recall, or neuropsychological responses, shows that people hold unconscious biases not just toward other ethnic groups but also with respect to gender and all manner of other groupings in our social world. The differences are higher typically in people who are openly discriminatory in their thinking, but also invariably show up with even the most ardent liberals.[7]

So just because people don't like to flaunt their views Mortimer-style these days—this does not mean they *do not* hold underlying views about group differences. However, before we jump to the conclusion that everyone is full of irrational stereotypes, there is an interesting twist to the unconscious bias data. Black people in the earlier example also show evidence of holding the same biases, but a bit less strongly. In fact, a whole host of research on both conscious and unconscious stereotypes shows that often, but not always, the group itself shares the views that others hold about them. In general, while people differ in the values they attach to particular qualities—generally valuing the traits they possess over those with which they are less associated—they nevertheless often agree on what qualities their own and other groups possess. Why should this be so? Is there a conspiracy to envelop everyone with a global false consciousness to which we have all succumbed?

One strong strand within psychological research of group perceptions holds that some, but not all, stereotypes have a kernel of truth to them.[8] This states that people formulate views of other groups because of certain tangible bits of data and evidence rather than picking them out of thin air.[9] It's a theory substantiated by the finding that many stereotypes seem to reflect people's observations of extreme or salient events. Simplistically, if you see a lot of Indian children in the Spelling Bee finals, you might think all Indians have a penchant for learning to spell complicated words. This is almost certainly a false view, but as will be discussed in the India chapter, there may be some cultural influences that drive success in such a competition for Indians. The stereotype is therefore both untrue and true at the same time. Stereotypes often arise from reading about different types of memorable events, portrayals of whiz kid geniuses, or quite simply the kinds of people who pop up on the TV. These extreme manifestations often do result from differences in the group mean of an attribute being skewed a bit—hence the kernel of truth notion.[10]

The unconscious bias research, plus the kernel of truth evidence, suggests that simply pretending there are no differences and that all views that express such differences are infused with a false consciousness is quite simply trying to push psychological water uphill. Even if the conscious mind succumbs to the effort, the unconscious brain will most likely rebel. A much better course of action is to recognize the reality of some differences, but to try to get people to value differences more—that is, encourage them to more actively examine their models of what is good or necessary for success. This is where unconscious bias can really lead to a false consciousness and cause leaders to fail to leverage the power of diversity. In fact, there is something of a paradox to some of the arguments around diversity. At one level proponents of a diversity agenda want to minimize any suggestion of difference; but at another level they also want to get people to value different approaches more. The latter can only make sense if differences exist, and if people recognize and actively celebrate them.

Greater Similarity and Difference at the Same Time

It would not be entirely true to say that people are always more different than one thinks or that prolonged exposure to a culture invariably leads to a heightened sense of difference. It only does so in certain respects. In other areas, people can also be equally surprised by similarities, which had been underestimated from a distance. There are many respects in which people everywhere are just humans going about their daily lives with the same hopes, drives, anxieties, instincts, and foibles as everyone else. From a distance, certain stereotypes and assumptions about differences that we hold can evaporate the minute one connects with a different culture. It is important in international business to see the person beyond the race. Simply ignoring differences is sometimes not a bad strategy at all, and sometimes firms tread too softly and self-consciously when engaging other cultures, tiptoeing around imagined sensitivities and differences. However, the point is to be alert to both greater similarity and difference at the same time.

We witnessed firsthand this paradox of greater similarity and difference when working for one of our global companies. This client had commissioned us to run a series of in-depth and groundbreaking personal development workshops for managers. As is the case in many of these workshops, there was an emphasis on personal disclosure, reflections on one's values and purpose, as well as extensive feedback from participants—the kind of intervention that gets routinely caricatured by television programs like *The Office*. Cynicism aside, we had in actual fact created an event that was quite powerful and at times even moving for participants. We ran it initially in Europe and the United States with great success. The managing director of the company's Africa division heard about it and said that he wanted to try it in his region as part of his long-term plan to develop local senior managers for the top posts.

Most thought that this was a step too far and that the company's African managers would find the experience somewhat perplexing at best—but most likely downright weird. However, the MD was proud of what he and others had created in the Africa division and persisted. After a degree of corporate handwringing, and mildly skeptical, we set off to Nigeria to run the first workshop for a group of managers picked from across the African continent.

It was clear from the moment that we touched down at Lagos airport that we had to reset some of the normal instincts and precepts that one ordinarily uses to navigate daily life. Simply getting into Nigeria proved to be a feat in itself, requiring the navigation of numerous arbitrary checkpoints, all aimed at fleecing us in some way. After having navigated one of these simply to get onto a horizontal moving belt, my heart sank when I saw a gaggle of semi-official looking individuals waiting to interrogate us at the end of the moving section. We had been led to expect this and told to smile and say, "I'll bring something for you next time." Astonishingly, this platitudinous and self-evidently unlikely promise more often than not did the trick. This was a regular pattern that we found in dealing with a lot of official and semi-official people in Nigeria then and also subsequently in trips to other parts of Sub-Saharan Africa. We were able to overcome initial wariness and at times overbearing sternness by telling a joke or attempting some form of personal connection, the impact of which was typically to release extremely high levels of responsiveness and personal warmth.

Once out of the airport, we were hit by what every visitor experiences—the joy and vibrancy with which people deal with each other on a daily basis in Africa. Quite simply interactions take place with more vivid color, emotional expressiveness, intensity, and laughter in many parts of Africa. This is both refreshing but at times also a bit overwhelming, especially if you come from a more restrained culture. Our sense of relief at having survived the airport experience and entering the country, was tempered by a wariness introduced by the realization that we had armed escorts in front of and behind us as we set off for our hotel. We wondered why such extravagant security was necessary. The truth is that Lagos, like many parts of Sub-Saharan Africa, is just not that safe. The caution shown by Western companies around security is well founded and not just a reflection of paranoia at operating in an unfamiliar environment. The jarring juxtaposition of great friendliness and warmth at one level, with an underlying feeling of threat at another, is something that plays on one's mind in many parts of Africa. We often found that a seemingly benign situation could unpredictably develop a threatening edge, just as a problematic encounter could easily dissolve into indifference or, more confusing at times, joviality.

Contrary to expectations, African managers took to the program like ducks to water. They showed a level of drive and commitment to the exercises that we had not encountered. There was also an openness and a robustness of exchange that at times even made us wince with its directness. The African leaders engaged in exercises that we had worried they might find silly or meaningless with a level of gusto and passion not witnessed before. The managers also performed extremely well on the case studies and other exercises. However, we did notice that if there was no allocated leader in the group discussions, participants tended to debate until they reached *complete* consensus—no matter how time-consuming this proved. If they made a decision at all, they did so only when the allocated time was about to run out.

However, just as we were concluding that African managers were just like those in Europe—but maybe even more driven—certain small but intriguing differences started to emerge. Participants were required to fill in some personality questionnaires at the end of the first day. We gave these out and told people that they typically only took 20 minutes or so and they should then break for the day. We left them to it, but after two hours, an anxious administrator came to get us and informed us that the African managers were having difficulties with the questionnaires. Perplexed, we returned to the room to find a number of them under considerable strain, sweating, and looking quite agitated. The group was treating these psychometric questionnaires—which merely tapped individual preferences and had no right or wrong answers—like an exam. What's more, word had got round that we were endeavoring to cross check responses across items as a test of honesty. Rather than reacting to each item naturally, the managers were going back each time over all their previous answers in an effort to avoid the inconsistency they thought we were trying to catch people on. Such cross checking was vaguely feasible at the start, but after you had completed about 50 or 60 items, it became a highly stressful kind of 10-dimensional Sudoku.

After the three-day program finished, we had the opportunity to visit some of those managers at their place of work—which was something of an eye-opener. Magically, it seemed that the collaborative and consensual leaders we had seen in the workshop who had had difficulty converging on a decision had transformed overnight into highly confident, driving, larger than life figures barking instructions furiously at their subordinates and conveying an impressive sense of decisiveness and efficiency. Often a certain degree of gratuitous insult was thrown in with the instructions: "Why did you do that, you fool?" or "Don't make such a stupid mistake next time." This was our first encounter in Africa with what has been termed the Big Man syndrome—an expectation that leaders should be huge personalities conveying confidence and certainty at all times. The subordinates appeared to take this highly directive and less than fully respectful behavior from their leaders in their stride and, if anything, seemed to get some reassurance and comfort from it. The transformation was remarkable for its sheer scale and rapidity. It was also disorienting given that we were psychologists who were supposed to have been able to get under the skin of surface impressions and uncover such latent tendencies.

The point of the above story is clear. Many expectations about differences across cultures are simply not true and on occasion even the reverse of what one might expect. Like executives everywhere, the African leaders were motivated to be the best that they could be, and, if anything, more driven and keen to learn than their Western counterparts. The curious episode with the psychometrics was in fact partly a reflection of their desire to perform well. However, there also lurked profound differences beyond the surface similarities. There were radically different attitudes toward the application of institutional rules—as our experience at the airport had demonstrated—as well as a wholly different and complex approach to the exercise of power in different settings. Relationships and trust also appeared to be built in very different ways. In their own milieu, the behaviors and instincts of the African managers were also profoundly different from how they acted with us. Gradually, we got to know and understand better some of the similarities and sources of difference. However, after a week or so we left with the thought that one all too frequently experiences on holiday. You have had a great time, the locals have been welcoming and at one level you have connected with them, but you are nevertheless left with the feeling—driven by subtle cues that you can't quite put your finger on—that a completely different world exists outside your orbit of managed experiences. You are left wondering, "Have I understood this place at all?"

The Globalization Challenge for Business

At one level, many businesses—particularly multinationals—would feel that they have been operating globally with success for considerable periods of time. Yet if you scratch the surface, the new multipolar world that is emerging is creating significant challenges and asking deeper questions of businesses that consider themselves to be globally minded.

The first point is that there is no such thing as a global company. Every significant company that I come across operating on the global stage has a culture that is distinctly rooted in its place of origin. The senior leadership teams of such organizations are often literally a pale reflection of the geographies in which these companies operate. One sees an increase in diversity with the growth of emerging markets. However, even the individuals who make it up the hierarchy tend to be socialized into the dominant host culture. Genuine diversity, inclusiveness, and the capacity to build ways of working that take the best from a range of global cultures have eluded just about every multinational.

A second point is that there can be a degree of common understanding between executives at senior levels in a business who have often been educated at elite universities or international business schools. However, there is also a tendency to underestimate the genuine differences in outlook and orientation at lower levels. International executives who do not develop a nuanced understanding of the cultures in which they are operating can exhibit significant blind spots about what is truly going on at deeper levels within the organization. How initiatives land and are executed in reality can be a far cry from what executives have intended or indeed what they think is happening. Governments and regulatory authorities also typically operate to the drumbeat of a local culture—presenting unforeseen barriers and developments that can catch many multinationals off guard.

Another point is that virtually all multinationals, particularly, Western ones, complain of significant and sometimes insurmountable challenges with regard to talent levels in different parts of the world. While there is some truth to this, the perception arises at least partially from applying a narrow set of lenses for looking at people. One of this book's intentions is to encourage executives to think more deeply and appreciatively about difference. Doing so in an authentic and genuine, rather than a platitudinous manner, requires real appreciation of some of the underlying causes of difference. Similarly, if your implicit notion of development is to inculcate executives into your dominant, core, cultural precepts, you are likely to be disappointed by the returns emanating from such investment. Releasing potential in different cultures requires nuanced and sophisticated interventions that go with the grain of the local cultural DNA.

Many of these issues point to a deeper challenge that global companies need to engage with: The ecology of the global business environment is changing fast. The analytical, process-oriented, organized, and structured approach that is the default setting of many Western multinationals may increasingly prove to be too slow moving, inflexible, and cumbersome in a dynamic and fast-moving world where the unpredictable currents of change require a more intuitive, emergent, and flexible set of responses. The frequent complacency around their core cultural values that many Western companies exhibit appears to emanate from a lack of realization of the depth and strength of the ecological changes in the global business environment. In fact, as will be explored later, some of the themes of this change may play to instincts that are more deeply rooted in non-Western cultures. However, companies from these emergent cultures also need to adjust their mindset as many step onto the global stage for the first time. A provocative and honest understanding of the strengths and weaknesses of one's cultural default settings in the new multipolar world is essential for all players.

Defining Cultural DNA

This book is about how the people in eight of the world's regions—Sub-Saharan Africa, India, the Middle East, China, Europe, North America, Latin America, and Australia—look at things, which I refer to as each region's *cultural DNA*. Before we go further, however, it is useful to say a few things about what is and what is not meant by the term *DNA* as used here. The first point to note is that in spite of the use of the biologically laden term, DNA, the focus is on the deeply grained aspects of a culture that are replicated over generations rather than biological differences. Occasionally, this cultural DNA springs from biological factors; but it arises more often from the environmental challenges that each culture faced historically or the predilections of the original founders who moved to that part of the world.

In fact, the idea of DNA comes from work in the area of organizational culture. Like many others, we discovered—after years of working with organizations to help evolve and change their cultures—that significant change requires time and is inherently a slow process. Over time, this has led to the idea of organizational DNA emerging as an explanatory concept for why things can be slow to change. The idea of organizational DNA centers on the proposition that all organizations are guided by deep, underlying assumptions, beliefs, and ways of working that their members faithfully replicate and pass on to other generations. Often, this organizational DNA reflects the original founders' predilections, and the business and environmental challenges that the organization faced early on in its history. Over time, these core instincts become deeply embedded, guiding just about everything that goes on—including the organization's response to new challenges.

In addition, we have developed a clear and somewhat radical view on just where this organizational DNA resides. Rather than sitting mainly in organizational structures or processes, it actually resides within the employees themselves and their way of looking at the world. The nature of the business that an organization engages in determines the kind of people they need to recruit and the organizational culture required. Over many years, members of the organization undergo a process not too different from natural selection. Only certain types of individuals are attracted to an organization in the first place. They lay the foundation for the culture and attract similar sorts of people to it—reinforced by the natural inclination to recruit in one's image. Those who do not fit the culture, but nevertheless make it past these filters, frequently end up being "tissue rejected" unless they adapt. One way or another, the organization's processes, structure, and decision-making instincts come to mirror the predilections of its dominant core of people. Efforts at change that go with the grain of the DNA can typically work, but anything that requires a significant alteration of people's underlying instincts is hard going, to put it mildly. Organizational DNA is a combination of the underlying psychological instincts of a company's people as well as the systems, processes, and ways of doing things that those people have developed and to which others joining the system are acculturated over time.

The genesis to thinking about this book was the question: If this can happen for organizations, could not the same process also be true for nations? As we shall see, most major global cultures have actually arisen from very small founding groups of people who originally migrated into that part of the world. Once there, the early migrants encountered very different environmental challenges and created societies focused on solving different problems. These factors helped shape different psychological instincts that eventually came to represent the cultural norms for that society. Those who did not conform either self-selected out through migration or did not succeed in the culture. In organizational terms, this is akin to somebody hitting a glass ceiling at a relatively low level because they did not fit. I would argue that the same processes that led to the rise of organizational DNA have, albeit at very different time scales, operated to shape national cultures. By DNA, we are referring predominantly to the fundamental psychological building blocks that eventually formed the cultural norms of different societies. In Richard Dawkins' terms, memes rather than genes.

The application of this type of DNA analysis to eight of the world's significant cultures raises some obvious questions. The first is that one cannot just aggregate into one entity the myriad subgroups, states, and nations that exist in many of these regions. In fact, there is considerable evidence that just as nation states within broad regions have distinctive psychological and cultural attributes, so do regions or even individual cities. Research shows that cities develop clear characteristics over time through the processes of acculturation and self-selection. However, a lot depends on your level of analysis. At one level, France and Germany are very different, as is the northern Indian state of Punjab from, let's say, Kerala in the south. However, when you really start looking at all four together, you quickly realize that the two European countries share a lot in common and are different from the two Indian states.

This is exactly what the World Values Survey found when data collected across almost 100 countries was analysed. Overall, nine distinct regional clusters were revealed—the eight above minus Australia, plus Europe split into Catholic, Protestant, and Orthodox (Russia/Eastern Europe) areas.[11] The Globe survey of 62 countries also found broadly similar clusters.[12] Geography and, to a lesser extent, religion define these clusters. Not a single country in the world sits on its own or in a cluster that is radically different from where it is geographically located or where most of its people come from. At one level, this is not surprising; but at another level, these findings point to a deeper truth. If a country's culture is purely dependent upon the vagaries of its unique history, specific rulers, or the institutions that people there created in isolation from their environment, one might not expect such tight geographical clusters to arise. This pattern can only arise if ecology, climate, and the movement of ideas and people from one place to another are the fundamental drivers of cultural DNA. The exceptions to this power of locality simply prove the rule. For example, the Anglo-Saxon countries cluster together. Australia and New Zealand are outliers from others in their broader region. If you want to understand the culture of these countries, you are much better off looking at the UK—where the bulk of the people originated—than to neighboring Papua New Guinea or Indonesia.

Some of the analysis below will, despite the above point, cover differences within the regions, as in the case of the Eurozone countries that have succumbed or not to the currency crisis discussed earlier. These differences fit neatly into the European clusters defined by the WVS. In many of the regions, there are often one or two significant cultural divisions—for example, in India between the north and the south or in the United States between the northern and southern states. In all these cases, I will argue there are powerful migratory or ecological reasons for the existence of these differences that lie deep in the past when the relevant regions were being settled.

A Word About the Evidence

Three broad sources of evidence are used to build the case for what constitutes the DNA of different cultures: primary data, secondary sources of information, and explanatory research.

Most of the primary data centers around the evidence accumulated over 25 years of working as CEO for the psychological consultancy YSC, which has 20 offices globally covering all the regions analyzed in the book. Our core work involves getting under the skin of both people and organizational culture—which we have been doing globally across the world for decades. As a consequence, our different offices have developed finely tuned instincts for what really makes people and organizations tick in different parts of the world. We have also systematically assessed 30,000 people working in a range of organizations across the world, which gives us a deep source of data and information to draw upon when forming hypotheses about cultural differences. In addition, a core feature of the data that the conclusions presented are based upon is a painstaking analysis of over 1,700 in-depth reports, approximately 200 from each region, which contain the strengths and development themes identified for executives in each culture. This gives us sound insights into the positive qualities, as well as issues, that leaders from each culture need to be mindful of as they negotiate the ecology of the fast-changing global business environment.

I have also accessed the considerable research conducted on cultural differences over the past few decades, employing a variety of methodologies such as value surveys, behavioral experiments, and personality instruments. Following the seminal work by Geert Hofstede and his colleagues, there have been several detailed and extremely comprehensive surveys of values across the world's key cultures.[13] The Globe study of 62 countries involving over 900 organizations, mentioned earlier, is one of the most important. The World Values Survey, mentioned earlier, is also an important source of data. The work of Michael Minkov, which extends the Hofstede constructs,[14] and Shalom Schwartz are also accessed.[15]

However, values are only one part of the story. Such inquiry can only touch the surface of differences in how people think. I have also drawn substantially on behavioral experiments and observations conducted by researchers across different cultures. Surprisingly, for a psychologist, I have been much less persuaded by evidence using standard personality instruments, as these frequently produce nonsensical results when it comes to cross-cultural comparisons. This is largely because a high proportion of personality tests implicitly or explicitly ask respondents to compare themselves to the people around them. By their very nature, many such instruments therefore cannot be used for teasing out differences across cultures. Last, but not least, I have drawn upon the observations of legions of anthropologists, sociologists, historians, and travelers who have drawn strong psychological conclusions about the cultures that they have engaged.

Much has been written about cultural differences. However, there has been a limited effort to explain *why* such differences exist in the first place. This is one of our main objectives: to get underneath the skin of differences and to provide an explanation for why they might exist. Here, there have been extensive breakthroughs that provide a foundation for understanding the roots of differences between cultures. Over the past decade, analysis of mitochondrial and *Y*-chromosome DNA has enabled us to build a very precise picture of how and when groups populated different parts of the world. In a field that was at best murky and speculative before, there is now a high degree of precision and convergence that I will draw upon extensively when seeking to explain cultural differences. We also now have a much sharper lens, driven in part by advances in analysis of ice cores, on the profound climatic challenges that have affected modern humans since they arrived on the scene 200,000 years ago. The modern concern with global warming can perhaps create the false impression that our environment in the past was some kind of stable, unchanging nirvana for humans. But nothing could be further from the truth.

Furthermore, while ecological and historical processes have been the main drivers of the cultural DNA of regions, there is increasing evidence that genetic features may also have a role to play. A wide range of genetic investigations, which will be reviewed later, suggest there has been rapid and intense evolution since modern humans left Africa that affects a diverse range of attributes, such as food tolerance, disease resistance, and energy metabolism. From the point of view of psychological differences, there is now extensive evidence that profound variations across different groups in some of the genes determine both the level and uptake of key neurotransmitters. These findings are relatively new and still in the process of being tested and replicated. However, some differences do appear robust. For example, the serotonin transponder gene, which affects the level of serotonin in the brain by influencing the same functions that the drug Prozac impacts, has both short and long allele versions. Individuals with the short alleles are more prone to anxiety and depression following negative life events. A variety of other behavioral and psychological traits are also associated with the presence of short alleles. Now something like 80 percent of people in China have the short allele versus 40 percent in the United States and 25 percent in South Africa.[16]

Similarly, a gene called *DRD4*, which influences dopamine levels in the brain, also has short and long alleles. Individuals with the long alleles are more adventurous, novelty seeking, independent minded, rebellious, as well as hyperactive—and something like 75 percent of South American Indians possess the long allele version. The figures for the United States are in the region of 30 percent and in Europe 20 percent or so. In China the rate of the long allele is close to 0 percent.[17] Similarly, large differences are seen in genes that influence the opioid system, which, as well as being associated with perceptions of pain and well-being, is also associated with emotional reactions to disruption of social bonds. When northern Europeans see Italian or Spanish soccer players react as if they have been mortally wounded at the slightest physical impact, it may not just be histrionic acting out—the poor guy writhing on the ground to boos from the crowd may actually be biologically more sensitive to pain.

The latter point illustrates something more important. If a small number of the differences observed between cultures reflect such biological factors, it may be wiser to recognize this fact rather than to pretend otherwise. At the very least, this can absolve individuals from personal blame, as well as lead to greater empathy, when their reactions or behaviors are not in accordance with what other groups expect. In addition, overwhelmingly most genetic adaptations, as will be reviewed later, arose first because of cultural change, which then drove differential selection; a kind of culture-gene coevolution.

Why Bother with Differences?

Even if differences exist, why bother focusing on them as opposed to what we have in common? We are in many senses a co-operative species—but once we introduce even small group differences, elements of wariness, suspicion, and frequently hostility ensue. Social physiologist Henri Tajfel graphically illustrated this in his minimal-group experiment in which he was able to engender surprisingly high levels of intergroup rivalry and discord simply by artificially dividing people between those who liked a particular artist and those who did not.[18] Anyone who doubts the power of trivial group differences to elicit powerful emotions can simply observe the dynamics between groups of teenagers at high school or go and see a soccer match just about anywhere in the world.

Another thing that makes discussion of group differences sensitive is that there is an automatic belief that merely identifying differences involves ordering groups of people hierarchically. People who repudiate all talk of difference seem to do so because they actually hold the implicit, but unacknowledged, view that in any comparison non-Westerners will come out for the worse. If, however, you accept the argument that different groups' psychological instincts are actually finely tuned to the environment in which they are required to survive—and that fundamentally all groups have qualities that play out for good or ill in different situations—discussing differences becomes less emotionally loaded.

Nothing illustrates the gravitational pull of immutable hierarchical thinking better than the whole controversial field of intelligence quotients (IQ) and race—which is the natural place many go to when thinking about group differences. Books like *The Bell Curve*[19] and, more recently, *A Troublesome Inheritance* fall into this trap.[20] The first point to make is that standard IQ scores, thought to be relatively fixed in populations, have been changing quickly the world over—the so-called Flynn effect. James Flynn found, for example, that IQ scores had risen by about three points per decade for several decades—this may seem small but actually makes a massive difference over just a few decades.[21] Diet, the spread of technology, control of infectious disease, as well as familiarity with IQ tests themselves, have all been hypothesized as leading to these improved scores. Different groups show different levels of this effect, and some developed countries appear to have stopped improving. It is likely that many developing countries will continue to post sharp rises and, until things have leveled out, nobody can make accurate statements about intergroup differences.[22]

More importantly, there is inevitably a danger in applying tests developed in one culture to others that might see the world very differently. Each culture's intellectual orientation is finely attuned to the ecology of the environment and the survival challenges that that culture has faced. Therefore, nobody is more or less intelligent than another in a fundamental sense; they are just different. The analytical/logical/structured approach so beloved by Western academic researchers is only one way of looking at intellect. It ignores wisdom, judgment, creativity, and emotional intelligence, as well as intellectual flexibility. The ecology of the new global environment will lead to a greater convergence of scores with respect to standard Western measures, as well as leading to many non-Western modes of intelligence becoming more and more valued and appreciated—thus challenging the notion of hierarchy.

Another reason for focusing on and helping to explain differences is to aid cultures in developing greater levels of empathy and respect for each other. Psychologically, since humans are one of the most social species in the animal kingdom, the development of empathy is one of the most important tasks that a person faces. Surprisingly, if one maps brain size against body mass, most species fall on a fairly tight curve. There are a few species that are clear outliers in that they have much bigger brains than their body size would indicate. Humans are one, and apes and dolphins are others. The clue to what is common lies in the two nonmammalian species that have much bigger brains than they should; ants and bees. All the outlier species are highly social. This leads to a natural conclusion that at least in part our large brains exist as tools for navigating our interpersonal environment.

There has been much research in recent years on the importance of mirror neurons in our brains that fire sympathetically when we observe people doing things or experiencing certain emotions. These were accidentally discovered by the Italian researchers Giacomo Rizzolatti and his colleagues at the University of Parma while studying the firing of individual neurons in the brains of Macaque monkeys as the monkeys reached for food. The researchers found to their surprise that some of these neurons started to fire when the monkey saw the experimenter reach out for the food. Thus was born the idea of mirror neurons, that is, neurons that fire sympathetically when we see an action or an emotion in others.[23] At some level we experience the same neuronal activation that the person we are watching does, and this drives both learning and empathy.

Many believe that research on mirror neurons represents one of the most significant recent breakthroughs in psychology. It is possible that as much as 10 percent of the neurons in the human brain may have mirror neuron type properties. Neuropsychologist V. S. Ramachandran says, "These are the neurons that changed the world," and argues that the significant presence of mirror neurons in humans is the very basis of our culture and civilization.[24]

However, what is really shocking about mirror neuron research is what happens when we observe people from groups different from our own. In one experiment, psychologists showed white people videos of a white hand being pricked by a needle. As expected, people's reactions showed evidence of mirror neurons firing in the relevant parts of their brains. But when the same people saw a black hand being pricked, there was little—and in some cases virtually zero—evidence of sympathetic neuronal response. Interestingly, when the experimenters showed a hand that had been painted purple being pricked, the relevant neuronal system dutifully fired in the expected manner. The failure of the mirror neurons to react to the black hand, therefore, reflects an awareness on the part of the white subjects that it belonged to someone from another race. Interestingly, those who scored highly on a test of unconscious bias showed virtually no mirror neuron activation in the case of the black hand being pricked.[25] Numerous studies have replicated these findings across different groups, and the suppression of neuronal empathy when one observes other groups is now an established fact. This research is saddening, but it does start to make sense of huge swathes of our sorry, human intergroup history—slavery, the Holocaust, and Rwanda to mention but a few. This research also indicates that one of the core objectives of this book—the development of intergroup empathy—is not an irrelevant or unimportant task in our global world.

A second objective of the appreciative approach to difference that is the focus of this book is to get people to question their implicit hierarchies. It is natural if you come from countries that are prosperous to develop a view of your superiority; sometimes this can be overtly held but, more commonly, it is an implicit view that is best not aired in public. Conversely, those at the other end of the spectrum often develop an unconscious sense of inferiority or inadequacy—although, again, this is not necessarily obvious on the surface, as many people from the cultures that are "on the back foot" express an overt sense of nationalism, pride, and display a surface confidence that may not always run particularly deep. I suspect that when you lift the lid, the underlying reality is that Westerners still feel superior and people from other cultures are playing a psychological game of catch-up in terms of their confidence and self-esteem. In fact, this is exactly what the work on unconscious biases cited earlier illustrates.

One of the motivations for writing this book is to attempt to level the playing field. While the analysis of the DNA of European and American societies identifies some clear attributes that have given these societies an edge over others in the past, it also unearths certain profound weaknesses that these societies must address if they are to retain their edge. Moreover, one—although not the sole—factor that has given Western societies an edge over others is their historical capacity for organized violence against other ethnic groups—something which I will argue is embedded more in the DNA of the West for a variety of reasons than some other world cultures. This is something that will be increasingly difficult for Western societies to leverage in today's world. In short, while other societies can learn something from those aspects of Western society that have led them to be successful, they do not have to be intimidated by their success.

However, if other societies are truly to catch up, they need to appreciate both the underlying strengths and also the limitations that their own cultural DNA creates for them in the emerging new world. While I have tried to stay positive, some parts of my analysis for all societies will make for uncomfortable reading. In fact, I suspect that most people will agree with the analysis of other cultures but likely become defensive about certain aspects of their own. This is not just because people only want to hear positives about themselves—which is, to some extent, true. In a very real and profound sense, one's own way of looking at the world feels like the only way, because everyone around you shares it. It is difficult to step out and question your core beliefs from inside your own frame of reference. However, as we have found in our work with individuals and organizations, an honest external mirror is often what is needed to move forward.

Having apologized in advance for likely reactions—it is time to move on to the analysis of each culture. We start our journey by examining the United States, as the relatively recent movement of people to the continent can be tracked with greater certainty, and the arguments help to illustrate principles we will use later. We then move to Sub-Saharan Africa, where the human journey began, and track the movement of people from our common home to different regions in the world.

Chapter 1

America—The Change Makers

A merica today is still the world's most powerful country, both in terms of the size of its economy and its military muscle. Even more important than this, however, is the soft power that the country exercises. In particular, after America and its allies won the Cold War, there was an implicit sense in many parts of the world that American values and ideals would become the global norm. It was this sense that persuaded the political economist Francis Fukuyama to prematurely call out the *End of History*, on the basis that fundamental debates about values were over and we were all marching toward an American future whether we recognized it or not.[1]

The American model also seemed to have triumphed in business. The idea that free markets should create the champions of the future through Darwinian selection became widely embedded. Other notions took hold, too: push relentlessly for ever higher targets and differentiate aggressively on the basis of performance; never rest from change; let companies outsource to the lowest cost providers around the world. American executives who went abroad did so on the front foot and led predominantly through American leadership values. The country's business schools were also teaching leaders from around the world how to manage their companies, and American heroes, such as Jack Welch and Louis Gerstner, were the doyens of the global business community.

Just a few decades later, however, the world looks very different. American business values are no longer the default setting for executives around the world. The global financial crisis that struck in 2007 has had a particularly significant impact on the credibility of the American business model. A short while ago, America's banks, ratings agencies, and insurance companies were seen as highly sophisticated operators in complex markets. Now many believe they had either no idea of what they were doing or were malevolently self-serving—neither judgment is flattering. While the American reward culture has created enormous wealth for some, many feel senior leaders have been excessively rewarded, often for indifferent performance. The model is also under question internally. Decades of economic growth have barely touched the living standards of the bulk of the American population and there is a sense of weariness and latent resentment among many in the workforce. Outsourcing may have benefited company profits—but whole sectors of American society have lost out or live on the precipice of insecurity.

American leaders wrestling with lower economic growth at home must think globally, now more than ever before. However, they can no longer go around the world simply teaching other people how to sing the American business tune. They have to adjust to a multipolar business world with all its complexities and contradictions. This requires American leaders to understand other cultures and flex their own approach as never before. On a day-to-day level, an American executive has to deal with a bewildering range of nationalities either within a firm or in global markets. Increasingly there is a chance your boss will be from a culture with which you have had only fleeting experience before.

More generally, America has lost its sense of omnipotence. People around the world instinctively recognize that other ideologies and values for how life should be organized are now on offer. In America itself, this has created a sense of ambivalence and uncertainty. American exceptionalism has always been deeply rooted in the national psyche; as such, the idea that others could genuinely overtake the country—rather than pretend to and then fade away, as did the Soviet Union or Japan—causes disquiet. America is in an uncertain mood where, psychologically, a lot of things are up in the air. The rest of the world is equally uncertain as to how Americans will adjust to a new multipolar world. Which of the myriad of potentially conflicting values that constitute its cultural soup will get stronger, and which will get weaker?

Founder Effects

Understanding America's psychological DNA provides some clues to answering the above questions. This DNA arises chiefly, but not only, from the fact that the early history of America was created by distinct groups of people who migrated there for very particular reasons. To understand American cultural DNA one has to understand the psychology of the myriad groups that founded the country.

The importance of founder effects can be illustrated by a simple story. Recently, researchers led by Deborah Neklason, of the Cancer Research Institute in Utah, achieved a breakthrough in their understanding of one cause of colon cancer in the United States.[2] The team studied an extended community in Utah where 5,000 people were stricken with an unfortunately high rate of colon cancer. Whereas the chances of developing the disease is something like 4 percent by the time one reaches 80 in the general population, close to *two thirds* of people in this particular community were found to be at risk of developing the disease. A specific genetic mutation was identified as being responsible for this heightened vulnerability.

Fortunately for the researchers, Utah—by virtue of its Mormon heritage—keeps quite detailed genealogical records. The researchers were therefore able to trace the source of the mutation back across a number of generations—which caused them to make an extraordinary discovery. There is another extended community in upstate New York that also has exceptionally high rates of colon cancer and the same genetic mutation. Tracing back the records of both, they found the inheritance paths began to converge. Eventually, they led to a common ancestral couple, Mr. and Mrs. George Fry, who arrived in the New World onboard the *William & Mary* around 1630. The Frys had four children, of whom one was the source of the extended community in Utah and another for the one in upstate New York. The authors concluded that the elevated risks of colon cancer in both these extended communities emanated from a single founder genetic mutation that Mr. and Mrs. Fry had brought with them—along with their hopes—to the New World. The authors also speculated that there were almost certainly many other extended communities across the nation who could be related to Mr. and Mrs. Fry, for whom the risks of colon cancer would be similarly elevated.

What this story illustrates is the powerful way that the exponential mathematics of procreation can lead to founder effects being amplified within a population. Quite simply, when a population has arisen from a clear founding group, there is a strong chance that many biological and psychological characteristics will be passed on to later generations, thus leading to differentiation from other populations that have different founders.

The Peopling of America

The peopling of the Americas is essentially a two-part volume with a short prologue and a longer and more complicated main story. The prologue concerns the original peopling of the American continent by modern humans some 10 to 15 thousand years ago. These modern humans settled, populated, and established ecological footholds that remained in place for thousands of years on the American continent. Unfortunately, these original human settlers were decimated by the arrival of European migrants over 500 years ago. To understand modern American cultural DNA one must therefore understand who settled there and why in the recent past. Unlike the settlement accounts for other regions, this is a story around which there is a lot of detailed information.

Although various parts of North America were populated by small colonies of Spanish, French, and Dutch settlers, substantial settlement of the Americas early on involved various migrations out of Great Britain and Ireland. This is well documented in David Hackett Fischer's book, *Albion's Seed*, and I rely extensively on the research described there for the early part of the story.[3] According to Hackett Fischer, four significant communities were driven by political developments or economic necessity to seek their fortunes in a vague and undefined land that lay at the other end of a forbidding journey across the cold, grey waters of the Atlantic.

The first significant community was that of the Puritans, who formed a strong movement in Oliver Cromwell's New Model Army. Unsurprisingly, the Puritans' stern and unyielding belief in a simple life and rejection of all pomp and ceremony did not endear them to the English aristocracy. Not unnaturally, as the fortunes of the different parties in the civil war fluctuated—when Charles I was in the ascendency—there were aggressive and wildly popular purges of Puritans. Many of those who were unwilling to quietly shed their beliefs and melt into the background decided to migrate to North America and set up base in the Boston area. By 1640, there were 20,000 people predominantly from a Puritan background in the area, which expanded by 1700 to 100,000, and to a million by 1800. This initial population was the root community from which Massachusetts, Connecticut, New Hampshire, upstate New York, and northern Ohio were eventually populated.

The early Puritans believed they had found a simple and ordered universal model for how the world should be organized. They were vehemently committed to a disciplined, pious, simple, and ordered way of life as a means of keeping man's sinful nature in check and for establishing a compact with God. As will be illustrated later, the aspirations around creating a moral "city upon a hill," utilitarian instincts, commitment to the idea of salvation through work, and attachment to a simple and ordered moralistic society had, and continues to have today, a significant impact on American cultural DNA.

A second, significant religious order that settled in the North American continent early on were the Quakers. The Friends, as they called themselves, believed in seeing the best in people and in extending the hand of friendship to others. Unfortunately, they found many responded to their well-meaning overtures with an iron glove. In particular, powerful sections of English society rapidly took against this new order once they learned that the Quakers were not enthusiastic about paying tithes to the established church. Perhaps also their peacefulness and reluctance to fight back elicited, through some paradoxical psychological process, unusual levels of animosity.

William Penn, an early convert to the Quakers, had been granted by the Crown an area that was subsequently to be called Pennsylvania, in payment of a debt that had been owed to his father. Weary of the hostility and difficulties that his peaceful and tolerant order attracted in England, William Penn decided to set up a kind of human experiment in his newly acquired land, creating a community of Friends that was free from the many forces that buffeted the religion in his homeland. The vision was radical, and fortunately for William Penn, the early Quaker settlers found the Native Indians were relatively peaceful and welcoming. William Penn's experiment attracted considerable attention in England and, between 1675 and 1725, something like 25,000 Quakers flocked to the colony, principally from the North Midlands, but also from Wales.

Like the Puritans, the Quakers had a strong work ethic and a belief in "serving God with one's talent." Their belief in wealth creation, not for its own sake, but as a service to the community, seeing possibility in people, and a desire to place all people under a universal umbrella of harmonious coexistence are all important strands of influence with respect to American cultural DNA. Eventually, Quaker communities were a significant source of the populations of the eastern parts of Virginia, large parts of the Delaware valley, and the state of Maryland, as well as Ohio.

The Puritans and Quakers constituted the first significant European populations to settle the northern part of the United States. Hackett Fischer describes the first significant southern community as the Distressed Cavaliers. Like the Puritan migration, their movement was driven by the ups and downs of the English Civil War. Just as conditions improved for the Puritans in England with the victory of Oliver Cromwell, so they deteriorated for members of the landed aristocracy who had supported the Royalist cause. This class of people suddenly found themselves on the wrong side of the line that granted authority, power, and patronage in Great Britain. The dimming of privileges proved particularly challenging for the second sons of such families. Many went to the Caribbean and a host of other places but a number ended up in Virginia. They brought with them their servants and indentured labor. Between 1642 and 1676, 40,000 decided to seek their fortunes in America, and this community was responsible for populating significant parts of Virginia, Southern Maryland, South Delaware, and coastal North Carolina.

The Distressed Cavaliers were in some senses the polar opposite of the Puritans and Quakers. Simplicity of lifestyle was not for them and they hankered after the trappings of privilege and the good life. As a community, though, they were bounded by a strong sense of honor and a commitment to supporting others of their class. However, they were inherently hierarchical and saw themselves as a class apart from the servants and indentured laborers that they brought with them. An interest in the good life made tobacco farming a natural area of economic activity for these settlers. They also had no compunction around importing vast numbers of slaves from Africa to help them support a somewhat leisurely but privileged lifestyle. Whereas the Quakers, and to some extend also the Puritans, had made efforts to extend a hand to the Native Americans, this group predominantly regarded the indigenous inhabitants as an irritating presence that had to be removed from their rich farmlands and plantations.

The fourth and final community that also settled predominantly in the south did so in the western hinterlands rather than the coast. This was a community from the border country between England and Scotland, as well as areas surrounding the Irish Sea, including Northern Ireland itself. In the seventeenth century, this was an area characterized by small but fiercely independent communities. The borderland migrants were driven to America in large part by a fierce desire to preserve this independence, which was being steadily eroded by landed gentry and a mercantile economy encroaching on their territory. In terms of scale, this group constituted one of the largest early communities into America; it is estimated that, altogether, 250,000 people went from these regions. Their initial point of entry was often Pennsylvania and other parts of the Delaware valley. However, the already settled Quaker communities rapidly recognized that the newcomers had very different values and encouraged their swift onward movement to the Appalachian Mountains; eventually this group settled in the mountains and hills of Maryland, Virginia, the Carolinas, Arkansas, and eventually Georgia, Oklahoma, Texas, and other southern states.

The cultural DNA of this community had been forged by a constant history of warfare in the border territories and the ensuing rise of clans and local chiefs. Another significant influence was the relative difficulty of working the land, with consequent emphasis on animal husbandry and pastoralism. These communities were fiercely independent minded, self-reliant, and hard to coax into any form of collective endeavor. A strong feature was an inherent belligerence, allied with a culture of blood feuds and retributive violence, which arose from the clan-like structure of the borderlands. Although independent minded, this group was inherently conservative and resistant to new or alternative philosophies. As Hackett Fischer notes, they also brought with them "the ancient border habit of belligerence to other ethnic groups" and were strongly xenophobic—not just against other races but toward any outsiders.

The above four communities created distinct cultural values in the areas in which they settled and, by virtue of their early arrival, set down a blueprint for American cultural DNA. Relationships and friction between these communities were also a significant dynamic of the early history of America and continue to this day. Two examples in particular illustrate this dynamic. The first is from history, and the second from recent psychological experiments.

The American Civil War was essentially and fundamentally a battle between two distinct groupings of cultural DNA. Although a southerner by birth, Abraham Lincoln's ancestry was almost completely Puritan and Quaker. His sober and prudent manner and strong underlying sense of moral conviction were characteristics typical of these communities. When he ran for president on the pledge to stop the expansion of slavery outside of the southern states, he swept the board across the north of the country but carried virtually no states settled by Distressed Cavaliers or the borderland migrants.

When the Civil War eventually broke, the north had far more resources than the south. However, both the Distressed Cavaliers and the borderland migrants had a much greater familiarity with warfare and violence. The Civil War itself was fought out between a northern army that essentially resembled Oliver Cromwell's New Model Army—with its emphasis on professionalism rather than social standing—whereas the south was led by swashbuckling, independent-minded characters who fought for honor and freedom.

To this day, one can see the same fault lines across American culture. When outsiders express dismay at the vehemence with which, in particular, the south resists efforts at gun control, they would benefit from recognizing that the right to bear arms and to rely on one's own resources for protection was one of the fiercest emotional drivers for the borderland migrants' decision to uproot in the first place.

The second example comes from psychological experiments conducted by the psychologists Richard Nisbett, Dov Cohen, and others in 1996 on how individuals from different parts of the United States react to the challenge of being physically or psychologically provoked.[4] The team found significant differences in how northerners and southerners responded to provoking episodes, such as

somebody bumping their shoulder or being called names. Southerners were quick to move from higher levels of initial friendliness to
greater hostility when such affronts occurred. The team also found
that cortisol levels—which are related to feeling stressed—rose in 79
percent of the southerners after being bumped and in only 42 percent of northerners. The researchers ascribed these differences to the
honor culture that existed in the pastoral communities from which
these groups originally arose and which they had re-created in the
Appalachian Mountains.

While these initial communities set the cultural tone for America as a whole, including differences between regions, the other
significant community was, of course, the slaves from Africa. Something in the region of 12.5 million were brought to the New World
under horrendous conditions between the years 1525 and 1866. However, only a tiny proportion, perhaps in the region of 500,000, from
1620 through to 1865, ended up in North America, the rest going
to South America and the Caribbean. Though ports of embarkation
were in West Africa, many of the slaves came from the interior of
the continent, predominantly sourced by African leaders who were
complicit in the slave trade. They were either members of tribes
who had been overrun or were relatively powerless members within
their own communities. These communities brought with them many
aspects of Sub-Saharan cultural DNA, which over time has enriched
the American cultural soup.

Following the initial settlement by the communities from Great
Britain and the slave trade from Africa, a series of migratory waves
rolled into the country and added to the mosaic of American cultural
DNA. First, a movement of people from Northern Europe occurred
throughout the nineteenth century. Germans were particularly prominent. A number were political refugees following failed revolutions
in 1848, while others belonged to radical Protestant sects. Others
were agricultural workers. Today people of German descent constitute roughly 17 percent of the American population—a greater
number than those who claim Irish, English, or African ancestry.
The founder effect of the English speakers explains why English, not
German, is the official language of the United States, and perhaps why
in all national culture studies, the United States clusters with England,
not Germany. At about the same time, the Irish famine caused large

numbers of Irish Catholics to move to Boston, Philadelphia, Detroit, Chicago, and New York.

A second wave of significant migration across the nineteenth and twentieth centuries came from Italy, Greece, Poland, and Lithuania. This was a dispersed and varied set of people driven in large part by economic considerations—but also, as in the case of the Jews from Eastern Europe, virulent persecution. In many ways, these Southern and Eastern European migrants were culturally quite different from the various Northern European settler communities, and created strong enclaves in which they congregated, while buying into broad aspects of American culture—particularly, the American dream.

Since World War II, the migration of Hispanics has been a dominant theme. People of Spanish descent now constitute considerable proportions of certain southern and western states. Their arrival has started a process of changing the underlying cultural DNA of the American south. More laterally, there has also been a significant stream of migration from Asia. Although varied, this migration has one feature that was not always evident in other migratory communities. People coming from Asia often do so in substantial measure because of their technical or professional skills or qualifications, and in many cases they constitute elites within their own countries.

Some obvious points arise from the above account. First, it's clear that significant numbers of people were attracted to America by a desire to preserve their distinctive religious or political beliefs in the face of serious persecution. They believed in something and were not prepared to bend like trees in a gale in the face of serious pressure to conform. Second, a fierce drive to escape poverty or to seek economic advancement characterized many migrant communities. Third, no other major region in the world has absorbed so many diverse ethnicities and nationalities as America has in its relatively short modern history. For the most part, while newcomers have swiftly been socialized into key facets of American values, their diversity has been respected. The earliest communities, having escaped strong forces pushing them to conform or drop their beliefs, were not inclined to start doing the same thing to others.

The themes created by the above patterns have sometimes reinforced each other to create powerful cultural forces within American society. An example is the Puritan and Quaker religious belief in salvation through work, that likely added fuel and potency to the drive for economic betterment, resulting in an attitude toward work that is quite distinct from that which exists in Europe. At other times, as in the American Civil War, these forces have created schisms in society. The particular mix of these different forces has also helped shape a myriad of subcultures within the overall mix. This extends to individual states and even cities. For example, Nevada was substantially populated as a result of a silver rush in the 1860s, as the discovery of the precious metal led a legion of opportunists, chancers, and gamblers to try their luck in the state. People are still trying their luck there, and Nevada's global reputation as a center for the gaming industry is a consequence of this early pattern of settlement.

At other times, some of these currents have run against each other and created contradictory elements in American cultural DNA. We see these between individualism and community, radical change versus conservatism, the pursuit of morality versus the pursuit of money, and reaching out versus withdrawing from broader engagement. Let's now examine the psychological themes that constitute the American mindset.

Positivity

A European executive of an American-founded consultancy firm told me a story of the clash between the two cultures that illustrates a gulf with respect to emotional mindset. The firm had underperformed the market for many years. Eventually, the leaders decided to pull in all the consultants from around the world for a global get-together in Miami. The European consultants, expecting a sober review of problems, were surprised to find that the meeting felt more like an evangelical gathering. When the CEO articulated highly ambitious goals for the future, they noticed that he glossed over the fact that these new aspirations represented a significant inflection from the results of the recent past. Most of the audience seemed also to ignore this inconvenient truth.

The executive I spoke to had gently asked at the end of the presentation what changes the firm might make to achieve these results. That evening, his regional manager took him aside and told him that the CEO was "fuming mad with him." In fact, the CEO was going around the conference vociferously complaining of the European's negative attitude, whom he accused of "going around like terrorists lighting fires all over the conference." The so-called European terrorists were completely taken aback by how their behavior had landed.

Many global cultures share the view that Americans are constitutionally positive and optimistic. In the world of work, engagement scores vary quite systematically across the world. Like the sun, they follow an east to west trajectory. For example, a survey by management consulting firm Aon Hewitt in 2013, covering an extensive range of global companies, found that only 16 percent of Asia-Pac workers showed high levels of engagement, compared with 18 percent of Europeans and a full 24 percent of American employees. Latin Americans were the most enthusiastic, with 33 percent highly engaged.[5] Many years back, when we opened an office in the United States, we encountered serious issues providing feedback about people's strengths and development needs—many American managers reacted to our assessments as if we had poured a bucket of icy cold water over them. We learned over time to convey our messages more carefully and with a philosophy of building on positives. Our global 360-degree feedback business, which has run tens of thousands of surveys globally, finds Americans rate both themselves and their colleagues much more positively than Europeans do. People from the Far East also do, but this is likely due to hierarchical respect.

Although Americans are distinctively renowned for being positive, there is in fact a bias toward optimism in all humans. Psychological research on people's explanations for events shows an overwhelming drive to take personal credit for success but to ascribe blame conveniently to others or external events. Optimism bias is a well-researched phenomenon in psychology that involves overestimating one's chances of succeeding at just about anything, including academic, social, career, or sporting success. Related is the *above-average effect,* where routinely vast swaths of the population consider themselves to be above average in intelligence, attractiveness, earnings, charm, popularity, or even luck.[6] We would live in a nirvana surrounded by happy, healthy, beautiful people, if everyone's self-images were even vaguely accurate. Cross-cultural research shows that the nature and extent of these biases do indeed vary across cultures. Americans, for example, are more prone to self-serving attributional biases, optimism bias, and the above-average effect compared to East Asians. Europeans are closer to Americans, but when differences are found, they are less optimistic than their cousins across the Atlantic.[7]

These differences also show themselves at all levels of American life—from the discourse at a political level, which is overwhelmingly oriented toward themes of optimism and positivity, to the incomprehension of American filmmakers when Europeans produce films that do not have a happy ending. Consider the packaging of oneself for interviews or just the simple day-to-day behavior where Americans routinely smile more and greet each other with greater positivity. The burgeoning self-help industry in America, which dwarfs that which exists in other cultures, rains an unending supply of positive advice upon people on how they can better themselves, fix their marriages, become wealthier, and live longer. These attributes of American society are not just a modern phenomenon. As long ago as 1750, Benjamin Franklin wrote, "Sorrow is good for nothing." Just about every successful American presidential candidate has made it his task to frame an agenda in positive terms. Recent examples are Ronald Reagan's *Morning in America* video, Bill Clinton's "There is no problem that America faces that cannot be solved with what America has," to Barack Obama's "Yes we can."

What are the roots of this increased bias toward positivity in American cultural DNA? I believe this was deeply embedded in the early phase of settlement of the continent. Unless you were forced to go to America, as was the case with the African slaves, actively choosing to cross a murky and forbidding Atlantic Ocean for a very dimly understood land nearly 3,500 miles away was not something for the fainthearted. In fact, 15 percent of people perished on the journey alone and even more once they reached the promised land. All this meant that a trip across the Atlantic was literally like rolling the dice, knowing that you would die if you got a one. Vessels bearing people to America soon came to be known as coffin ships. Choosing to go to America essentially required one to be an optimist—someone more inclined to see possibility rather than peril, hardship, or even death as a potential consequence of your choice. The same has applied to many subsequent people making the decision to migrate to the United States.

Psychologists have long known that some people have a more positive outlook than others; the reason why, however, has been a mystery. Numerous family and twin studies have indicated that there is a strong genetic component to always seeing possibility in situations. More recently, advances in genetic research have begun to tie down just what genes may be responsible. One candidate gene is the serotonin transporter gene, different variants of which determine the level of free serotonin in the brain. Serotonin is a plausible candidate for involvement in optimism, given the efficacy of serotonin-boosting drugs in the treatment of depression. There are two significant alleles of the transporter gene, the short and the long version. As noted earlier, a number of studies have shown that having the long version may be associated with greater optimism and resistance to stressful life events. Elaine Fox, a specialist in the field of optimism, has shown, for example, that people who inherited two long versions—one from each parent—attended much more to positive than negative images presented on screen, whereas others were more balanced.[8]

Oxytocin, which has been found to be associated with maternal bonding, empathy, and interpersonal trust, has also been studied in this context. Shelley Taylor and her team looked at genes associated with the *OXTR* receptor gene, which determines how receptive neurons are to oxytocin. At one locus of the *OXTR* gene, there are three alleles: *AA*, *AG*, and *GG*. The researchers found that people with at least one *G* scored significantly higher on measures of optimism, mastery, and self-esteem. Other lines of inquiry have also shown that people can tell whether someone has *AA*, *GA*, or *GG* simply by rating traits like emotional expressiveness and likeability. However, there is some evidence that while oxytocin may increase trust levels within in-groups, it may actually increase distrust toward out-groups. Similarly, other research indicates that individuals who are *GG* or *GA* for the receptor gene may need higher levels of social support and trusting early environments for their well-being.[9]

While a lot of the preceding findings are new and need to be more widely and consistently replicated, there is substantial emerging evidence linking both the serotonin transporter and oxytocin receptor genes to optimism, mastery, and trust, as well as sensitivity to negative events. There are well-known differences in the alleles of both these genes across cultures. As noted earlier, the long version of the serotonin transporter gene is most common in Africa, where 75 percent have the variant. The comparable figure for Americans and Europeans is 60 percent, and for East Asians 20 percent. With respect to oxytocin, it appears that the *A* version appeared after humans had left Africa. So virtually everyone in Africa is *GG* but only about 16 percent of people in the Far East are *GG*. The figures for Europeans and Americans are 50 percent.[10] These global rates chime eerily with higher levels of happiness and optimism in Sub-Saharan Africans and much lower levels in people from the Far East, with Europeans and Americans somewhere in between, but closer to Africans.

However, while genetics might explain some differences between Americans and East Asians, this cannot entirely explain the gap with Europeans. The self-selection for positivity factors unrelated to serotonin and oxytocin is a partial explanation. However, this tendency has likely been reinforced as well by a virtuous cycle driven by success in the new environment. As arduous and life threatening as the journey across the Atlantic was for the early pioneers, those who made it had good cause to view themselves as lucky and successful. These settlers rapidly moved to get a foothold, escape British control, and—in less than 200 years—settle the whole continent by establishing flourishing communities and cities. In this headlong expansion, optimism and success reinforced each other again and again. Even when they encountered severe problems—such as the 1930s' Depression—there was always the sense that things could be fixed. Franklin D. Roosevelt's "We have nothing to fear but fear itself" was classically rooted in this aspect of American DNA.

We can see this positivity throughout American business. In our database, a full 35 percent of American executives—the second highest level of all groups—were seen as having a strength in positivity/emotional resilience compared to say only 19 percent of Indian and Chinese executives. European executives were also reasonably positive, with a score of 30 percent. Globally, only Latin American executives were stronger than Americans in this area. This attitude is evident in all aspects of the culture of American companies, ranging from how leaders are expected to appear, the spirit they exhibit in engaging with problems, and the tone of leadership conferences. A sense of innovation and entrepreneurism is also evident in many U.S. companies. Consider the fact that bankruptcy—something seen as a severe embarrassment in many cultures—is relatively accepted in the United States. You just dust yourself off and go on to your next brush with destiny or failure. The ability of businesses to set stretch goals—a target that is beyond the company's current abilities—as well as being open to new ideas, is also evident in many American companies.

While a mindset of positivity is mostly a virtue, it can create issues—especially when Americans are dealing with cultures that are much more driven by avoidance of failure. Lack of pace and caution can frustrate American executives, while those on the receiving end of the American positive mindset can internally resent the setting of impossible stretch goals or the airbrushing away of genuine problems. Other cultures can also experience American positivity as inauthentic, which can hinder the ability to make a genuine connection with others. One of the most common observations that our consultants report is that in spite of their reputation for openness, American managers are sometimes the hardest to assess—because it is so difficult to penetrate that protective layer of learned positivity. In fact, only 11 percent of American executives were rated as having a strength with respect to "emotional openness and authenticity," the lowest level of all global cultures, with the exception of Africa. In addition, 19 percent were perceived to have a development need in this area compared to a global average of less than 10 percent. In addition, when it came to honest self-insight, only 3 percent of American executives were strong and 19 percent had a development need. Only Latin American and Indian executives were weaker with respect to grounded self-insight globally.

At a personal level, positivity can also be a double-edged sword for Americans themselves. If you are not feeling internally positive, it can be tiring and wearing to constantly present an upbeat image. This issue also begs the question of how deep the projected positivity actually runs. The idea that, if you are positive, then good things in life will come to you has a bitter alter ego. If you are not experiencing good things, then it must be because you have been negative and pessimistic. You start to blame yourself for becoming ill, for example, or for not being able to beat cancer with a positive attitude. Similarly with work, underneath their high engagement scores, our experience is that there is an unexpressed sense of weariness, fatigue, and cynicism among American employees. Such a gap exists in most cultures, but in the United States, the need to project a constantly upbeat image makes this issue more pronounced.

As Barbara Ehrenreich notes in her book *Bright-Sided*, there are societal issues that a culture of unrelenting positivity can create. The first and foremost of these is that you can risk getting ahead of yourself as a country. You might wade into situations whose complexity you have not anticipated, as has occurred with many external interventions by America. You can also blot out things that are uncomfortable, and metaphorically airbrush them from the mental picture that you have of your country. Since the American economy became dominant, the country has delivered the global economy a number of spectacular boom-and-bust cycles. The latest, credit-fueled economic crash that much of the world has experienced was in no small measure due to the collective irrational exuberance of American banks, regulators, investors, and consumers.[11]

There is another aspect of positivity that needs to be considered as America enters, potentially, a more difficult and challenging future. What happens when a country finds that the positive engine of optimism that powered the genuine success described earlier starts to stutter? This has happened for short periods before; but how do you react psychologically if it is more enduring? While many in American society are still adhering to an ideology of positivity, there are also powerful undercurrents of resentment and frustration. The Tea Party movement, the rise of extremist political sects, or the now all-too-frequent rampages of crazed gunmen are all potential signs of the puncturing of the culture of optimism. To be sure, there have always been vast swaths of the American population that have not been able to fully partake of the American dream. But, in earlier times, there was always enough to make the dream a realistic vision for the many rather than the few. What if this changes? Americans would probably regard these questions as unduly negative. America has always responded to crises and come through, and a mindset of *there is always a way* gives the country much to draw upon.

Embracing the New

The depth and extent of religious belief in the United States is something that catches people by surprise, even though it is well known that Americans have a greater gravitational pull toward religion than other regions in the world. The sense of religiosity hits you immediately upon picking up newspapers or switching on the TV. There are over 1,600 religiously oriented TV and radio stations catering to the American thirst for religious connection and uplifting of the spirits. Over 40 percent of Americans attend church weekly, and close to two thirds claim to do so at least once a month—compared to fewer than 10 percent for weekly attendance in the UK. Over 75 percent of Americans say that prayer plays an important role in their lives and 80 percent say they have never doubted the existence of God.

Religion infuses all aspects of American life. For example, it is frequently considered electoral suicide for an American politician not to openly proclaim his or her faith. In Europe, and particularly in Northern Europe, politicians are encouraged to keep their faith under wraps, lest it scare the voters.

The cultural roots of this religiosity in the United States are obvious from the early account of the initial founder communities that settled America. Compared to many other migrant communities, such as Canada, South Africa, or Australia, the American migration had significant numbers of people who went for religious reasons and, at times, also for political freedom. However, these people were also radicals. When one talks about the original Puritans, Quakers, the various German Protestant sects, or indeed the German revolutionaries, one is talking about people who had a fundamentally radical set of values that almost always challenged the existing status quo in their countries.

While sections of the original founder population, such as the Distressed Cavaliers or Irish Catholics, went for predominantly economic rather than ideological or religious reasons, they nevertheless also made a disjunctive choice in life. The decision to migrate to a place that no one really understood—without a fixed or ordered society—could only have been made by people who were prepared to disrupt their lives. You were reacting to whatever was going on around you and saying these problems can only be fixed if I seize this opportunity of making a once in a lifetime choice. If you were indecisive, change averse, or content to play it safe with what you had, then you were unlikely to have rolled the dice in this way.

One sees this dynamism reflected in many ways early on in American life. In the religious sphere, new ways of connecting with God, referred to as awakenings, regularly swept the country. The first great awakening began in the 1720s and lasted for about 30 years. It consisted of preachers, such as Jonathan Edwards and George Whitefield, rejecting the turgid and theologically dense sermons administered in favor of a much more emotionally charged tone, which created a more vivid sense of immersion and experience for the audience. This was associated with a strong sense of rejecting orthodox and hierarchical religious observance for a much more open and democratic ethos. Not unnaturally, many historians believe that this initial great awakening was a precursor to the American Revolution itself. Since then there have been at least three more periods of emotionally charged awakenings, each impacting society more broadly, that have swept the country.

This dynamism is evident even today. An extensive survey by the Pew Forum in 2008 covering more than 35,000 Americans found a huge churn in people's religious affiliation. The survey found that something like 44 percent of adults had switched religious affiliation, moved from being unaffiliated with any religion to embracing religion, or dropped out of religious observance. The survey also found extensive fragmentation and diversity as being increasingly characteristic of American religious life.[12] Even outside of religion, American life is peppered with cult-like organizations that bring together believers in all kinds of generally new ideas. When we look at this—along with the history of various American revivalist movements and the rollercoaster of religious sects that have multiplied across the American landscape—it's clear that something in American psychological DNA predisposes people to believe in *something*—but that this something is open to dynamic change.

This simple and obvious fact has had an enormous impact on how American individuals, companies, and indeed the society as a whole cope with challenges and embrace change. A perfect example of this is the rapid and confident decisions that Americans made when the recent financial crisis emerged—whether around injecting money into the system or saving certain banks and letting others go to the wall. Compare this to the indecisiveness with which Europeans faced up to the Eurozone crisis. A constant theme in the dialogue between American and European officials was frustration on the part of Americans that the Europeans were just not seizing the problems by the scruff of the neck and making active choices about how to solve them. Meanwhile, Europeans saw Americans as gung-ho shooters from the hip who preferred action to thoughtfully considered steps.

We can also see this openness to change across American business. In global surveys of innovation, American companies top the league. Close to 40 percent of companies in the 2014 *Forbes* Most Innovative 100 are American. Europe has a similar size economy but only 25 percent of companies on the list, while Asia-Pacific is even worse, with only 16 percent. This innovation happens across all spheres of activity and not just in Silicon Valley or Wall Street. Whether it is new forms of retailing, military technology, aviation, or fast food, America sets the tone. Another feature of this strength is that American companies are able to execute innovation fast. Like the earliest pioneers, they are prepared to be bold in turning thought into action. In our research, over 40 percent of American executives had a strength in action orientation, the highest score globally. While having the capacity to be intellectually innovative, their European rivals struggle to translate this creativity into action.

However, while American society can be highly innovative, this may happen through radical disjunctive change rather than more continuous steps. In fact, as will be argued in the next section, there is a relatively high psychological need in Americans for holding a clear schema that provides certainty of belief. This schema can be dropped, but the need for clarity can lead to resistance to change on a day-to-day basis. Despite American strength in radical innovation, American executives in our database were found to demonstrate only average strength globally with respect to improvement and change orientation; a kind of continuous-improvement mindset. The resolution of this paradox naturally takes us to our next psychological theme.

Assimilation over Accommodation

A while back a client of ours asked us to look at a whole range of highly successful global organizations to identify common cultural patterns that might explain their success. We found three clear themes in the companies studied compared to their less successful competitors. All the successful companies had aggressive performance cultures. Surprisingly, however, they also combined this with an equally strong focus on *coaching*. The third thing they shared in common was a clear cultural signature. American companies such as GE, P&G, and Coca-Cola were almost cultlike in the strength of their culture—which gave them great strength in terms of internal alignment, executional effectiveness, and knowing who to recruit. Such companies also invariably promoted from within. This observation points to a deeper reality about American psychological DNA: the need to hold a clear schema and to socialize people into that worldview.

Many outsiders who engage America commonly encounter a precise script and routine one is expected to follow—across a myriad of areas. Processes like checking into a hotel, ordering a drink in a bar, boarding a flight, or just about every other day-to-day activity involves dealing with people who engage you in a friendly but scripted and semi-robotic manner. If what you say and how you say it is not in line with expectations, then you're likely to face incomprehension and a sense that you have completely failed to get through. One female executive explained to me how she had to repeat her request for a gin and tonic four times before finally finding the right intonation that allowed her to be understood. One might think that this is natural when speaking a language with a different accent. However, I have rarely heard Americans in England complain of a difficulty in getting through, whereas by contrast virtually everyone from Britain experiences this problem in America.

The clue to understanding both the above phenomena lies in the psychological concept of assimilation versus accommodation—developed by the renowned Swiss developmental psychologist Jean Piaget. Piaget posited that a child's development requires the creation of schemas for understanding the world. These schemas represent an individual's concept of reality or a map of preconceived ideas. Once these initial schemas are formed, they are developed through the twin processes of assimilation and accommodation. Assimilation occurs when new information is integrated into an existing schema and made to fit in with the original concept of reality. Accommodation occurs when new information causes people to adjust their original schema. For example, consider a small child's schema of things that float in a bath. Initially, a child might have learned that things that float in the bath are called toys. One day, the child drops a piece of soap in the bath and notices that this also floats. The child can assimilate this information and conclude that soap is a toy. Alternatively, the child might change the prior schema for what floats in a bath and conclude that besides toys, other things can also float. Essentially, assimilation involves bending external reality to the mental constructs that you have already and using new information to confirm these constructs. Accommodation means adjusting your internal mental models in response to new information and data.

In my experience, there is a strong psychological bias within American culture for assimilation over accommodation. Americans have clearly developed schemas for a variety of situations, and look to absorb things into these internal mental models. If things come at them that do not conform to their precepts, then they are inclined to reject the unfamiliar. For example, when it comes to team sports, Americans show little interest in many games that the rest of the world plays, preferring instead their own distinct locally grown sports, such as American football and baseball. Of course, I do not intend to be black and white here; clearly Americans, just like any other people in the world, engage in both processes of assimilation and accommodation. There's just more of a tendency toward the former in American culture.

The reason for this preference likely has roots in the original reasons that many people came to America. Those who came for religious reasons did so in response to intense pressure in their various European homelands to shed their beliefs. While many people eventually chose to follow a path of least resistance in the face of such pressure, those who wanted to preserve their schemas more or less intact did so by moving continents. Even the early migrants who came for nonreligious reasons were often driven by a desire to preserve a way of being that was under threat in Europe.

This tendency toward assimilation over accommodation manifests itself in many areas. The ease with which outsiders can feel the sense of disconnection and lack of comprehension noted earlier is an example at a micro level. It also shows itself in the speed with which people from the UK who are living in America start calling mobiles "cell phones," petrol "gas," and ask for the "check" rather than the bill in restaurants.

It is evident as well in how American executives operate. In our assessments, only 8 percent of American executives had a strength around empathy and listening skills, whereas 20 percent had a development need in this area. Only African executives were weaker in this area. In addition, only 16 percent of American executives had a strength around intellectual flexibility compared with averages of 30 to 40 percent for most other cultures.

Much of American business success abroad also seems to stem from firms that have found a formula for success that they then roll out worldwide. McDonald's, Kellogg's, Heinz, Marriott, and many, many other U.S. brands are based on the launch of products and a standardized business model scaled up around the world. These companies show very little accommodation in their approach. European multinationals in similar sectors to the preceding ones, such as Unilever, Cadbury-Schweppes, or Nestlè, tend to be much more flexible around adjusting their models as they engage different parts of the globe. A particular feature of the American market also leads to this difference: When a nascent successful business starts to expand, the initial challenge is to enter markets in other states. Such expansion requires little adaptation and a model of tight replication for managing growth often is reinforced. In other parts of the world, expansion pushes firms very early on to think about non-familiar markets.

As a consequence, American firms operating abroad typically show strength in implementing their values and creating cultural clarity. However, there has been increasing criticism within the United States of the lapse into cultism that many strong organizations seem to promote. In many cases, employees are expected to absorb everything uncritically and to give enthusiastic endorsement to a firm's values. The gatherings of such firms can feel like over the top rallies that stifle dissent and seduce employees into forsaking their personal lives for their work—often without too much compensatory reward. The recent emphasis on employees bringing their full selves to work, openly exhibiting high engagement levels, and identifying closely with their companies has, if anything, accentuated this sense of uncritical acceptance. However, in my experience, while executives can enthusiastically embrace, say, the Coca-Cola way, if a better offer from Pepsi comes along, emotional commitment can shift to the new player in a nanosecond.

This orientation can also land badly when engaging other cultures, such as Europe and India, where people desire more flexibility. A CEO of an Indian business, which had been owned by a British company but was then taken over by an American global giant, said, "It is chalk and cheese. There is no room for discussion. I feel I have just been taken over by a cult." In a sense, this represents the propensity for holding a schema at the level of business once it has been shown to be successful and taking pride in not changing it or accommodating to different contexts.

This psychological theme also explains why overseas firms find it so difficult to penetrate the American market. Legions of firms have failed to crack the American market after setting out optimistically. The barrier of "it's not invented here" is a real issue—whether you are a professional services firm, bank, or retailer. Unless you are a global luxury brand selling on the basis of uniqueness, businesses seeking to prosper in America must carefully adapt to the precise preferences of American customers. At one level, you could say that this amounts to the exercise of economic power and leverage. However, even the mightiest foreign companies face issues of the kind described above when operating in America—likely due to powerful underlying psychological processes.

The preference for assimilation is also the underlying cause for the overwhelming sense of parochialism that overseas visitors experience when connecting with America. In spite of the global reach of American cultural soft power and military hard power, virtually all visitors are struck by how insular and America-centric news is in the United States. The fact is reflected in American knowledge and interest in the external world. For example, a recent survey found that despite having fought two recent wars with Iraq, close to 50 percent of Americans were not able to locate the country on a map. Some Americans are surprised that English is spoken in the UK—assuming, one supposes, that the early settlers of the continent created the language. The common statistic that a third of Americans do not possess passports and that more than half have never traveled abroad is another feature of this parochialism.

These inclinations do not arise because Americans are not inquiring, intellectually lively, or inventive. Frequently, they are all these things. As we saw earlier, there is a greater tendency to embrace disjunctive change at a societal level in America than just about anywhere else in the world. Rather, the extent to which Americans are interested in exploring and adapting their mental schemas, particularly with respect to information and data from other parts of the world, is more questionable.

Indeed, the whole history of how migrants are absorbed into the United States illustrates the supremacy of assimilation over accommodation. While a large number of Americans are hyphenated—in other words, they see themselves as Italian-American, Greek-American, Indian-Americans—it is clear that wherever you come from, you are expected to voluntarily absorb and make your own American values. You are expected to join the melting pot. Paradoxically, this means that new settlers are required to mentally accommodate themselves in order to assimilate to the norms and expectations of American society.

There may be a natural inclination to assume that the tendency to assimilate is counterproductive, that it smacks of intellectual rigidity and lack of receptiveness to external influence. However, it can also be a force for good. The strict adherence of the early settlers to their ways of communicating, living, and getting along together has helped create a distinct cultural identity across the United States. In business, too, preserving your schemas and being clear about your identity, cultural values, and how your products and services should look creates clarity as well as potential confidence in the consumer base.

The psychological reluctance to accommodate would be a more serious impediment to progress in America if there wasn't also the ability to adopt a new schema when change is required. Whether it is at the level of politics, business, or religion, Americans are very good at this kind of disjunctive change. However, it typically represents the adoption of a radically new schema and the two forces may actually complement each other rather than be contradictory. That is, the ability to change disjunctively may arise precisely because one also has the capacity to maintain a schema intact for quite a long time—driven in part by the implied tolerance of ambiguity that an accommodative approach to life inevitably requires.

However, as America plays out its global role in a context where other powers are emerging, there is plenty of room for missteps and error if your predominant orientation is assimilation rather than accommodation. This is demonstrated in the sheer surprise Americans show when others are not open to American values in the way they naturally expect. The expectation that vast proportions of the Iraqi population would enthusiastically embrace Western values after the overthrow of Saddam Hussein is an example. One of the most successful global colonialists of all time, the British, recognized this and trod a fine line between preserving British traditions and values versus adapting and working with local rulers. Americans need to appreciate that they cannot simply export their values with the same ease with which they set up Coca-Cola plants or factories for building iPhones.

Mammon: Tamed and Untamed

When Sigmund Freud made his trip to America to give his famous lectures on the history of psychoanalysis, he was not particularly looking forward to his encounter with the country. Traveling with his colleagues, Sandor Ferenczi and Carl Jung, he said before the journey, "The thought of America does not seem to matter to me, but I am looking forward very much to our journey together." Freud had been tempted to make the trip by a financial offer he could not refuse. Central to his antipathy toward the United States was the belief that Americans had channeled their sexuality into an obsessive concern for money. Going to a country toward which he had expressed vociferous antipathy for financial gain must have created the kind of internal conflict that Freud was famous for analyzing in his patients. Rationalizing later, he commented with rare emotional intensity, "Is it not sad that we are materially dependent on these savages, who are in no way a better class of human being?"

Ironically, despite his offhand and distant manner on the tour, Freud's lectures were a great success. American positivity meant that his subtle hostility mostly went over the heads of his hosts. As a result, psychoanalysis took off in America in a much bigger way than it ever did in Europe. American openness to new ideas and the well-embedded cultural desire for self-improvement made American audiences naturally more receptive to Freud's revolutionary psychology than the cautious and skeptical Europeans.

Freud's observations on the preoccupation that Americans have for money is, of course, a commonplace stereotype held both inside and outside the country. Alexis de Tocqueville noticed this in 1831 when he visited America.[13] "I know of no country where love of money has such a grip on men's hearts," he wrote. Virtually anywhere that you turn in America today, you notice a different attitude toward money, especially if your reference point is Europe, less so if you have been immersed in the commercially intense Far East. If you switch on the television, and just randomly go through the hundreds of channels, you will find that close to a third of them are showing advertisements at any time. The nature and quality of the advertising is also instructive. It is rare to see many concessions to artistic creativity or efforts to create a mood or sense of beauty. Viewers are instead hit by short, rather forceful admonitions extolling them to buy something because it is cheap or has this or that feature. The jarring legalistic disclaimers commonly appended at the end also add to this sense of overdone functionality.

The ubiquity of tipping is also another distinctive element of American life. Most other cultures view this act as a discretionary reward for good service and not some kind of inalienable human right. A colleague once described how he was chased out of a restaurant and followed up the street—not because he had failed to give a gratuity, but because the 10 percent tip considered more than adequate in the UK was felt to be insultingly small. Although service relationships in any society are inevitably transactional, the fact that such relationships almost always carry with them an expectation of financial reward in America means the aura of money is always hanging in the air. In all walks of life, whether it is higher education, healthcare, or the conduct of political campaigns, money is much more directly evident in America than just about anywhere else.

Americans, too, embrace this picture of themselves. There is collective ennui about overconsumption in society, but few seem to want or feel they can get off the treadmill. The trend for consumption seems to be getting stronger. For example one survey showed that between 2005 and 2007, 62 percent of young people said they wanted lots of money, compared to 48 percent in 1976 to 1978. Ironically, the percentage that didn't want to work hard also went up, from 25 percent to 39 percent.[14] More recently, there is evidence that people in America increasingly recognize that money does not equate with happiness; however, this does not seem to stop people from still wanting more of it.[15]

Paralleling the attitude toward money is the role of work in American society. Americans simply work harder and longer than people in other countries that are comparable in terms of living standards. A study by consultancy Mercer found that many countries in Europe give employees between five and six weeks off a year when one combines vacation with holidays. American executives are often visibly taken aback when they discover that most of Continental Europe shuts down in August. Americans do not have any nationally defined legal requirements for holidays at all. The norm is for people to start with two weeks' vacation, which then gradually increases with tenure.[16] But even then, it's common to see an unexpressed cultural pressure for *not* taking one's full leave in many firms. Americans are not unique in this attitude. Mercer found that many Asian countries had a similar attitude to holiday leave. But what distinguishes American culture is that, relative to its wealth, people work much longer and have far fewer holidays than say, Scandinavians, whose income levels match American wages.

What explains this attitude toward money and work? An obvious point is that one of the main reasons that many historically chose to leave everything and everyone they knew behind was because of a burning desire for economic betterment. All voluntary migrant communities show this enhanced drive for material success; the only difference is that America is globally unique in terms of the extent to which it is composed of such groups. Collectively, this creates a critical mass of people who are unusually focused on material advancement as the lens through which personal success and the success of others is evaluated. The second reason is that both the Puritans and Quakers had a deeply held view that honest work was a religious duty and the basis for one's compact with God. Idleness broke this relationship and constituted a sin rather than being a personal choice one made between work and leisure. The notion of salvation through work was embedded in the early fabric of American culture, especially in the north.

The work ethic shows itself in many features of American life. Global leaders who attend Harvard Business School are frequently shocked at the level of effort and application that the programs require. "I was expecting to be worked hard, but did not think I would get hardly any sleep for three weeks!" exclaimed one executive, used to the more relaxed tempo of European college life. Harvard was set up by the early Puritan community in New England, barely a decade after their arrival. The Harvard laws of 1643 and 1700 established the new college as a highly disciplined center of learning and virtually all of its early leaders, although curiously not the first president, who was quickly removed, were Puritans. They instilled a strong and rigorous work ethic that still lives on today. Yale was itself founded by dissenters from Harvard who felt that its Puritanical values were not being enforced strictly enough.

While some like Freud might hypocritically view American materialism and the work ethic that accompanies it as unbalanced, there is another side to the coin. The honest and direct relationship that Americans have with money perhaps creates a straightforwardness around the material impulse that other cultures seek to airbrush. American organizational culture's no-nonsense focus on end goals also encourages an honest clarity about business life—and, for good or ill, this orientation shows up in many places. In our research 45 percent of American executives had strengths around commercial thinking, the highest score out of all regions, with the exception of the Middle East. In the Globe survey, Americans achieved one of the highest scores out of 62 countries surveyed on performance orientation.

In researching value dilemmas, Charles Hamden-Turner and Fons Trompenaars asked global executives what they would do with an employee who had served a company exceptionally well for 15 years, but whose performance had deteriorated, and was unlikely to improve. The options were "Dismiss the employee regardless of age and previous record" or "Show understanding and tolerance and take previous contribution into account." Over 75 percent of Americans were happy to fire the underperforming individual at once. The figures for European executives ranged from 30 to 40 percent. However, only 20 percent of Japanese or Korean executives were prepared to bite the bullet in this way.[17]

Of course, the gravitational pull of money and the unrelenting demand for even more time and commitment at work can have some corrosive implications. We see an underlying sense of guilt that one is not doing enough—or that you have dared to go for lunch when you could have been doing even more work—emerge in many leaders during coaching. Underneath the commitment to work bubbles a resentment born of the fact that real wages have barely moved for the vast bulk of the working population for decades, while they have skyrocketed for those at the top. This unexpressed resentment can hinder productivity, and many leaders from outside the United States complain of a culture of *presenteeism*—that is, physically showing up on the job but not fully performing. The over-reliance on money as a motivator can also make American leaders neglectful about tapping into other sources of drive or recognizing that the motivational calculus of people in other parts of the world is different. The fear of losing a bonus or one's job can also make American workers more compliant and less inclined to challenge corporate orthodoxy than one might expect given the directness that is also a feature of American culture. Often this directness is much more evident in external or downward dealings than in upward internal relationships.

American lawyer Thomas Geoghegan was surprised when he went to Europe, and saw the lifestyle and working conditions that people enjoyed there. This turned to shock when he calculated that, once social benefits and shorter working hours were taken into account, Americans were barely better off. This prompted him to write a book, *Were You Born on the Wrong Continent?*, to tell his country folk the sorry truth about their reality.[18]

More broadly, as Kenneth and William Hoffer point out in their book *The Puritan Gift*, American business has come to be dominated by Taylorist number-counting experts and finance men over the past hundred years—a trend that is only just being reversed.[19] Experts in the science of business rather than people have come to dominate corporations, reducing whole areas of industry, such as car making, to a shell of their former selves. Interestingly, this numbers-driven approach also applies to many American sports, where there is often an intensive focus on a plethora of statistics. The money motive untamed has also led to a crash in not just the value, but also global reputation, of many firms on Wall Street. I argued in my last book,

Meaning Inc., that the future belonged to firms that thought more widely about their purpose, were passionate about their people, and were led by those who had more than a passing interest in the products they were delivering for customers. The money motive untamed can ride roughshod over these sources of strength. Some of America's most successful companies, such as many Silicon Valley stars, owe their success to putting the money-people in their rightful place and behind those who care about the product.

However, a significant feature of the pursuit of material success in America is that it is balanced by an equally strong countervailing moral drive. This itself is an expression of the moral and religious sentiments of many founding communities. The psychoanalyst Clotairer Rapaille has also argued that "money as proof" is what drives the materialist impulse in American society. That is, it does not matter for its own sake but as proof of worthiness. The way in which you have acquired money, therefore, counts. Inheriting it or illegitimately earning it does not cut any ice. Once you have demonstrated proof, you can also give the money away as it has served its function.[20] So while American leaders can be highly results oriented and not shy about pushing for enormous packages, they also outdo executives from just about anywhere in terms of their philanthropy. Nationally, the United States is also extremely generous. Few countries in history have resisted the temptation to economically milk defeated nations after victory. The Americans by contrast poured huge amounts of money into Europe and Japan following World War II, and have done so with many other countries more recently.

In fact, a dynamic interplay between materialistic and moral forces has been the motor behind many significant events in American political and corporate history. The Unionists and Confederates, the robber barons and the antitrust drive, prohibitionists and bootleggers, the Great Depression and the New Deal are all reflections of this interplay. While all cultures experience a tension between moral concerns and materialistic values, a distinctive feature of American cultural DNA seems to be the *intensity* with which these two drivers intermingle—at times supporting and at other times opposing each other.

This moral countervailing force is significantly focused on levelling the playing field for all actors in the economic sphere. It also finds distinct expression in the legalization of many areas of life that other cultures seek to manage more informally or through relationships. Strict rules around equality of treatment and fairness at work, including a strong sense of political correctness, arise from this tendency. The sue at a drop of a hat attitude of some Americans, and a tendency for juries to award exorbitant damages, are also a natural consequence of the legalistic expression of morality in the context of a highly materialistic culture.

After having let the materialistic genie run riot for a few decades, the pendulum is swinging back once again in American today—and the moral legalistic countervailing forces are reasserting themselves, on a variety of fronts. External scrutiny and regulation are now one of the chief areas of focus for American leaders. The moral backlash, not just against Wall Street, but also big corporations, corrupt politics, and the power of big money in all walks of life is now once again bubbling to the surface as it has done before on many other occasions. This modern taming of mammon is a trend that all business leaders operating in the country will need to adjust to and appropriately support.

The Triumph of Functionality

When one visits America, one is struck by how well everything works and is designed to make life easy. Vast and broad highways dominate the landscape; the supremacy of getting people quickly to where they want to go overrides everything. Expansive shopping malls make parking and shopping so much easier than in typical European city centers. The bars, eateries, and cafes in America typically operate with efficiency to provide you with good food and service. A lot of things in America are designed to get you from *A* to *B*, whether this represents geographical movement, nourishment, and rest in a hotel room, or the satisfaction of any other basic human need.

There is, however, another side of the coin to this functionality. Virtually all the people I know who love America are themselves intrinsically practically minded, efficient, and purposeful individuals. Invariably, those who have a more aesthetic bent and a greater drive for things to look and feel good find America less enticing. Although Americans may not recognize it, outsiders tend to experience an overwhelming and pervasive sense of *functionality* triumphing over aesthetics. Whether it is design of airports, freeways, buildings, hotel rooms, restaurants, or everyday objects such as fridges, irons, washing machines, American versions just seem less aesthetically pleasing. Did someone in America once get a bulk discount on sepia-tinged paint? Because much of the country seems to be enveloped by these somber tones.

The roots of this functional approach to life lie in the same factors that were posited for the material impulse in American culture. The drive to improve one's life in a concrete and pragmatic manner was, and continues to be, an important motivator for migration to the country. Furthermore, a core tenet of Puritanism and many of the other early religious denominations centered on decrying an excessive focus on form over substance in all walks of life. Simplicity, a focus on the basics, and a suspicion of flowery show or adornment were early values within American culture. The task of creating a functioning industrial society from scratch in an incredibly short space of time inevitably also favored a functional and practical approach to life.

This triumph of functionality has a pervasive impact on business culture. In particular, it leads to a strong practical focus and a results orientation. A full 40 percent of American executives exhibited strength around action-oriented thinking in our assessments, the highest of all regions studied. Americans get to the point fast in business and can be frustrated by cultures that are more elliptical in their mode of operating. American corporate culture also favors brevity with respect to presentation. Business books in America usually include readily accessible lists of practical tips that one can imbibe without necessarily bothering with the less useful—that is, longer—bits. The European luxury of exploring a topic for its own sake generally lands poorly in the American context.

A values dilemma that Charles Hampden-Turner and Fons Trompenaars posed for executives focused on exploring their fundamental view of an organization. Respondents were asked to choose between two views: "A company is a system for performing functions and tasks in an efficient way" or "A company is a group of people working together, the functioning of which is dependent on these relationships." About 75 percent of American executives chose the first option, while 30 percent of Asian leaders and 40 to 50 percent of Europeans shared this view. This fundamentally different perspective has an enormous impact on how just about everything in business works and arises ultimately from the functional orientation of American cultural DNA.

Functionality does not just influence how things look or how businesses operate; it's also evident in the way people speak. Americans typically use language in a direct, pragmatic, and no-nonsense manner, as a funtional tool for communication. This different attitude toward the use of language is only really appreciated by those who have had substantial experience outside of America. Catholic priest Dwight Longinecker spent close to 25 years living outside of the United States and he commented upon his return:[21]

> *I do love my home country and I'm glad to be back. However, there is a certain aspect of America that I still find difficult. It is a vague and uncertain quality; something I have never heard defined before but I think I can give it a name: literalness. America the literal … the English use language as a poem, even when they are being practical, the Americans use language as a tool, even when they are being poetical. This is what I mean about the literalness of America.*

I remember being struck by this difference when studying at Oxford. I was friends with a number of Americans and watched some of them perform in debates. The English approach was to try and entertain the audience, be creative, witty, and ironic. Losing elegantly was considered something of a triumph. The Americans meanwhile had been competitively schooled in debating and taught to make as many points for their view as quickly as possible in a machine-gun-like manner. This literal approach was a shock to the English and rarely led to the expected victory for the Americans, who often felt perplexed at having lost out to wacky individuals advancing flimsy and insubstantial arguments. The widespread view that Americans "do not do irony well" may also arise from this functional approach to language.

While this functionality means that many things work in a simple and straightforward manner, the lack of attention to aesthetics, or the importance of other aspects of life, can also lead to problems when Americans engage the rest of the world. American products can struggle in the global marketplace in areas where aesthetics or other nonfunctional attributes are valued. For example, American manufactured products such as cars, washing machines, or kitchen appliances tend to travel less well globally than their German or Italian counterparts. American business culture itself can also sometimes be experienced as lacking in soul or insufficiently attentive to the human elements.

However, when the world wants fast food or coffee delivered efficiently, it is often American firms that are favored. Even the success of Google, Amazon, and Facebook arises in no small part from the simplicity and ease with which customers can access their services. Brands, like Apple, which combine superb functionality with elegant, admittedly British-driven design, become world-beaters. However, this combination is not seen as frequently as one might expect. Aesthetics and design sense are also much more prevalent in the outward facing areas of America such as New York, California, and Miami rather than in the core. Marrying functionality with these influences is likely to be a powerful strategy for American firms' ability to engage global consumers as they become more discriminating in their tastes.

Increasing Plurality

While American cultural DNA has strong tendencies around assimilating people to clear, overarching values, these norms themselves have built-in acceptance of diversity. American politics are also diverse, at least when compared with many European countries. No European country has had a nonwhite leader. Additionally, the exceptional success of many new migrant groups, such as the Indians, Lebanese, Nigerians, Iranians, and various Far Eastern groups, attests to the fundamental openness of American society. As Amy Chua and Jed Rubenfeld mention in their book *The Triple Package*—while there is sound recent evidence that upward mobility has declined for many sections of American society, it is alive and kicking for many of America's new minorities.[22]

The roots of this acceptance of diversity have already been alluded to earlier. The plurality of groups escaping persecution that constituted the early founder communities were never going to be that inclined to throw their weight around over others. Independence and freedom from suppression was what drove them abroad, not power over others. Similarly, as other groups joined the melting pot, their early experiences of being outsiders made them broadly accepting of others that came later. The American sense of comfort with radical change has also helped the country cope with its constantly evolving plurality. There is much greater wariness toward outsiders in Europe, China, or the Middle East, for example, driven in part by fear of change.

A kind of communitarian individualism is also apparent in American cultural DNA. That is a fundamentally individualistic psychology, bounded by defined communities that one was either born into or has chosen to join voluntarily. Americans can be both conformist and highly individualistic at the same time; that is, they can conform when in a group to which they have bonded, but be highly individualistic if not committed, or when breaking an allegiance to find something new. This is different from the free-for-all individualism one sees in parts of Europe. Outsiders can also find America difficult to penetrate socially if they do not fit into a natural group and be surprised by the drive for conformity they find in people.

In U.S. business, this plurality leads to a greater diversity of leadership than one typically sees in other cultures. American companies today can be led by all manner of nationalities. In 2014, four of America's most iconic companies, including Microsoft and Pepsi-Cola, had Indian-American CEOs. Hispanics, African-Americans, Lebanese, Asians, and various European nationalities are all increasingly visible at senior levels in U.S. multinationals. This gives many American companies a great edge in the global market place, as people see partial reflections of their own culture when dealing with them. Going forward, this will also help American companies to moderate their natural tendency to simply roll out the American model when venturing abroad.

It also gives rise to a much greater internal variability within the United States than many from outside expect, given the relatively uniform projection of American culture externally. The Human Resources Director of Tesco Clare Chapman, felt that one of the reasons for the lack of success of their Fresh & Wild model in the United States was that "We completely underestimated the variability within America." The formula was extensively researched in and around the Los Angeles area. However, even expansion to northern California, Arizona, and Nevada threw up big differences in consumers' tastes and predilections. Similarly, organizational cultures can vary tremendously between regions, especially when one gets below the surface. The different settlement histories of individual states create distinctive micro cultures everywhere. The parochialism of American local papers and the lack of a significantly dominant national newspaper are reflective of this fractionation.

This plurality gives the United States great strengths in the new, emerging multipolar world. It also gives the country the feel of a dynamic cauldron of ideas and approaches. However, there is also a price to be paid for this increasing plurality. Compared to many other cultures, the ever greater lack of a dominant cultural frame means that relations between communities have to be regulated by something other than a common and shared set of values. Step forward the legalism of American culture, which seems to be designed to fill this vacuum. This legalism has become more and more pronounced over time and is now a source of considerable bureaucratic delay and for what outsiders see as a ridiculously overregulated culture of control in many aspects of life.

A second issue is the increasing difficulty, as the plurality of communities grows, of different parts of the whole to find common ground. The United States is now more politically polarized than ever before. Legislative gridlock and an increasingly shrill dialogue that completely bypasses the other point of view is a natural consequence. The tendency of parts of the whole, such as the business community, to pursue their own interests at the expense of the wider good is another. Extracting the value out of plurality, while reducing its harmful effects, has always been an acute tension within the U.S. mindset, but more recently the task has got a whole lot more difficult.

Looking Ahead

Many of the themes implicit in the American mindset combine to create a culture of change makers—which is perhaps the country's greatest gift to the world. Positivity, tolerance of plurality, preparedness to take risk, pragmatism, and indeed the emotional desire to find and believe in something new, all combine to create a deep-seated tempo and dynamism around change. This gives American companies a great edge in the fast-moving world of global business. The country's openness to talent from around the world also means it has a natural self-corrective mechanism for ensuring that it evolves and stays relevant as new powers emerge.

However, Americans would benefit from stepping back and looking at themselves from the outside as others might see them. This would make the country less complacent about the quality of people's lives and the environment more generally. For all the self-help literature that abounds, Americans do not always pause to take a deep and authentic look at themselves—and they will need to do so as they enter a more emotionally complex era. Many questions could be neglected when the country was surging forward, but now deeper reflection—that moves beyond the default option of positivity— is required.

Most importantly, in order for American business and the country itself to prosper in a multipolar world, U.S. citizens will need to curb their tendency to assimilate everything to domestic frames of reference. Psychologically, the future will also require the country to develop a greater capacity to live in a world of greys rather than absolutes. The tendency to withdraw when the world cannot be engaged on its own terms has always been a strong default option within the United States. In response to the economic crisis, many American firms, as well as investors, have chosen to pull back from their global ambitions and focus instead on home. The same may happen with respect to the country's willingness to be, and pay the price of being, the global policeman. Developing the capacity to engage the wider world flexibly, leveraging its plurality even more, and exercising both economic and military power thoughtfully and with an understanding of other people's perspectives will be necessary if America is to avoid the disappointments that may naturally lead to another cycle of drawing away.

Yet despite these questions, the United States has much deep strength in its cultural DNA to draw upon in response to future challenges. In fact, the capacity to change is a meta strength that equips the country for many things that the future might throw its way. The speed with which the country has bounced back from the global financial crisis or the rapidity with which the world's energy market has been transformed by American shale production are two examples of the distinctive U.S. ability to confront issues through embracing radical change. Those who write off America as last century's superpower underestimate the sheer capacity of the country to reinvent itself.

Chapter 2

Sub-Saharan Africa: Under Nature's Shadow

The external perceptions of Sub-Saharan Africa are in a state of flux. In the past, affection for the evocative beauty of the continent and the vibrancy people show in their daily lives has coexisted with the view that this part of the world is hampered by horrendously corrupt governance, vicious diseases, intractable tribal conflict, and, as a consequence of all these and many other problems, stagnant economic performance. These negative feelings in people's minds are corroborated by graphic images of poverty, the unpredictable behavior of some African leaders, and many other disturbing vignettes. Internally, the soaring hopes that people had following the independence of various African countries almost without exception hit the brick wall of reality a long time ago. Much of the writing of notable post-independence African authors, such as Chinua Achebe, Wole Soyinka, and Ayi Kwei Armah focuses on surfacing and exploring this collective sense of disappointment.

Yet as investment bankers would say, the stock of Sub-Saharan Africa is on something of a rebound. Many countries on the continent have astonished the outside world by delivering robust economic growth and improvements on a range of indicators. In recent years, countries such as Rwanda and Ghana have been some of the fastest growing economies globally—all of which is helping to lift millions out of poverty. On many indices of human development Africa has shown robust forward movement. Slowly and surely, governance standards are also improving. While this is often a "two steps forward, one step back" process, it *is* nevertheless progress. More broadly, there is a shift in the confidence of the region. Long used to feeling on the back foot and patronized by the outside world, there is a spring in the step of people in many parts of the continent.

And the outside world has noticed. Fund managers who piled into the BRIC (Brazil, Russia, India, and China) emerging economies in the last decade are increasingly extolling the virtues of Sub-Saharan Africa. The West, China, and India are all now competing ferociously for economic opportunities on the continent. While this looks like a version of the scramble for Africa that the European powers engaged in long ago, this interest is not all about capturing African mineral or energy resources. It is also about meeting the needs of the new African consumers. Furthermore, Africa is not just waiting for outsiders to help take it forward. Long dependent on global companies for any large-scale economic activity, Africa is now producing its own successful enterprises in fields as diverse as telecommunications, brewing, and food manufacturing.

People with direct experience of Africa have always had a sense of the drive, dynamism, and desire for progress that many countries show. Long used to staffing their businesses with expatriates, multinationals are now moving to Africanize their leadership. In the past, the head of the Africa region for a multinational company tended to be a quixotic, somewhat semi-detached figure who would occasionally be seen in a safari suit at HQ trying to persuade skeptical senior executives on the merits of the opportunities that existed on the continent. Today, the leader of the African region often sits on the operating board, being seen as central to achieving the company's targets and exuding a degree of swagger flowing from the delivery of positive results.

Africa is therefore no longer a marginal outlier or a footnote on the world stage for national governments or companies as they pursue their global ambitions. As the continent gets integrated, though, questions about the cultural DNA of the continent assume greater significance. Is this resurgence just a dead-cat bounce driven by a global resourcing boom whose impact will dissipate as some of Africa's traditional problems resurface? Why is the continent still plagued by bad governance, internal violence, and tribal conflict? Will Africa's educational institutions and people-development strategies produce talent at the pace required? A lot of these questions assume that Africa's future lies in absorbing external values.

However, we can also pose more positive questions. What can we learn about how to live life and relate to each other from Sub-Saharan societies? Why is the sense of joy so evident in Africa missing from many other parts of the world? How can businesses harness the creativity and entrepreneurialism with which people live their day-to-day lives?

The answers to these questions require a deep understanding of the psychological DNA of the continent and the factors that have driven this DNA. This also requires us to turn back history and understand how Africa was populated by modern humans, as well as seeing the distinctiveness of the challenges that people who live on the continent have long faced. This requires us to go back much further in time with Africa than with any other region of the world.

How Modern Humans Populated Africa

In his thoughts on the origins of our species, Charles Darwin speculated that the first humans most likely arose in Africa. This was not a popular view in Victorian England where the need to justify the colonial oppression of other races led, almost unquestioningly, to the assumption that Europe must have been the source of such a dramatic evolutionary shift of gears. Ever the rationalist, but a cautious one, Darwin did not retract his views but neither did he press his point—he had stirred up enough controversy already.

Finds in Kenya show the presence of modern humans around 180,000 years ago. In no other part of the world do we find evidence of modern humans anywhere close to this date. In fact, although there was a small colony that died out in the Middle East 115,000 years ago, the first sustained movement of people out of Africa only occurred 70,000 years ago. The mitochondrial DNA evidence also suggests that all humans had a common ancestor—the approximate mutations clock dates this to about 200,000 years ago in Africa. The *Y*-chromosome evidence also points to a common male ancestor in Africa around the same period.

The African continent has a dozen or so mitochondrial DNA lines and has far greater genetic diversity than any other region in the world. In fact, Africa has more genetic diversity than the rest of the world put together. Much of this diversity parallels linguistic boundaries; there are over 2,000 ethno-linguistic groups in Africa. In fact, the continent contains a third of the world's languages. This diversity is another piece of evidence that points to an African origin for modern humans, as genetic diversity decreases the further one gets from any source population of a species. However, other features of the African landscape have also helped preserve this extensive differentiation—and this diversity has had a major impact on African cultural DNA.

Subsequent genetic analysis of African populations, in particular by Sarah Tishkoff and her colleagues, indicates that there are nine ancestral clusters in Africa that are closely related to modern linguistic divisions.[1] Mitochondrial analysis is helpful in outlining how Africa was populated. The original mitochondrial line is referred to as *L1*, and this is the source of all lines anywhere. There is debate as to where *L1* arose—southern Africa is a possibility. However, it appears that East Africa was the place where the line expanded and there was a movement of *L1* to central Africa and back possibly to southern Africa about 120,000 years ago. About 100,000 years ago another divergent line appears, *L2*, probably also in East Africa. *L2* populations moved to western and central Africa 30,000 to 70,000 years ago. Yet another line, *L3*, also seems to have arisen between 70,000 and 100,000 years ago in East Africa and is now spread throughout Africa. One offshoot of *L3* is the source line for all humans outside of Africa. The *Y*-chromosome data are consistent with a movement of people out of East Africa into other parts of the continent, as well as a splinter group moving out to populate the rest of the world.

The above population movements spread hunter-gatherers throughout the continent. Remnants of these populations, such as the Khoisan of South Africa and the Hadsa and Sandawe of Tanzania, remain dotted about Africa. However, later movements have predominantly shaped modern African population structures. About 15,000 years ago some of the humans who left Africa and settled in the Middle East started to feel the pull of their original home and returned in small waves, mixing with local inhabitants, and bringing their agricultural and herding technologies. Five out of the 14 population clusters identified by Sarah Tishkoff have Saharan or Middle Eastern connections. However, these intruders from the north seemed to know that the desert or semidesert was their natural abode and did not penetrate deeply into Sub-Saharan Africa. Jared Diamond, author of *Guns, Germs, and Steel*, argues that this north–south challenge in Africa, associated with dramatic shifts in the ecological environment, was a major barrier to the diffusion of agriculture.[2] In much of Eurasia, it was relatively easy for agricultural innovations to move along an east–west axis. The crops that fueled the agricultural revolution in the Middle East, such as wheat and barley, struggled in the tropics, while the domesticated animal livestock found African wildlife just too ferociously wild.

It was left to people who had developed agriculture locally to settle the Sub-Saharan regions and force the hunter-gatherer populations into niche environments deep in the tropical rain forests or the interior of deserts in the south. About 5,000 years ago on the Nigerian–Cameroon border, an agricultural people who had mastered the art of cultivating yams, oil-bearing palms, and perhaps also bananas arose. Around 3,000 years ago these early African agriculturists started to expand eastward and to the south. On their eastern journey they picked up cereal cultivation and cattle rearing, as well as iron technology. Around 1,000 years ago this expansion gained momentum and in one of the most rapid replacement movements of all time, Bantu speakers pushed into much of Sub-Saharan Africa, replacing or interbreeding with the existing hunter-gatherers. Today there are over 500 Bantu-related languages, such as Swahilli, Shona, and Zulu, spoken in different parts of Africa. However, as this multitude of languages suggest, regional diversity was preserved despite this replacement movement. As well as bringing new agricultural techniques, this Bantu sweep was responsible for the diffusion of a number of specific cultural practices and values throughout Sub-Saharan Africa.

Nature's Crucible: The Forces Shaping Africa's Cultural DNA

The way that humans populated the continent points to a variety of factors that have affected African cultural DNA. The first point is that

Africa is our natural home. Nearly two thirds of the 200,000 years or so that modern humans have been around was spent in our African homeland. There is therefore a bit of Africa—and potentially quite a large bit—in all of us. In the accounts of business leaders, certain themes emerge with some persistence and regularity with respect to different parts of the world. When it comes to Africa, people posted there come up with things like "Africa gets under your skin," or "Africa touches your heart," or "Africa gets into your blood like nowhere else." Perhaps we react in this way because at some level it is actually true—Africa *is* in our blood.

The prevailing consensus is that it was either in east Africa or southern Africa, rather than the west of the continent or the central tropical rain forests, where modern humans first burst onto the scene. Certainly, all modern humans outside of Africa can trace back their origins to east Africa, as this was the jumping-off point for the original global beachcombing jaunt that our ancestors embarked upon 80,000 years ago. When researchers look at the kind of climates and landscapes that people prefer, regardless of whether they live in the freezing tundra of Iceland or in the Saudi Arabian desert, there tends to be a bias toward landscapes and temperatures that prevailed and still exist in east Africa.

While our African origins can help explain, in part, our landscape and climate preferences, a more important point in terms of influence on psychological DNA is that East Africa is the place where modern humans spent two thirds of their time since coming on the scene. This is in substantial measure where we evolved our natural instincts. While some of those who left Africa also found environments that were relatively suitable for humans, others did not. They found themselves, or rather chose to fight for an existence, in places like the Arabian Desert, the Tibetan highlands, or the freezing wastelands of northern Europe and Siberia. The natural instincts that served us well in our original homeland would undoubtedly have needed to be modified in these unfamiliar and strange settings. I will argue that this critical fact helps explain some important features of African cultural DNA, most notably in areas such as attitude to controlling the environment, the use of power, and the approach to human relations.

A second significant feature influencing African cultural DNA is that there is much greater genetic diversity in Africa than in other populations. It is not surprising to find some elevation of variability at the home location of any species or subspecies that then goes on to inhabit broader territories, which is the case in Africa. Only one mitochondrial line out of 30 or so made it out of the continent. What is surprising is that studies of genetic diversity routinely find that there is more variability in Africa than the rest of the world put together. This is an astonishing fact, given that 6 billion of the 7 billion individuals populating our planet live outside Africa—yet it's true. This fact arises from the small founder population that set out from Africa to populate the rest of the world, but probably also due to some significant genetic bottlenecks that affected the early development of African humans, leading to a severe restriction on diversity that subsequent population growth was not able to overcome.

The impact of a high level of diversity has been accentuated by the heightened level of pathogen threat in Africa. The reasons that make Africa a hotbed of species origination and proliferation also make it a petri dish for pathogen creation—something that early European explorers discovered to their cost. Expedition after expedition into the interior was laid waste by a profusion of tropical diseases. It was not uncommon for parties of several hundred to be reduced to a handful within a few weeks of traveling. This eventually prompted Europeans to move to a model whereby they paid locals to go into the interior in search, for example, of slaves. Our ongoing arms race with invasive organisms has been one of the most powerful engines driving human evolution in the past. Recent research indicates, however, that this battle has also impacted social behavior and attitudes toward out-groups in certain cultures. Specifically, it appears that regions of the world with high pathogen threats developed cultural patterns that emphasized tight social bonding, avoidance of contact with external groups, and general suspicion and wariness toward those outside of one's circle.[3]

A consequence of both the preceding factors is that many other global cultures are more naturally set up for homogenization, with perhaps the exception of India, which also has a combination of high diversity and pathogen presence. These factors naturally lead to a push toward cultural fragmentation with smaller rather than larger units of social organization. Sure enough we find a profusion of clans and tribes in Africa, in many cases with distinct cultural and biological attributes. There are over 2,000 languages and ethnic groups in Africa, and loyalty and identification within these groups run deep. European colonizers took great care to understand these differences, and used this knowledge to play games of divide and rule. However, they were less careful about the way they left—and for the most part, headed for the exit doors in a disgruntled and unseemly rush. In many cases the Europeans left vast states that had suited them, but which pulled disparate ethnic groups into what people hoped would be a magical, new sense of nationhood. The Congo, for example, which is the size of Western Europe, has close to 250 ethnic groups and languages among its 80 million people. Nigeria has over 500 living languages within its borders. Many of the political and economic difficulties facing Africa stem, in part, from the imposition of artificial national structures on countries embodying extremely high levels of genetic and cultural diversity.

This presence of extremely high levels of diversity both between and within countries is also a common observation of business leaders operating on the continent. Doing business can vary enormously from place to place, perhaps more so in Africa than elsewhere. In addition, this means that the rotation of African leaders within the continent, which is increasingly being pursued as part of Africanization, is not always an easy process. It is not straightforward to transpose a Nigerian leader from one part of the country to another let alone to another country on the continent, without encountering some difficulties either of acculturation or acceptance. In terms of product acceptance, management style, and social orientation, Africa is a complicated mosaic of small groups.

A third broad factor that I believe has influenced African cultural DNA is perhaps less obvious. In spite of the fact that Africa is a natural home for us, this is not necessarily the same as it being an easy environment for humans. All the things that make Africa our original habitat also make it a welcoming home for an extremely diverse and varied range of plant and animal life. Ultimately, there is only one source of energy for the earth, and that is the sun. All other natural energy sources, such as oil and coal, are essentially forms for storing this energy in plant and marine life deposits. Africa quite simply gets more of this ultimate source of energy than most other places—unrelentingly so at times. Every day, more energy is pumped into Africa than just about any other part of the world. In places where water is not an issue, this has led to an explosion of plant life and a huge array of animal species—something that's evident in the lushness of the deep organic and earthy scents that hit you upon touching African soil.

Of course, this abundance creates challenges as well as opportunities. Beyond the obvious risk of pathogens and predators targeting humans, there is the sheer difficulty of holding back plant life—an ever-present threat, especially in tropical Africa, of everything turning into bush. It takes some work to clear a field in Europe, but not a Herculean effort to keep nature at bay thereafter. In many parts of Africa, this is a Sisyphean challenge and one that many people might be inclined to back away from. In terms of climate, the sheer energy that the sun pours onto the continent creates unpredictability and extremes. People living in cooler climates rarely have to worry about cyclones, hurricanes, or violent strong storms that can wash away everything before them.

It is often simpler to live with the power of nature than to try and control it when it comes at you with the energy and ferocity that Africa is able to conjure up. While northern Europe is a difficult environment for humans, it is challenging in a more predictable sense. Once one has worked out a way of living there, unforeseen daily events are unlikely to knock one's equilibrium. The unpredictability of life in Africa and the greater challenge of gaining control and retaining control of the environment are important elements of understanding the cultural DNA of the continent, especially around psychological attitudes toward time, mastery of the environment, and planning.

Another factor that has influenced African cultural DNA is the population dynamics that specifically arise from the unpredictability discussed above. Any species in the animal kingdom faces a fundamental choice when it comes to raising offspring for the next generation. What should the procreation strategy be? Should one raise large numbers of offspring and send them out into the world in the hope that at least some will survive? Or should one be more circumspect, produce fewer children, put more parental investment into care, and hope that a higher proportion survive? Biologists call these choices the *R–K spectrum* and argue that different ecological pressures influence where a species sits on this spectrum. Environments that are benign but unpredictable typically lead to a preference for R strategies. If you think your offspring do not require too much protection, but also feel that unforeseen, cataclysmic events could cause premature death, or the turn of fate could unleash a bountiful era of plenty, then it makes sense to put a lot of chips on the table. The reverse applies if high levels of investment are needed or the environment is inherently fairly predictable. Humans, unlike other species, can make conscious choices about these matters.

The pattern of a relatively benign but nevertheless highly changing and unpredictable environment is exactly what prevailed, and to some extent still prevails, in Africa today. Psychologist J. Philippe Rushton argues that Africans are culturally—as well as more controversially biologically—more R than Europeans who, in turn, are more R than East Asians.[4] Fertility rates support this view. For example, Niger tops the list of global fertility rates with an average of 6.86 children per woman. Nineteen of the top 20 countries in the world in terms of fertility rates are African. The only exception to this is Afghanistan, a country where one presumes years of endemic uncertainty and unpredictability have also led people to invest in having large numbers of children.

The fact that Africa has probably had historically and certainly today a population structure heavily skewed toward youth also impacts its cultural DNA. This pattern creates great vitality and is a potential source of future talent, consumers, and overall economic dynamism. However, a powder keg situation can arise when the energy and optimism of youth hit the brick wall of frustration that societies that are languishing economically deliver to many of their young people. The world's press circulates countless stories of armies of young children terrorizing many African countries, prone to casual and almost unthinking violence. The root cause of these armies may not be obvious, but it may lie deep in African DNA and the gravitational pull of certain life strategies, particularly, when times are uncertain and difficult. The value people place on life in Africa may also arise in part from this and not just the level of poverty on the continent.

These five factors—Africa being our natural home, huge levels of diversity, high pathogen threat, the sheer difficulty of predicting or controlling the environment, and the preference for R-life strategies—have driven many of the distinctive psychological themes within African cultural DNA. They have created profound strengths in the underlying psychology and culture in Sub-Saharan Africa, which are a source of hope for the continent. However, they also highlight some challenges that will need to be negotiated as Africa takes its rightful place in the world. There are many aspects of this DNA that others can learn from, and Africa has much more to teach the world than is commonly recognized.

Community and Beyond

The head of the African division of a major multinational once reported to me an experience that initially mystified him, but which helped him gain a deeper insight into African relationship culture. Given the growth in the African market and its future importance to the company, he was promoted to the top executive leadership team. When he made the announcement to his people, he noticed that the African leaders expressed an unusual level of personal pride and satisfaction at his elevation. They kept talking about it, went around with an extra spring in their step, and insisted on wanting to acknowledge it at gatherings. At first, the Managing Director thought they were just managing upward well—if not a little too enthusiastically. After a while, however, it dawned on him that in a very deep and profound way, the African managers felt that *they too* had been promoted. In this sense, they did not see a difference between the MD and themselves. His elevation was their success, too. He began to understand that one's identity in African culture does not stop and start at the individual level. Rather, a person exists wrapped in a deep set of relationships and connections with others. The idea of an individual being an island is an alien concept to the African psyche.

On the Hofstede dimension of individualism–collectivism, African societies typically score strongly as collectives—but not as collectivist as Far East societies. There is a subtlety here that simply rating societies on a single dimension fails to capture. The Globe study has two dimensions relevant to this area: in-group and institutional collectivism. The former refers to the strength of ties to one's immediate social circles and the latter to commitment to wider social and organizational institutions. African societies score highly on the first, but achieve some of the lowest scores globally on the second.

Michael Minkov's dimension of exclusionism versus universalism, which looks at how widespread one's relational net is thrown, is relevant here—as African societies are some of the highest in the world on exclusionism. This data and considerable experience on the ground indicate that Africans are typically highly collectivist in their immediate team and within defined groups and tribes, but much more wary of other groups or wider identification. So while the African exists in a world where he or she feels intimately connected with others—often to the point of not seeing themselves as an individual at all—beyond their immediate community lies a world that needs to be treated more cautiously; a world of strangers and potential threats from others.

Here the very opposite of common interest and collectivism operates. Due to the colonial creation of vast states with huge levels of tribal heterogeneity, the rapid growth of urban conurbations, and the increasing presence of cross-border multinational companies, this is the world into which many Africans have simply been catapulted without too much preparation. Not surprisingly, in comparisons of global levels of national trust—posing a question such as, "Generally speaking would you say that most people can be trusted or that you can't be too careful in dealing with people?"—African societies score among the lowest in the world. Typically, only 20 percent of people say they can generally trust others in African countries. By comparison, this figure is over 60 percent in the Nordic countries, 36 percent in the United States, and 38 percent and 52 percent, respectively, in India and China.

The reason for the existence of this tight in-group orientation, coupled with distance and suspicion of out-groups, lies in three aspects that strongly influence African cultural DNA. These include the extremely high level of genetic, linguistic, and cultural diversity that characterizes the African continent; high pathogen threat; and the relatively late introduction of settled agriculture, which has meant that the ensuing concentration and development of large-scale collectivist societies has occurred relatively late in many parts of Africa.

This sense of interdependence at the group level is evident in many business practices. In South Africa, in particular, the notion of *ubuntu*—a word that literally means humanness—is often emphasized in business but also in society more widely. The South African historian Michael Eze sums up the core of this philosophy: "A person is a person only through other people. We create each other and need to sustain this otherness together."[5] This sense of interdependence creates a strong emphasis on teamwork and the collective good of one's immediate group—which can lead to a strong drive to employ members of one's clan or tribe. Western leaders can regard this as nepotism without truly appreciating the strong sense of seeing one's identity as being part of a broader group that drives such behaviors. This is why many successful Africans who live away from their community typically downplay their achievements for fear of being inundated with requests for help.

The pressure to provide for others can also be the root cause of ethical violations in companies. A problem that small African entrepreneurs face when they set up business is that members of their community simply want whatever goods and services the business offers for nothing. An African manager once told me how his father's efforts at setting up a shop were ruined because he could just not bring himself to say no to the countless members of his extended family who descended on his shop wanting the products for free.

There is plenty of evidence for this community orientation in African leadership culture. Our own analysis found that a full 51 percent of African leaders have an identified strength around working with and developing their teams, compared with only 24 percent of European leaders and 25 percent of American leaders. There can also be a reluctance on the part of African business leaders to drive a decision unilaterally in their senior teams, however authoritarian they are in the wider organization. It's not uncommon to debate an issue until the group reaches consensus—even often over a prolonged period. This tendency shows up in our data, too. A full 25 percent of European leaders and 23 percent of American leaders had a development need around intellectual openness and inclusive thinking, a dimension that looks at how actively one engages other people's opinions when formulating views. Only 9 percent of African leaders had a development need in this area, the lowest score globally.

This orientation also has an impact on how performance is judged. Success is often pinned on individuals in Western business cultures—something that can make people in African business contexts feel uncomfortable. There is a natural inclination to see everything as a team outcome, which means that conversations on individual performance or lack of it have to be handled carefully. Gary Watson, a consultant based in South Africa who works across Africa on human resources-related areas, says:

> *Many African markets are characterized by individuals that strongly relate personal identity to group identity. People in Africa tend to shy away from direct confrontation in the workplace and holding an individual accountable in a public forum only results in a passive-aggressive response. Taking people aside, exploring reasons for failure, and offering assistance is far more effective than admonishing them or threatening them on an individual level.*

This sense of human interrelatedness is a deep source of strength in African culture more widely. When disease strikes parents down, other relatives or the wider community typically bring the bereaved children into their fold, looking after them as their own. If fortune smiles on the member of a community, it smiles on the whole community in a very tangible sense. A successful African is expected to take his or her community with them and to give and share without so much as thinking about it. African politicians, who do not mind taking the toughest of actions dealing with opposition to their regimes, frequently cannot bring themselves to remove members of their community who come to camp in the gardens of their mansions. In an analysis of power shifts in African societies, Michela Wrong reports how coups and regime change are rarely just an individual grab for power in Africa, but rather are seen as an opportunity for another tribe to enjoy the fruits of office: "It's our turn to eat now."[6]

However, the other side of the coin—lack of connection to wider entities—also has an impact. When individuals are catapulted into the wider world, other tendencies can take over. It can be tricky to move local managers around Africa because acceptance outside one's own community is only slowly learned. Whole departments can form an identity and then develop mutual wariness or hostility with other groups that have also forged an identity, often around clan or tribal lines. Consultants in our South African office report that African leaders are often at sea when it comes to forming close relationships at a distance, or knowing how to navigate relationships or exert influence in a global organizational structure. Some tend to treat outsiders from other parts of a company with wariness and simply tell them what they think they want to hear.

There are wider consequences, too. The failure of many African states to gel as a nation, the high levels of ethnic and intertribal violence, and the level of crime that exists in large African cities likely stem from this breakdown of identity, so dependent on relatedness, as people are catapulted into unfamiliar worlds.

One answer for organizations is to progressively broaden people's identification with the whole business—not just people's own narrow area. Starting first at the unit level and then broadening to country, regional, and global levels of identification takes time, but reaps considerable benefits eventually. It is also helpful to have people meet others outside their area for relatively prolonged periods of time to build trust. At the national level, interventions or symbolic actions that drive national rather than more local identification are necessary to activate the *ubuntu* mindset. However narrow people's points of reference, a sense of interrelatedness exists and is a diamond waiting to be polished and made relevant to the context that many Africans find themselves in now.

Naturalness: Expressed and Denied

As many multinationals have moved from an expatriate to a local model of leadership in Africa, they have sought to put in place more coherent programs for developing African talent. At the highest levels, this typically means giving high potential leaders the opportunity to go to HQ, typically in the United States or Europe for Western multinationals. While such rotations can be broadening, they are not without risk. Not infrequently something akin to a personality transplant can take place on the flight from Africa. Confident, outgoing, and emotionally open executives can suddenly go into their shells and become a pale shadow of their former selves, appearing lost and ill at ease in their new environment. Rather than turbocharging their career, such assignments can leave both parties with what is often an unexpressed sense of disappointment. This does not always happen; some executives land on their feet. However, this experience was so common for one company we worked with that they put such assignments on hold until they had worked out a better way of ensuring success.

The inner experience of engaging a wider organizational culture can be jarring for African leaders. Thinking that they are part of a welcoming family that will open up to them, some find the experience of the new culture socially off-putting. "I felt I had had a bucket of cold water poured over me and my first thought was these people are so unfriendly. I wondered what I had done wrong. Then people started to tell me to speak up and that confused me even more," one leader told me before dissolving into laughter about the whole experience of visiting HQ. Another African woman executive who had worked in the UK for some time said, "I just cannot get used to how cold people are ... this makes me seem cold in return."

These reactions make sense. Anyone who visits Africa will immediately notice the openness and warmth with which people go about their daily business. It becomes obvious just standing on any street corner in virtually any part of Africa that there is a different tone to the way people relate to each other. Greetings are typically effusive to the point of being melodramatic. Back slapping and physical contact is not only accepted but seems, in many instances, to be required. The overriding feeling that one gets in Africa is that laughter is everywhere. Indeed, the African division of one of our clients, Diageo (which has a big beverage business in Africa), identified *joy* as one of the distinctive features of life in Africa—and therefore one of the main themes that they acknowledge and seek to honor culturally within their African business.

However, this naturalness of emotional expression is only really evident when one sees Africans relating *to each other*. Those who arrive from the West are greeted with a certain wariness by locals. People may want to be open and warm but are not sure how you are going to take it. This can lead to caution until the rules of the game become clearer. Even a small joke, or sincere attempt at lightheartedness, releases a huge level of relief and helps almost instantaneously to ease and lubricate relationships. It serves as a signal that people can be themselves—an opportunity that is typically seized upon with enthusiasm and also relief. I've talked to many Africans who travel or who have migrated to Western countries. One of the most pervasive experiences that they describe is the jolting shock they feel when confronted with the reserved, restrained, and cool reaction of Europeans and Americans. This can put their naturalness drive in reverse and prompt a much more cautious approach to emerge.

There is tangible data to support these observations around restraint. Our analysis of African leaders working for the most part in multinational companies found that only 11 percent had an identified strength around emotional openness and authenticity, the lowest figure out of all regions globally, where comparative figures were in the 25 to 30 percent range. Surprisingly, the data indicated that African leaders tended to have low scores across a range of interpersonal qualities, the opposite of what we might have expected. Nearly 15 percent of African leaders were identified as having a development need around being engaging and building relationships easily, by far the highest figure globally. A full 21 percent were also identified as having a development need with respect to forming close, deep bonds. The figures for other cultures were in the 3 to 5 percent range with others. Thus, in global companies one sees the opposite of what one might expect standing on the streets of an African town.

Within Africa, there is evidence that this naturalness is an embedded aspect of the cultural values of many but not all African societies. In an extension of their original model, Hofstede and his team identified two additional dimensions in addition to their original four: one of these they termed *indulgence-restraint*. Societies high on indulgence were characterized by "a perception that one can act as one pleases, spend money and indulge in leisurely and fun related activities." High indulgence societies were also typically happier—and unsurprisingly, there was a tendency for wealthy societies to be higher on indulgence given the emphasis on leisure. Yet despite this, many African countries scored very highly on this dimension as well. Out of 93 countries, Nigeria was fourth highest, Ghana tenth, and South Africa twenty-fourth. Only three Sub-Saharan countries were below the world average; Rwanda, Zimbabwe, and Burkina Faso. These three exceptions illustrate the earlier point about this naturalness dimension; just as with executives dropped into Western settings, in conditions of perceived threat, it can go into reverse.

The naturalness of people on the continent is not only expressed in human relationships. The distinguished Polish journalist Ryszard

Kapuściński, who spent the bulk of his life writing about and reporting from Africa, witnessed the following scene after a man blew a
whistle in a street:

> *I couldn't believe my eyes. Instantly the street filled with people. In
> a matter of seconds they formed a large circle and began to dance.
> I don't know where the children came from. They had empty cans,
> which they beat rhythmically. Everyone was keeping the rhythm,
> clapping their hands and stomping their feet. People woke up, the
> blood flowed again through their veins, they became animated. Their
> pleasure in their dance, their happiness in finding themselves alive
> was palpable. Something started to happen in this street, around them,
> within them. The walls of the houses moved, the shadows stirred. More
> and more people joined the ring of dancers, which grew, swelled and
> accelerated.*[7]

The immediacy and vibrancy of many types of African music and
dance is reflective of this naturalness. So too is the natural creativity that one sees in the way people communicate. There is another
point to the episode described above: There is much less of a barrier
between the performer and the audience in Africa. The restrained,
passive, and somewhat wooden absorption of a piece of music or
theater—with the associated terror of inadvertently making a noise
or having one's phone go off that is so common in the West—is
alien in the African context. Performance is something people participate in actively, whether it is in a formal setting or on the street,
at church or at a work gathering. Even in cinemas, African audiences are not reticent about providing a running commentary on
the events unfolding onscreen or engaging in a one-way dialog with
the actors.

In communities with African roots outside of the continent, reactions to important events also exhibit this naturalness and theatricality.
The play acting that the sprinter Usain Bolt engages in before a critical race, as well as his trademark lightning bolt gesture following
victory, is not something that one would expect from, for example, a
Chinese sprinter.

One reason why naturalness might be a psychological theme
for Africans is relatively simple and straightforward—people in
Sub-Saharan Africa are more natural because their culture has
evolved in a part of the world to which we are at some level all

naturally suited. The roots of our emotional patterns and orientation toward relationships evolved in an African context. When we moved away from this context, we had to put more of a barrier between what we might naturally *want* to do versus what we actually *do*. Survival in the arid deserts of Arabia, the steppe lands of north Asia, or the frozen wastelands of northern Europe required an inevitable suppression of certain natural instincts. The everyday notion of warm and cold personalities captures this intuitive understanding.

There is another more recent aspect to explaining differences in this area. Hofstede's team noted that indulgence was highest in societies that had, until recently, been pre-agricultural and those that were post-industrial. Societies that had been or were still highly agricultural were highest on restraint. They argue that, because intensive agriculture requires strenuous work, discipline, and tight social organization, it offers limited opportunities for self-expression. Societies with a stronger legacy of hunter-gathering or horticulture are therefore less burdened by the psychological demands of intensive agriculture to which more advanced modern societies with service-dominated economies are reverting.

Increasingly, however, Africans face a challenge with respect to this aspect of their cultural DNA. The world is moving fast and changes that took place over thousands of years for people in some other parts of the world have been telescoped into a few decades for Africans. The disruptive shock is particularly acute for people from Africa who have migrated to more economically developed economies or executives who are thrown into the unfamiliar world of the multinational corporation. The sheer unfamiliarity of the environment pushes the naturalness engine into reverse, but the underlying yearning still exists. It is not unusual for people to resort to a behavioral pattern of repression, oscillating between periods in which control is released. A great deal of writing on the African or the Black experience in Western countries focuses on how pressure can build up inside people. This pattern was so apparent to author Ken Pryce when he examined the West Indian experience in Bristol, England, that he titled his book *Endless Pressure*.[8] The relatively high levels of mental illness, drug use, and crime levels found in many communities of African origin in the West may not simply be a reflection of poverty and socioeconomic status. They may also arise from tensions created by having to manage the drive for naturalness in environments where its expression may not be particularly well accepted or tolerated.

There are lessons for both international businesses operating in Africa as well as for local people themselves. Western businesses and schools, for example, can have a natural tendency to drive prescriptive behaviors that can feel overly suffocating for those whose cultural roots lie in African societies. Indian and Chinese leaders, coming as they do from societies with very high restraint scores, tend to find such pressures much easier to embrace. Businesses that operate in Africa itself can all too often create a culture that represses naturalness. Those like the firm Diageo—which embraces joy as a distinctive theme in its African operations—release more energy and creativity.

Multinationals could also do much more to support executives who move from African cultures to other regions to keep them from undergoing an aversive shock and retreating to their shells. As noted earlier, many African leaders operating in multinationals need help to ensure they show the best of themselves when managing relationships outside of their comfort zones. Overseas executives operating in Africa can also release energy and reduce pressure by simply modeling a lighter touch and being more expressive themselves. Executives from cultures where social restraint is more valued can fail to connect with locals because of this tendency, something that is already proving challenging for Chinese nationals operating in Africa.

More broadly, as African societies go into the next phase of intensive agriculture or industrialization, or encounter internal problems and tensions, one may see this attractive and appealing source of great creative potential in their cultural DNA decline. Hanging on to this naturalness is important for people's own sense of wellbeing, as well as for Africa's contribution to global culture. It is especially essential for releasing creativity, and for developing warmth in relationships—qualities that are profound sources of strength within African cultural DNA and that need to be nurtured rather than allowed to dissipate.

In the Moment

A while back executives at one of our pharmaceutical clients were taken on a trip to Kenya to help them understand how their company could cater to the distinctive needs of this important emerging market.

Part of the visit entailed visiting a hospital. Outside the hospital the executives noticed a number of ambulances in various states of disrepair. Some were badly dented, others had doors missing, and all seemed rusted and had flat tires, if they had wheels at all. The executives assumed that these were disused vehicles, perhaps cannibalized to ensure the operation of the main fleet.

While they were there, the hospital received a call that a young girl who lived some distance away had been burned in a domestic accident and needed to be brought to the hospital with urgency. At this point the executives realized that the dilapidated vehicles they had seen were not some disused discards waiting to be ferried to the scrap heap, but actually constituted the main fleet. The hospital workers set to work with gusto putting wheels and tires on one vehicle to enable it to function. It appeared that no one had had the foresight to prepare any of the vehicles for what clearly was not an unusual demand for an ambulance fleet. Although the executives were shocked by this demonstrable lack of planning, they were also deeply impressed by the speed with which a vehicle that had previously looked to be well past its sell by date was made serviceable and dispatched to collect the girl.

The above example illustrates a point. The sheer difficulty of controlling the environment in Africa—combined with the fact that failing to do so is not so immediately fatal as in some other environments—leads to an important dimension of African cultural DNA: living in the moment. In response to the challenges of a high energy, biologically prolific, and unpredictable environment that cannot be easily tamed, people on the continent have had good cause to develop an instinct for taking things one step at a time, "as they come." Planning for the future in a precise rather than more diffuse sense, has, at least in the distant past, been relatively more difficult in Africa than in many other parts of the world. People are more resigned to the vicissitudes of fortune and there is an internal acceptance of the futility of humble humans attempting to control the vigorous and rampant natural world around them. This promotes a stoic approach to life, deep resilience, and inherently high levels of day-to-day flexibility.

There is plenty of evidence for the idea that in the moment is a significant element in African cultural DNA. In our own analysis of leaders, 42 percent of African leaders were considered to have strengths around "intellectual flexibility," the highest score in the world. By comparison, only 16 percent of American leaders were considered strong in this area. However, 49 percent of African leaders were seen to have a development need around long-term strategic thinking, again the highest scores globally. By contrast, only 28 percent of American and 29 percent of European leaders were identified as having a development need in this area. Only 17 percent of African leaders were assessed to be strong in the area of strategic thinking. The comparable figures for American and European leaders were 24 and 29 percent, respectively.

The second of the dimensions that Hofstede's team added to their original four was *long-term–short-term orientation*, based on the Chinese Values Survey. In addition, Michael Minkov identified a similar dimension using the World Values Survey. While the precise nature of the constructs varies, African nations tend to score strongly toward the short-term end of the spectrum in all of them. For example, Ghana is the second most short-term oriented society out of 93 countries in the World Values Survey; Nigeria the fifth most and, out of the bottom 20 countries, 6 are in Sub-Saharan Africa. Using the Chinese Values Survey construct of long-term orientation, the only two Sub-Saharan countries out of 23 studied were Zimbabwe and Nigeria, which respectively scored fifth and second from bottom. Although a different construct, African societies also score very low on the Globe measure of future orientation.[9]

Experimental research going back over 50 years or so, predominantly in the United States, on the concept of delayed gratification—or in popular parlance, the marshmallow test—also alludes to such differences. In fact, the first study on the subject by Walter Mischel was in Trinidad where the researchers found huge differences between Black and Asian respondents, with the former much more likely to prefer a smaller reward now to a bigger one later.[10] Subsequent research has also tended to confirm this pattern. For example, African-American and Mexican 10-year-olds are much more likely to prefer $10 now to $30 in a month's time or a smaller present immediately to a bigger one in the future.[11]

Some researchers have tended to put value labels on these reactions without appreciating that a bird-in-hand strategy makes perfect sense in many unpredictable situations. Rather than being a fixed orientation, the perceived predictability of the environment influences people's behavior on such tests. For example, children will readily pick up if the experimenter seems unpredictable or unreliable, and start preferring immediate rewards. Indeed, in the very original study in Trinidad, the researchers found that black children from single parent families—where the father figure was presumably an unpredictable presence—were much more likely to make short-term choices. The notion of taking rewards now is also something many traders playing the chaotic uncertainties of financial markets would understand. Being a strong futures discounter is a perfect strategy in the highly volatile and unpredictable casino world of financial markets.

This African tendency for living in the moment is evident in many areas of life. Outsiders frequently express surprise and disappointment at the way buildings and amenities that have been created with considerable effort and expense are simply left to decay in many African countries. In business, maintenance of plants or the creation and implementation of structured approaches to planning or financial management also suffer. Richard Dowden, a journalist for *The Economist* who spent much time reporting on Africa, comments that when Africans handle machinery or appliances, they will use something until it gets broken and only then worry about repairing it. He does not see the concept of preventative maintenance as being strongly embedded in African culture. Ryszard Kapuściński observes that if a path or a small road is cleared and a tree falls across it, Africans will typically choose to walk around the tree until a new path or small road is created rather than removing the obstacle. In his writings of his life in Uganda, Paul Theroux describes how he was shocked walking through a park when his fellow novelist and mentor V.S. Naipaul remarked, "Some day all this will be bush." Theroux's accounts of Uganda on his return decades later are full of disappointment at what had happened to things he had cherished and remembered with affection—the library where most of the books were either mutilated or missing, broken doors and windows left unrepaired, and all manner of amenities left to decay in the face of the relentless march of nature.[12]

This is not to say that Africans do not work hard or care. Indeed, just about every observer of the continent sees huge levels of tenacity and resilience on the part of Africans in the face of incredibly difficult life conditions. It is simply that Africans are frequently wise enough to ensure that they expend energy and effort on managing for today as opposed to preserving, planning, or building for an uncertain tomorrow. And this tendency makes perfect sense given the environment that existed historically in much of Africa. Africans were not wrong to be pessimistic about controlling their environment. Rather they were being entirely realistic, adaptive, and flexible.

The unpredictability and futility of controlling the environment has also had a profound influence on the value attached to time in African culture. If you are trying to live in harmony with your environment or trying to escape the vicissitudes of fortune, time at one level becomes less important—or more accurately, is only important for people who have a linear goal in mind, who want to impose themselves on their environment, or change their surroundings in a systematic manner. For such individuals—which is most of us in the modern world—this desire to achieve something or go somewhere means that time is a precious resource measured out, to use T. S. Eliot's language, in coffee spoons.

African philosopher John Mbiti believes that the orientation toward time in Africa is fundamentally rooted in the presence and absence of events rather than having an independent existence; that is, time passes only when events occur. So, if nothing happens, then no time has passed. In Mbiti's view this leads to an orientation toward time in which there is "a long past, a present, and virtually no future." In this context, future events are only anticipated in as much as they fall within the rhythm of natural phenomenon, such as daily fluctuations or the ebb and flow of the seasons.[13]

The relaxed approach to time is evident everywhere in Africa. People will happily wait for an inordinate amount of time for a bus to fill up for its journey or for a car to be fixed. A colleague who lives in South Africa and runs leadership workshops across the continent finds that the starting time for the workshops is something of a lottery, dependent on when people decide to arrive. As a consequence, she routinely plans to begin two or three hours after the stated start time. Although people working in Western businesses are acculturating fast, it's not unusual for even a senior African business leader to simply not turn up for an arranged meeting, sometimes without subsequent apology or explanation. These experiences— understandably frustrating for Westerners—make complete sense if you don't have an attitude toward time as a precious resource. Paul Theroux notes that there is no word for hurry in Swahili, and that reference to such notions is typically made through words borrowed from Arabic. In his description of his journey across the continent, from Egypt to South Africa, he remarks, "Sometimes it seems as though Africa is a place you go to, to wait."[14]

The in-the-moment mindset creates issues for international businesses operating in Africa, and it's often necessary to reset one's expectations. The natural desire to create tight plans of action can seem theoretical and insufficiently pragmatic to African leaders who are aware of the unpredictable and unreliable context in which they operate. Embracing both patience and flexibility is helpful to leaders from outside. Giving local leaders the freedom to achieve things in their own way and to exercise their considerable creativity and capacity to pull rabbits out of the hat is also helpful. As an executive running a plant told me, "I know it can cause you to have a heart attack, but sometimes you just have to rely on things happening at 1 minute to 12." The instinct for structure and controls, while necessary in some areas, needs to be managed carefully so as not to slowly suffocate a business.

Westerners tend to regard the African attitude toward time and environmental control as something that needs to be corrected. But does it? The modern, fast moving, and unpredictable world of global business is coming to resemble the original African ecological environment more and more. Intellectual flexibility, creativity, and intuitive responses to new events are necessary for agility. Many Western executives can appear lead-footed in the face of such demands. African cultural DNA is ideally suited to these challenges. Rather than trying to squeeze their African leaders into Western straitjackets, many companies would do well not only to tolerate, but also learn from their African colleagues. The mindset also gives Africans tremendous levels of resilience in the face of what life throws their way. Virtually all the overseas executives one speaks to on the continent will comment on the daily resilience and flexibility Africans exhibit in the face of death, disaster, political turmoil, and all manner of other challenges.

There is another point, too. In the West, we try to squeeze as much as we can out of our day and worry about time slipping through our fingers. In short, we march to its tune. This creates a gnawing feeling that hangs around us, a constant worry that somehow we are not making the best use of our time. Treating time as valuable may help one achieve more than one would otherwise—but does it lead to greater fulfillment? Certain instincts toward achievement and time were necessary for many non–African populations in order to succeed in the novel and unfamiliar environments in which they found themselves. But now that we have successfully dominated our environment in most parts of the world, does it not make sense, at least partially, to revert to the more relaxed African attitude toward time?

This is not to say that the African approach toward time or living in the moment does not require adaptation either. Planning appropriately, valuing time, and recognizing the knock-on effects of one's actions on other people's plans are becoming increasingly necessary in the emerging African economy. Judging where it is appropriate to adapt and where one just has to recognize the reality of how things work is critical. More generally, a shift in perspective may be helpful as well. Countless AIDS workers will tell you that despite the horrendous risks associated with unprotected sex and repeated efforts to inform people of the Russian roulette that they are playing when they have sex without condoms, many Africans simply do not listen. The pleasure of unprotected sex is in the moment; but the consequences of it are far off and indeed often much further out than John Mbiti's unfolding future.

The maintenance of buildings, machinery, and infrastructure would also benefit from this shift. Although they do not necessarily consciously recognize it, many Africans operate with an underlying fatalism about their ability to significantly influence and control the world. Recognizing this pessimism as an out of date attitude, given the resources and technology that humans have accumulated, is necessary, just as it is important for many non-Africans to fight the inner demons that propel them into cycles of endless activity that do not yield the expected returns in terms of greater fulfilment.

Metaphor, Analogy, and the Connectedness of Things

All societies seek to understand events, explain the world around them, and find some kind of method in its madness. There is a powerful body of work in psychology that argues that much of our thinking about our environment is driven not by rationality, but rather by our desire to experience a world that seems more controllable—or at least predictable—than is actually the case. People do seem to have real difficulty accepting that anything around them is randomly determined. For example, if you give members of a group tickets with one being a nominal winning ticket, the winner's self-esteem goes up, despite the manifestly random nature of the exercise. Even more bizarrely, other members of the group start to think the winner is more attractive, intelligent, or powerful in some way. Many issues in social psychology, such as excessive victim blame for random events or a tendency to inflate one's capacity for reading others, are manifestations of this desire for a sense of control.

At a societal level, it is possible to segment broad belief systems about nature into two categories: those that comfort the human soul and help make sense of events that otherwise would seem capricious, versus those that aim to uncover systematically what is going on so as to gain greater levels of actual, rather than illusionary, control over events. Certain religious sentiments, superstitions, and magical beliefs fall in the former category. In the latter category sit the more analytic, experimentally tried and tested theories of mathematics, science, and medicine—ideas that genuinely help us to define, predict, and better control our world.

These systems of beliefs frequently sit in tension with each other or at other times act like an estranged couple, knowing the other party exists but studiously ignoring each other. Nowhere is this truer than in Africa today. Traditional, psychologically satisfying, and intuitively plausible forms of thought jostle uncomfortably with more analytically derived and scientific worldviews. Medically rooted strategies for fighting malaria sit alongside belief systems which suggest that injecting malaria victims creates an opening for the spirits that create the disease to escape—thereby risking afflicting others. Campaigns to educate people on the consequences of unprotected sex and the causes of AIDS coexist with beliefs that unprotected sex is natural, that women need sex in order to stay beautiful, or that one can get rid of AIDS by having sex with a virgin or a young child. Many modern Africans seem to recognize the validity and usefulness of scientific explanation of the world on one level. Yet at another, they cannot bring themselves to give up their beliefs about the world that make intuitive sense or which seem to provide more complete and holistic explanations.

The impact of traditional beliefs is more subtle today but nevertheless powerful. African leaders have an ambivalent attitude about meteoric personal success in business or professional life. People start to get suspicious if someone achieves too much too fast—how has this person managed to leave everyone behind, they wonder? Into this explanatory vacuum drifts the idea that the person has practiced or had recourse to some kind of juju, the catchall African term for magic of some kind. Charms, the storage of potions in pots, and the like are common, particularly in small businesses. This is considered normal practice, but there is a difference between good and bad juju. When success is extraordinary, there exists the strong possibility that the entrepreneur has strayed into bad juju.

Juju can play a part in many areas of African life. Explanations for ill health, accidents, or good luck often center on themes that smack of magical thinking. Football fans will often bring objects or charms to a match or dress up in ways to deliver good juju to their team and bad juju to the rivals. A Gallup survey in 2010 found that across Africa some 50 percent or so of people believed in witchcraft, a figure that rose to over 95 percent in certain Sub-Saharan countries, such as the Ivory Coast. West and Central African counties had a greater belief in witchcraft than Eastern African countries. One sees the impact of these beliefs in the business world as well. When things go wrong, people are reluctant to blame their immediate team—but can be motivated to find malignant influences from other parts of the organization. These beliefs can interfere with the drive to find more rational explanations.[15]

There also exists a view in African about how well other cultures understand this aspect of life. There is respect for Western scientific thinking, but also a belief that Westerners are blind to the power of deeper forces and how interconnected the world is. They see only one aspect of reality. The Chinese are wiser and skilled at soft juju. However, the people who win the gold medal in the art and practice of juju are the Indians. I had a conversation with a Ghanaian mini-cab driver in London about this. Apparently when India played Ghana in a football match, Indian juju completely outdid anything the Africans had. The Ghanaian goalkeeper saw multiple balls coming at him every time a shot was fired, phantom snakes were conjured onto the pitch, and the Indian goalkeeper had the capacity to develop, Shiva-like, numerous invisible arms, whereas the Ghanaian keeper had to make do with the more regular two. I pointed out to the driver that this juju can't help India much, as the country has pretty much one of the worst records in international football. However, he had an explanation for this. Indian use of juju had become so outrageous that FIFA had banned its use by the team—apparently, a certain amount of juju is acceptable to FIFA—but you have to stay within reasonable boundaries. Later when I tested out these ideas with other, for the most part, educated people in Africa, they laughed. Some said they had heard similar urban myths about India playing their own national team. However, they pointed out that even if a lot of people are now free of this type of thinking, many still believe that others believe it, and the hint of juju can be helpful in many instances.

The co-existence of these very different approaches to explaining the world arises from aspects deeply embedded in African DNA. The root cause is that the environment is genuinely more ferocious, unpredictable, and difficult to control. However, no human can just wait passively for the roulette wheel of nature to dispense its arbitrary verdicts. You at least have to make sense of things and have recourse to doing something to get even a tenuous grip on events when disaster strikes. As a consequence, at least with respect to traditional African thought, there is a bias toward belief systems that give a sense of comfort, the illusion of understanding and control, or at the very least some sense that the world is not a mad free-for-all.

Ryszard Kapuściński, has described the traditional world of the African as existing on three interrelated but distinct spheres. First, there is the natural world that surrounds everyone—weather, natural phenomena, the plants and living things that are around, including other humans. For many Africans, events in this immediate world are all interconnected. They exist in some kind of coherent whole. It is a world where analogy predominates. For example, if somebody is able to get a picture of you, they then have the means to control you or influence you because they have captured you at one level. A very powerful person is often imbued with special powers because it is natural that somebody of high status will have special aptitudes.

Behind this immediate world lies the world of the ancestors—all the people who have departed this world but who still exist. These ancestors sit metaphorically on one's shoulder watching and observing every move. They have certain expectations that one must be careful to honor. In many African societies, despite incredible poverty, families will do all they can to give their departed loved ones the required burial rites and funerals. Those departed become the living dead and retain their personal identity. The idea of not showing sufficient respect to them is anathema to many, regardless of the cost. When a person dies in Ghana, for example, there is supposed to be a burial ceremony on the third day, followed by funeral celebrations on the eighth day, and then celebrations on the fortieth and eightieth days, as well as the first year anniversary. Adherence to these practices can wreak havoc on a family's finances.

Beyond the world of the ancestors lies the spirit world. This, argues Ryszard Kapuściński, is the most shadowy world of all—but it is from this world that nature and most living things derive their energy. In the face of mishaps, you are much better turning to the wizards, sorcerers, and witches who really understand and can influence this world than trusting in Western mumbo jumbo that falls at the first fence of understanding the interconnectedness of things.

An understanding of the interdependence of things and how the world one sees is influenced by the world of ancestors and spirits is provided daily to people through the graphic and poetic stories that are told at sundown across the continent around campfires, under trees, or on street corners. Africans are great storytellers and just like to talk. The traditional African worldview—populated by analogy, metaphor, and flights of imagination—lends itself to creativity and storytelling.

Herein, I believe, lies one of the great strengths of African intellect—the ability to paint evocative pictures with words. Trucks and buses across the continent are plastered with poetic slogans. Award-winning writer Ayi Kwei Armah was struggling at one time with the title of a book depicting the psychological disappointments of life in post-independence Ghana. Then one day at an Accra bus station he saw a vehicle with the words "The Beaytiful Ones Are Not Yet Born" inscribed on the back. At once he knew he had the perfect title for his book, and even preserved the misspelling of *beautiful* to reflect the title's street origins.

Africans like to talk. An East African saying, "The creator of mountains has passed away, but the creator of words is still at work," captures this cultural embrace of poetry, language, and stories. The explosive growth of mobile telephones, and their much greater penetration into African markets relative to the economic development of the continent, perhaps also reflects this desire for talking and connection.

Westerners judging African patterns of thinking through their own experience can be inclined to miss the tremendous power of intellectually seeing connection at all levels in the world. Indeed, much modern thinking—from chaos theory and quantum mechanics to Carl Jung's ideas on synchronicity—reflects a move in the direction of seeing complex causality and connection in the world. The lament of many companies that the African education system is not producing enough talent also reflects the narrow reference points around how intellect is judged. This tendency is reinforced by the application of intelligence tests that are overwhelmingly oriented to Western concepts of intellect. When Muhammed Ali was unsuccessfully trying to avoid the Vietnam draft, he failed to do so, in part, because of his poor performance on standard tests of intelligence. Yet anyone vaguely familiar with the evocative poems and epitaphs that he regularly produced, seemingly on a whim, might more fairly have seen a prodigiously creative and inspiring intellect.

Valuing the capacity of African leaders to communicate orally and mobilize others through evocative metaphors and stories would be helpful on the part of Western leaders. Certainly the whole notion of storytelling has become something of a bandwagon in Western business training.

Of course, there is also the other side of the coin. In our analysis, only 9 percent of African leaders were seen to have a strength around analytical thinking, the lowest score globally. Comparative figures for American and European executives were 52 and 44 percent, respectively. As multinationals Africanize their operations and locate a variety of operations on the continent, including research centers, African executives will need to develop their muscle in this area. Overdoing the analytical approach can be a weakness in today's business world, but some capability is helpful. Systematic effort is required to develop these skills, and overseas firms can risk creating a gap between expectations and reality if this does not occur.

The power of valuing different intellectual traditions can be illustrated by the following account from a colleague who attended an academic conference in South Africa. At the end of the day, a leading white expert in the field summarized the conclusions of the conference in an effective and systematic manner. As he sat down, a black African participant stood up and asked if he too could also have a word—an unusual request, since everyone thought that the proceedings had been concluded. The conference organizers reluctantly agreed, mostly to avoid the embarrassment of an outright refusal. The audience then heard an impromptu living poem that memorably and evocatively brought to life the two days of discussion. "It was brilliant, poetic, and compelling. Both interventions were powerful, but I remember the poem more," my colleague mused.

Perhaps African educational institutions could be less slavish in following Western methods and use, for example, oral methods and storytelling as a means of inculcating ideas and testing knowledge. For their part, Africans could endeavor to be less satisfied with ideas that simply pass the comfort of knowing test, and lift their aspirations about the level of control they can actually achieve now over events. They could take their natural orientation to see connections on to a more rigorous plane. As mobile telephony has benefited from the fact that Africa is relatively bereft of landlines, Africa has the opportunity to leapfrog to an intellectual orientation that the wider world is itself beginning to value.

The Big Man and His Alter Ego

Outside of their immediate team, where consensus and teamwork are generally evident, one sees African leaders project strong confidence, which can easily shade into posturing and bravado. Frequently leaders on the continent can be both paternalistic and caring about their people, while expecting high levels of respect and obedience in return. In fact, everybody is strongly attuned to signs of respect and disrespect when leaders and subordinates engage. These include implicit rules about how you challenge—or rather, *don't* challenge; how you signal respect; and how you are just expected to wait for prolonged periods to see your boss, knowing that the meeting may be entirely canceled on a whim without the slightest consideration of your feelings. People in an organization expect their leaders to show confidence and to command respect. In short, they expect them to act like the Big Man.

Things happen in African organizations when someone has power and exercises it. In the absence of this, one can get the illusion of alignment without the necessary follow-through. Many functional executives visiting from outside can leave after a few days thinking that what has been decided will get done only to be disappointed on their return. You either need to exercise power or invest time in building really strong relationships to have more than tokenistic levels of influence in many organizations.

This attitude toward power is evident in other areas of life as well—in the way, for example, people treat their servants or deal with the weak in society. Most of all it is seen in the way governments work. It is impossible to read any modern accounts of Africa without encountering the view that bad governance, corruption, and totalitarian rule have been the major impediments to economic and social progress within the continent. Occasionally, states such as Botswana and Ghana are cited as positive examples, but these tend to be very much the exceptions that prove the rule. Across large swaths of the continent, the term *government* generally conjures up an image of a small group of unelected leaders who have achieved and maintain their position through the barrel of a gun, rule capriciously and at times erratically, and whose motivation is to extract as much wealth for themselves, and their acolytes, as possible.

At the center of these cliques is generally a Big Man who sits at the hub of the state apparatus and to whom all power, privilege, and wealth in the country ultimately flows. American journalist Blaine Harden provides a graphic portrait of this archetypal African ruler. The Big Man frequently lavishes on himself a string of grand titles such as the "the father of the nation," "the boss," "the unique miracle," or "the vanquisher of the British Empire."[16] This Big Man's picture is everywhere, especially in government offices, on the bank notes of the country, but also on badges worn by his ministers. Television, radio, and the press are full of articles praising his daily activities or impressive insights that the Big Man has shown on local or global issues. Any number of stadia, schools, and hospitals are named after the Big Man. Frequently, this Big Man is assumed to have mystical and magical powers, which even the educated members of the country fear. He is all-powerful and consuming until one day he is deposed or killed by a younger or more ruthless version of himself.

African history post-independence has been full of such Big Men, the most notorious examples being Uganda's Idi Amin, Jean-Bédel Bokassa of the Central African Republic, Congo's Mobutu Sese Seko, and Robert Mugabe of Zimbabwe. One might think that these particular rulers represent an extreme manifestation of all that is not well in African governance. However, until recently such rulers have been very much par for the course. The continent is littered with autocrats who have been carved from the same mold, but have not been publicized by the Western media. The impact of these rulers on their countries is enormous and generally negative, often culminating in the complete ruination of the societies and the economies over which they preside. While some are semirational in their pursuit of self-interest, others degenerate into a twilight world of ostentatious consumption, paranoia, and strange beliefs.

The ubiquity of this pattern of governance across Sub-Saharan Africa, while being dispiriting, also raises a deeper question. Is there anything about African psychology and culture that leads to this mindset on the part of rulers? Here the historical pattern provides answers that are potentially contradictory. At one level, there is strong evidence within small tribal groups or clans of democratic checks and controls. While all such groups typically appoint a leader, there is a strong tradition within African culture for such leaders requiring ongoing permission from their followers to remain in their positions. Decision making in such groups is frequently highly consensual to the point of being laboriously slow.

However, the evidence would suggest that more repressive instincts come to the surface when leadership over larger entities is concerned. When Muslim explorer Ibn Battuta traveled to Africa in the fourteenth century, he was taken aback by the extent of abasement activities that African rulers expected from their subjects—such as throwing dust on themselves or crawling on the ground. Early European explorers who encountered African kingdoms were intrigued but also somewhat repulsed by the level of distance that existed between a ruler and his or her people. In some cases, subjects were not allowed to look at rulers on the pain of death, and there is much reportage of arbitrary and somewhat unusual servile rituals that many rulers imposed on their people. In fact, a large number of African leaders enthusiastically embraced the slave trade and, as soon as they knew that good money was to be made of it, worked vigorously to supply Europeans with what they needed.

Journalist Richard Dowden feels that there is something in African cultural DNA that helps create an environment in which the Big Man can flourish:

> *At the heart of African politics is an attitude to power. Power whether used for good or ill is widely revered for its own sake. The Big Man is given great respect because he has power. Many African societies traditionally had little sense of equality, and even today you can be shocked to see people prostrate themselves before their superiors. This does not just mean little people who line the roads to cheer the Big Man. Ministers who behave like gods themselves become lowly servants in the presence of their Presidents, bowing and hunching their shoulders in deference.*

On Geert Hofstede's dimension of power distance, many African countries emerge as having some of the highest scores in the world. Power distance, it has to be said, is not just about the power that those in authority accrue to themselves; it is also about what people let others get away with. In Africa there is a belief in authority and sometimes even quite deeply held superstitious beliefs about the mystical power that those in authority hold. Many African rulers play on these convictions and allow wild rumors to circulate about their prowess and their supernatural skills. Stories about cannibalism are also used to create fear in people. Rulers are frequently perceived by their subjects to have the power to know exactly what everyone is thinking and even at times to be able to control nature and the spirit world. As a consequence, despite appalling governance, one can count on the fingers of one hand the number of African rulers who have been deposed by popular uprisings like the Arab Spring.

So what explains this orientation toward the use of power in Africa? Hofstede and his colleagues provide some clues that point to the answer. Their research looked at power distance scores across more than 180 countries and put in a number of explanatory variables to try and explain these differences. The startling finding was that the best predictor of power distance was a country's distance north and south of the equator. If we take a line down from the northernmost parts of the world, one can see this pattern. Scandinavian countries are, for example, the most equal societies in the world. Britain and Germany are also fairly equal but less so than Scandinavian countries. But inequality increases as you go to the southern European countries. Witness what Silvio Berlusconi was able to get away with in Italy and still win elections. Further south in the North African Muslim societies, one sees a strong pattern of despotic rulers, but at least an effort by some members of the society, as in the Arab Spring, to dislodge these autocrats. In Sub-Saharan Africa, one sees rulers often scooping up large amounts of a country's resources with limited democratic or popular challenge. The only challenge such rulers face is from other versions of themselves who might try to get their hands on the levers of power themselves.

There is no sound explanation for why power distance scores should follow the pattern outlined above. However, it's likely related to the nature of the environmental challenge faced by different cultures. If the environment is one that requires control and shaping for humans to have any chance of surviving—and you have to band together to make this possible—then high power distance becomes a less viable option. In such environments, it is pointless to argue over the division of the cake; you are better off devoting your collective energies to working out how to bake one in the first place. Conversely, in environments where less human shaping is necessary or possible, one can imagine the culture focusing much more on how the spoils are shared and regulating these expectations through hierarchical cultural norms.

The dynamics outlined above were set in motion a long time ago in Africa. Being our natural home, it was a resource-rich environment for humans, where the cake had already been baked by nature. However, there is a modern version of this phenomenon that helps the argument—the so-called resources curse. Development experts coined the phrase to describe the destructive impact that a high level of resources (usually minerals or energy) that a particular country possesses has on a myriad of indicators. Quite simply, the more resources a developing country has, the worse its politics—and condition of the bulk of its people—seem to be. Less resource-rich countries often have better politics and income distribution. Compare Nigeria with Ghana, which has no significant oil, and you see the pattern. The central driver of the resources curse is, I believe, the fact that when a cake is already baked, people devote their energies to fighting over how it should be sliced and in the end some despot emerges. When there is no big shining cake to fight over, more inclusive instincts take over. The underlying dynamic behind the resources curse and the theory of power distance outlined above is one and the same, just on different time scales.

However, one cannot just stop this account of the use of power in Africa at this point. The Big Man, whether in business or government, has an alter ego, which is also rooted in African culture. The expectation for consensus and debate in smaller teams is also there. In my experience what is needed to activate this mindset is the sense that "this is my team." Once this assumption exists, then a markedly different attitude toward the exercise of power arises. The further one gets away from "my team" or "my people," the more evident is the unilateral and arbitrary exercise of power.

Even at the level of government one can see different types of leaders emerging with different mindsets. There are newer and more modern-minded leaders moving into government across the continent. Not many people have heard of Pedro Pires of Cape Verde, or Festus Mogae of Botswana, or Joaquim Chissano of Mozambique, all winners of the Mo Ibrahim prize for governance in Africa. What is interesting about these rulers is that they either come from small countries where a common sense of us is more possible or nations that won their independence relatively late and where the memory of the struggle is still alive, prompting an afterglow of nationhood. Of course, the best example is Nelson Mandela, who adopted a strongly inclusive sense of national mission following the struggle with apartheid. Big Men—and Big Women as well—with alter egos are arising all across Africa, representing one of the best hopes for the future of the continent. In fact, one of the interesting dynamics one sees in many African organizations is the challenge to older, more traditionally minded leaders by a newer generation of less subservient "upstarts." In business, as at a national level, it is encouraging an identification with the wider entity, rather than sectional interest, that releases this alter ego of African leaders.

Looking Ahead

Africa is moving forward in an unprecedented way, which represents huge opportunities for businesses operating on the continent. However, it will not work for Western companies to simply carpet bomb Africa with their cultures. Determining how to release the energy, joy, intellectual flexibility, and creativity that is so much a part of life in Africa is much better than stifling people through the imposition of orthodox corporate values. Respecting and working to broaden the sense of community that binds people together rather than labeling such behavior as tribal or nepotistic would also help Western companies to operate less judgmentally. Chinese and Indian companies operating in Africa also need to realize that, while their flexible ways of operating and understanding what value driven consumers want give them an edge, their introverted and socially exclusive modes of operating may store up long-term problems for themselves on a continent where open, natural, and warm human relationships are valued.

However, there will need to be certain shifts in the underlying assumptions that have governed life on the continent for Africa to take its place in the world. The deep pessimism about control of the environment that is the root cause of many cultural DNA themes needs to be replaced by a much greater sense of possibility that control is now possible. Surfacing, recognizing, and changing this core assumption would encourage a much stronger long-term orientation and lead to lay theories and practices about the world being more rigorously tested for the impact they have rather than the psychological comfort they create.

It will also be critical to expand the sense of community. Without such an extension, organizational and national life on the continent will always seem atomistic, somewhat paranoid, and full of intergroup rivalry and conflict. Such an adjustment on the part of leaders is also the key to unlocking better governance. These mental shifts will be needed if the current economic boom in Africa is to lead to sustained improvements in people's lives.

However, the rest of the world also has something to learn from Africa's cultural DNA. Knowing how to relate as humans, how to find joy day to day, and how to live in the moment rather than always chasing after tomorrow are things that many cultures lost sight of long ago. There is another broader point. Africa has always been a cauldron of activity and change, and this is the reason that virtually all advances in the human species have occurred on the continent. One sees this dynamism in the high birth rates, extremely youthful populations, rapid level of change, as well as less positively, in the wars and disease that are all such a part of life on the continent. Now that many people in Africa are embracing a sense of possibility, there is also a renewed level of drive. All this is creating a sense of dynamism across the continent and Africa has the potential to become the source of creative advancement for humankind, just as it has been for the large part of our evolutionary history.

Chapter 3

India: Beyond This World

India has the potential to perplex many who engage or seek to do business with the country. At one level it is a free, welcoming, and tolerant nation that embodies many of the values the modern world prizes—a surprisingly democratic outlier in the developing world, where authoritarian and despotic instincts for the most part still reign. The country's emergence as an economic and technological power supports these sentiments, giving the sense that the country must soon take its rightful place in the modern world.

At another level, however, India is a mind-numbingly bureaucratic and rigid society, difficult for an outsider to navigate, and a place where many leaders say doing business is harder than just about anywhere else in the world—including China, Africa, or the Middle East.

State-of-the-art campuses for IT and outsourcing companies can all too often be serviced by appalling infrastructure and sit in the midst of squalor and levels of environmental degradation that are difficult to fathom, but which locals seem to blithely ignore. Images of highly advanced satellite monitoring equipment for India's ambitious space program literally being carted to rural areas on rickety, bullock-pulled vehicles reinforces the sense of India as an incongruous, multifaceted place. Indians themselves can be confusing. On the surface welcoming, open, and warm, the capacity of Indians to be less than direct and to engage in opaque strategies can leave people confused and unsure as to where they stand in relationships.

India represents a bewildering range of races, religions, castes, and languages—all sorts of people coexisting together in a noisy, jangling, and, for the most part, warm-hearted harmony. Westerners who are drawn to India by virtue of its other-worldliness can all too often be jolted by the crass materialism, dishonesty, corruption, as well as sheer dirtiness of much of India when they first arrive. While the fainthearted may be tempted to give up at this point, India is a layered place, and philosophical profundity is also there if you know where to look and which type of guru to avoid.

Much of what perplexes about India can make sense when deeper psychological constructs are applied to its myriad contradictions and tensions. India's search for the truth behind the veil of reality and its tolerance of diversity means it has much to offer the world. However, the country's DNA also gives rise to some clear psychological weaknesses that need to be tackled if India is to truly flourish in the modern world. The high rates of economic growth, in large part driven by the fact that India is coming from a long way behind many other countries, can lead people to underestimate some of these problems or blithely sweep them under the carpet—a perennial hazard for the Indian mind. In fact, these rates of growth are already starting to slip as the gravitational pull of certain psychological instincts starts to take its toll again.

The Peopling of India

An understanding of Indian cultural DNA requires us to turn back to how modern humans settled the subcontinent and the challenges they faced in surviving in that part of the world. The evidence overwhelmingly suggests that the first movement of people outside of Africa, from modern-day Somalia to Yemen, was a beachcombing community that crossed the Red Sea some 80,000 years ago. The fact that the first human colony outside of Africa was in an oasis in the Middle East is oddly resonant with the Old Testament story—perhaps the ancient Hebrews based their account on some tribal memories reverberating from the distant past. Members of this community moved along the southern Arabian shores and the coastal strips of modern-day Iran and Pakistan, avoiding the forbidding deserts to the north before finding a congenial home in the lush conditions of the Indian subcontinent.

Contrary to what one might expect, India—*not* the Middle East—was the first major staging post for the out-of-Africa humans some 75,000 years ago. The high levels of genetic diversity and the presence in India of both mitrochondrial and *Y*-chromosome lines not seen in the Middle East and Europe point to India as being the next staging post. Europe and the bulk of the Middle East were populated much later, counterintuitively by a set of eastern movements from India rather than directly from Africa.

The Toba Event

However, just as the first modern humans had arrived in India and moved through to South-East Asia, the world experienced one of the most extreme environmental shocks of the past 2 million years—the Toba eruption. Precisely dated to 74,000 years ago, this super eruption in Sumatra sent a dense cloud of volcanic ash into the atmosphere, triggering global cooling. Because of prevailing winds, the Indian subcontinent was most severely affected. Excavations today across India routinely see evidence of a thick layer of volcanic ash directly attributable to the Toba event—in some areas this layer is several meters thick. In fact, many biologists believe that Toba was responsible for a sharp reduction in modern human populations everywhere. This extent of the global impact is debated, but it's clear that the Toba event was a devastating, ecologically redefining event in the Indian subcontinent—likely to have caused extinction on a wide scale. Genetic evidence backs this up: while India has a lot of diversity, there are certain lines that are present in Southeast Asia and Australasia that are absent in India, indicating a genetic bottleneck.

Stephen Oppenheimer believes India was repopulated from both the west and the east following the Toba event. Uniquely, modern humans advancing into India had one major advantage. Unlike just about any other modern human expansion, with the exception per-haps of Australasia—they did not need to battle and compete with earlier human species. However, the mass extinction also of other animal species meant that the early modern humans in India had to rely almost exclusively on foraging and plant life rather than hunting for their survival. When settled, volcanic ash is surprisingly fertile and plant life returned to the subcontinent fairly rapidly, but animal life took much longer to establish.

The above, of course, only represents the start of the process by which India was populated. The Indian mainland was then populated by a series of movements into the hinterland. Light has been shed on how this might have happened by David Reich and his colleagues, who have to date conducted the most extensive study on the genetic structure of populations spread throughout India.[1] The authors found strong evidence of all Indian populations being descended from two distinct ancient founder populations—Ancestral North Indians (ANI) and Ancestral South Indians (ASI). Although it is not clear when these populations diverged, it is possible that this happened in the distant past—perhaps as long ago as 60,000 years, just 15,000 years after the Toba event. Since then, there have reputedly been many periods when the two populations mixed together.

Virtually all Indian populations have traces of both root populations, with the ANI component varying from 40 to 70 percent. The ANI genetic structure is linked to patterns found in the populations of the Middle East, Central Asia, and Europe. However, this does not mean that the root population for ANI came from these regions; it is much more likely, in the early stages at least, that the regions to the north and west of India were populated by a movement from the subcontinent itself, with later flow backs occurring more recently. ASI genetic structure conversely is unique to India and not found anywhere else in the world. However, even in South India, people have some ANI roots as well. The only community in India whose genetic structure is solely ASI is a tribal community on the Andaman Islands, presumably an isolated group originating from the original founder populations that escaped ANI admixture because of its separation from the mainland.

It is important to note that this split of ANI and ASI happened long before the Aryan invasions into India that are believed to have led to the demise of the Indus Valley civilization. However, there is evidence that there was an increase in ANI and ASI mixing around this period. It is highly likely that this Indus Valley population had strong ANI roots as well. The study also puts to bed the idea of an Aryan-Dravidian genetic divide today, as both populations have a mixture of ANI and ASI, although in the distant past, long before recorded history, there was a north to south separation of populations.

Reich and his colleagues also found that there was strong evidence of genetic distinctiveness and separation in different castes going back thousands of years. The view that caste is a relatively modern invention or even one made acute by colonialism is a popular one; but this study and a number of other investigations now clearly suggest that the genetic separation of castes goes back to the dawn of history in India.[2] An important point established by the researchers is that in many other parts of the world, such as Africa and Europe, genetic segregation is evident across geography, but in India it manifests itself through horizontal stratification. Populations in India have lived in the same villages for thousands of years with virtually no gene flows between subpopulations. The authors also found that higher castes in India had higher ANI as a proportion of their ancestry, even when they lived in South India. There is some evidence that although it might have existed long before, about 1,900 years ago caste became more genetically fixed in India and the rate of mixing between different populations declined sharply.

The Forces That Have Shaped India's Cultural DNA

There appear to be three distinct forces that have combined with each other to profoundly impact Indian cultural DNA. The first of these concerns the impact of the Toba event with respect to eliminating competitor human species, as well as most other animals from the Indian landscape. The modern humans who settled India did not have to fight their way in, or at the most would have encountered fragmented and limited resistance from other species of humans who survived the extinction event. This was not the case in most other regions of the world. In Europe, for example, modern humans had a 5,000-year ecological battle with Neanderthals for supremacy. I believe that the selection pressure for skills related to fighting and warfare was significantly attenuated by this fact in India. Clearly these pressures would have returned over time as the populations expanded and as people fought for supremacy on the subcontinent—but the early impetus was less acute.

Furthermore, hunting was less available to modern humans as a survival strategy, forcing a focus on plant life. Although it may seem speculative to hang features on to events so long ago, the strong cultural values around nonviolence and vegetarianism that have been, as I will demonstrate later, such distinctive features of Indian cultural DNA through the ages may arise from this fact. In addition, a central feature of Indian philosophical thinking—the unity of all living things and the sanctity of animal life—also perhaps owes its origin to the need to protect the fragile early populations of animal life.

After Africa, India has the highest levels of genetic diversity in the world—something that has likely been an important factor in driving a key and somewhat reprehensible cultural institution in India: caste. Unlike Africa, where high levels of genetic diversity led to vertical separation of communities into tens of thousands of tribes, this diversity expressed itself in India—because of the limited barriers to geographical separation created by the early advent of settled agriculture—much more in horizontal segregation. India, like Africa, is also a high-pathogen environment that experiences the same pressures for tight in-groups and distancing behaviors from out-groups that such threats drive. However, humans in India had to devise elaborate forms of segregation while living in close proximity to each other. Many of the purification rituals and avoidance of contact behaviors within Indian caste life—including the whole notion of untouchability—may well stem from this need to maintain horizontal segregation in a high pathogen environment.

Finally, the combination of the lack of prior human settlers or competitor animal species, when combined with the relatively benign climatic conditions, likely meant that the early humans who colonized India were less challenged than modern humans just about anywhere else, at least for a while. The daily struggle for survival was easier here than many other places. Furthermore, these benign conditions continued for some time as humans enjoyed the lush, subtropical environment with fertile volcanic soil nourished by the clockwork appearance of monsoon rains. This I believe had perhaps the most fundamental impact on Indian cultural DNA out of all the factors mentioned above. The psychologist Abraham Maslow famously suggested that after humans satisfy their basic needs for sustenance and security, they start turning their attention to more uplifting concerns. At least some of the people who settled India were able to move up Maslow's hierarchy of needs more quickly than other human groups and concern themselves more with matters beyond the practicalities of life.

Buddha-like, they could metaphorically go on journeys of enlightenment without putting their lives at risk. India is the only global culture that has put thinkers, priests, and gurus as opposed to rulers, warriors, landowners, or commercial people at the apex of society consistently through the ages. I will argue later that, for both good and ill, many features of India's cultural DNA—such as its predilection for abstract thought, focus on introspection, concern with mastering the body, and neglect of the external environment—stem from this reality. Many of India's gifts to the world, too—such as Ayurvedic medicine, spiritualism, yoga, and the numbers system—also arise from this focus on the internal world of abstraction at the expense of more mundane realities.

Ahimsa

One of the most immediate impressions that visitors to India remark upon is the warmth with which people embrace outsiders and treat one as an honored and valued guest. It is a gentle kindness underpinned by respectfulness, courtesy, acceptance, and empathy. While people can be animated and noisy in their interactions, overt displays of bad temper or aggression are rare. The Indian roads are a case in point. Though anyone who has been there will tell you that they're noisy, chaotic, and something of a free-for-all, road rage is rarer than one might expect given that there is a never-ending stream of provocation for it. In Western countries, frayed tempers and aggression would accompany anything remotely resembling the Indian road system experience. When somebody—usually an outsider—reacts in a bad-tempered or aggressive manner, Indians get visibly discomforted and disturbed.

This abhorrence of aggression—as well as its frequent lack of efficacy—is also evident in business. A senior member of a significant Indian outsourcing company told me a story that exemplifies this point. At one point the Indian CEO had a meeting with the CEO of a significant American client. The American CEO and his entourage flew in big style on a private jet; the Indian contingent mostly went to the meeting coach class. As the American CEO entered, without too much preamble he launched into a tirade about how the outsourcing company was letting his firm down. Every time he seemed to have come to the end of his monologue, he remembered something else which then started him off on another bout of ill-tempered shouting. There was a long silence as he waited for his Indian hosts to react. Finally, the Indian CEO said, "Welcome to India, we are very honored to have you here." He then looked at his watch. "We have 90 minutes for this meeting and I see we have used up 45 minutes already," he observed. "Shall we get on to the agenda?" The American CEO, used to his aggressive tactics evoking panicked responses from people, was completely flummoxed by the total failure of his tirade to have any impact. This gentle stubbornness in the face of aggression is not an uncommon feature of Indian culture.

This underlying antipathy toward aggression I believe stems from the Indian concept of *ahimsa*, which literally means cause no injury—a principle deeply and widely embedded in Indian culture. It not only influences attitudes toward violence, but has also driven vegetarianism to a level not seen in other cultures, and affects Indian attitudes toward sport, negotiations, as well as deep views as to the purpose of business in society and how corporations should conduct themselves. Before exploring these areas further, it is worth appreciating how far back this attitude goes in Indian culture and where it comes from.

The Indus Valley civilization, one of the oldest in the world, dates back to 3,000 BCE. The archaeologists who stumbled across it and unearthed its long-lost remains were astounded by the scale of its large, geometrically formed cities. The cities had extensive public buildings and baths, as well as high-quality plumbing, and seemed to have been well-ordered. Perhaps not all cultural DNA features reverberate through time. As excavations of the Indus Valley continue, it has also become clear that this was a much vaster civilization than originally envisaged, with hundreds of towns and cities stretching from modern-day Punjab in India to the Pakistani Punjab, and all the way down the Indus to the Indian Ocean. However, a puzzling thing is that for such an extensive civilization, there is little evidence of forts or other defensive structures such as walls or moats. Neither is there much evidence in the remains of armaments or much depiction in its art or statues of warfare. It seems that the civilization was characterized by a lack of attention to military matters and was possibly much more peaceful than comparable societies in Mesopotamia and Egypt.

Puzzlingly, the Indus Valley civilization disappeared without trace relatively suddenly. The most widespread view is that it succumbed to pastoral, Aryan invaders from the northwest, who brought a more aggressive form of warfare to the Indian subcontinent. The speed of this collapse might have been due to its neglect of military matters. Another theory is that the so-called Aryan invaders were local inhabitants from neighboring regions who simply toppled a civilization that was in decline due to climactic changes and the desertification of much of its lands. Either way, the successors to the Indus Valley civilization were the creators of India's Hindu culture and traditions. Although more aggressive and warlike—their epics are full of tales of battles between kings and princes—this new culture seems also to have quickly absorbed some pacifistic instincts. One of the most famous texts of the Hindu scriptures is the Bhagavad Gita, a work embedded in the broader Hindu epic, the Mahabharat. The Gita is a sermon given by Lord Krishna to Arjuna just before the start of a crucial battle between the Pandavas and the Kauravas. Arjuna is wracked with doubt and concern about the forthcoming battle, not because he is worried that he might lose, but because he might win:

O Krishna, seeing my kinsmen standing with a desire to fight, my limbs fail and my mouth becomes dry. My body quivers and my hairs stand on end. The bow, Gaandeeva, slips from my hand and my skin intensely burns. ... I do not wish to kill them, who are also about to kill, even for the rule of the three worlds, let alone for this earthly kingdom.

Lord Krishna advises Arjuna that he has been caught up in the illusion of the world and that he does not fully understand the nature of living things. Since the soul is eternal, death is not what it seems; it only represents the shedding of the external manifestation of the soul. As a metaphor for life itself, Arjuna is implored to perform his duty and rise to the challenge of the battle, but to engage it in a way that recognizes that neither victory nor defeat matters much. The interesting thing to note here is Arjuna's doubts and unusual reflections on the wisdom of war or violence, certainly depicting sentiments that were alien to other rulers of that time or, indeed, subsequent rulers in Europe, China, or the Middle East.

We find other evidence of the abhorrence of violence as we move on in history. The Emperor Ashoka, who ruled and united much of India from about 269 BC to 232 BC, engaged in a number of wars. His early rule was characteristically violent for an emperor seeking to widen his reach. One of Ashoka's most notable conquests was the kingdom of Kalinga in the east of India, which had hitherto remained unconquered by his predecessors. However, once he had won this war, something unusual happened. He became consumed with guilt and his reflections after the battle of Kalinga are resonant of Arjuna's doubts:

> *What have I done? If this is victory then what is a defeat? Is this a victory or a defeat? Is this justice or injustice? Is it gallantry or a rout? Is it valor to kill innocent children and women? Do I do it to widen the empire and for prosperity or to destroy the other's kingdom and splendor? One has lost her husband, someone else a father, someone a child, someone an unborn infant.*

Ashoka turned his back on violence, embraced the notion of ahimsa and became a Buddhist. He devoted the rest of his time to public welfare, building roads, hospitals, and universities, and sending Buddhist missionaries to all parts of the known world. Ashoka took his nonviolence beyond the preserve of humans; he promoted vegetarianism, outlawed most forms of sport hunting and the branding of animals. He also set up hospitals for animals as well as for his subjects.

It would seem from the above that ambivalence, at the very least, or revulsion to violence, is an important aspect of India's cultural DNA. The concept of *ahimsa* comes through repeatedly in Hindu, Buddhist, and Jain texts. Through the ages sadhus, scholars, and sages have argued about the morality of war in India. Indian history since recorded times, in as much as it touches other parts of the world, is a history of invasion of outsiders into India—from the Aryans at the time of the Indus Valley civilization, to the Greeks, Mongols, and latterly the British. India, for its part, has sent out merchants, scholars, and religious teachers to the world, and made its impact felt through soft rather than hard power. When the British arrived in India they found the conquest of a vast subcontinent thousands of miles from their shores a relatively easy task, requiring only a modest number of British soldiers. When British rule was ended, it was not through violent insurrection. Many Indian liberation movements attempted this, but attracted only limited following. It took Gandhi, with his notion of nonviolence, to touch a chord with some of the deepest instincts in Indian culture to create a distinctive, historically unprecedented, nonviolent movement for change to force the British to leave.

While India, like most other societies, experiences violence at all levels—and can be particularly prone to intergroup, caste, and sexual violence—its culture does seem to be distinctive in how much it agonizes about violence. This attitude goes back to times before Hinduism took root and I believe is ultimately traceable to the impact of the Toba event. As explained earlier, the modern humans who moved into India following Toba did not have to fight other humans as they needed to just about everywhere else. Vegetation was relatively quick to recover, particularly given India's lush tropical climate and the fertility of volcanic ash, but animal life took longer. Nonviolence, with its associated sister sentiment vegetarianism, could well have been a feature of the very earliest human settlements in India following the Toba event.

One might ask from a psychological point of view: What is the fundamental characteristic that underpins *ahimsa*? Cultures that exhibit high levels of aggression may well require high in-group identification and strong levels of empathy suppression for out-groups. Group identification in India is caste based rather than territorially clannish; when one sees violence in India it is often based on caste or religion. *Ahimsa* also inherently arises from a holistic long-term orientation to the world, which recognizes the connectedness of things and the eventual corrosive impact of violence, however tempting it may seem in the short term.

This wider notion of *ahimsa* with respect to long-term orientation seems to have deeply impacted Indian business culture in a number of ways. One is the counterintuitive fact that while Indian businesses can seem (and are) highly commercially driven on the surface, there also exists a widespread view that business needs to think about its wider purpose in society. A McKinsey survey of international executives found (to their surprise) that 90 percent of senior Indian executives feel that business should have a broader societal purpose than simply making profits. The figure for American executives is 40 percent, and only 10 percent of Chinese executives endorse this view.[3] A study of Indian executives reported in the *Harvard Business Review*, involving executives at 98 Indian companies, found that Indian leaders put a much stronger emphasis on businesses having a positive social purpose and looking after their employees, than American leaders do. In fact, they put serving the interests of shareholders at the bottom of four areas of priority, whereas American executives put it first:[4]

> *Indian leaders have long been involved in societal issues, pre-emptively investing in community service and infrastructure.... More so than most Western companies, the best Indian companies have a social mission and a sense of national purpose because that helps employees find meaning in their work.*

When we were researching companies for our book *Meaning Inc.*, the best global example we could find for a true Meaning Inc. company was the Indian conglomerate Tata.[5] Companies like Infosys, Bharti Airtel, Max Vijay, and countless others all embrace a positive sense of societal purpose. The roots to this approach lie in the *ahimsa* DNA theme within Indian culture, an orientation that also leads to an emphasis on the people working in the business. The best Indian companies invest in people and their growth, as well as in creating a culture that embodies humanistic values. The HBR survey also found that twice as many Indian leaders thought that human capital drove business success, compared to American executives. Over 80 percent of human resources executives said that employee development was critical to business success, compared to just 4 percent in the United States. Indian employees expect their companies to invest in their growth.

However, these characteristics are not always evident in all Indian companies where commercial pressures and a hierarchical segregation of people lead to short-term considerations or a neglect of the human agenda. Firms engaged in the day to day struggles of surviving in an emerging economy do not have the same luxuries that Western companies can afford. However, in the long term even such companies would do well to understand that long-term legitimacy and acceptance in Indian society is likely to require them to embrace this core cultural DNA theme. Outsiders, too, can miss the humanitarian core that lies at the heart of many Indian companies, in part because such companies are also commercially aggressive and high performing, as well as operating in an environment where corruption is endemic. However, in order to truly connect with Indian executives—whether in negotiations or as a leader—having a broad, long-term view of business purpose and exhibiting people-centric values, as opposed to charging in aggressively or coldly, helps. *Ahimsa*—cause no injury—means that long-term partnerships are prized over the narrow pursuit of short-term interests. Displays of ill temper, as in the case of the American CEO cited earlier, diminish the actor in the eyes of the audience, however effective it may be in the short term. India's labor laws are notoriously restrictive for employers who want to sack people, and are a cause of justifiable frustration on the part of many in business. But they do arise from a consideration of wider societal needs. Navigating India's notoriously corrupt bureaucracy can be made easier if external companies are able to articulate a positive social agenda.

The notion of *ahimsa* also infuses interpersonal relationships, which in India are generally highly respectful, courteous, and positive. However, it can also lead to Indian leaders having a real difficulty in being direct, as well as an internal, but rarely overtly expressed latent criticism, of excessive directness in others. American executives, in particular, can be caught off guard by the lack of directness on the part of Indians and over time learn to pay attention to subtle signs of disagreement. One senior executive said to me, "Unless I get a full and enthusiastic Yes, I know the answer is No." Statements like "This is interesting," "I like it," "Let my team work on it," or changing the subject all mean that nothing is going to happen. Lack of attention to these signs can mean one constantly lives in a world of unfulfilled expectations as a leader in India. While this can be frustrating for many overseas executives, they can miss the point that this aspect arises from an Indian desire to be kind and not offend others.

On a broader front, the Indian concept of *ahimsa* can be seen as one of India's great gifts to the world, with other cultures only just now catching up with the idea that might does not equal right. Vegetarianism started as a significant movement in India and has rapidly caught on in other parts of the world. Buddhism, which has expanded to many countries in the Far East and South East Asia, is increasingly attractive to many in the West. Europeans and Americans, who perhaps have a long history of violence toward other races, are beginning to ask the kinds of questions about the rightness of their activities that the ancient Indians posed before their battles many thousands of years ago. On this dimension, India's instincts represent the future. Yet India itself has to nurture this aspect of its cultural DNA as modernity sweeps its society, and perhaps diminishes this traditional value.

However, there are also dangers in being out of sync with the rest of the world—which India can still be to some extent. Since time immemorial, India has been subjugated to invasions; no other culture in the world has succumbed so easily and so often to external aggression. Even recently in post-independent India, driven by Gandhi's ideology of nonviolence and Nehru's concept of nonalignment, India completely neglected its armed forces until it was rudely awakened by an attack from China in 1962. Months before the attack Indians were chanting "India China Bhai Bhai (are brothers)," completely unaware, or in denial of the fact, that forces were building up on their borders. The shock of the Chinese betrayal literally broke Nehru's heart and he died shortly after the humiliating defeat at the hands of China. Shocked into the realities of power in the modern world, India embarked on a massive program of rearmament.

However, the old instincts returned after a decade or two of this. Infrastructure development on the border was neglected, arms procurement slipped, bureaucrats made choices about arms purchases more on the basis of the opportunity they provided for graft than the needs of the country. Desperately needed programs for renewing the armed forces' equipment floundered in the corrupt labyrinth that constitutes India's arms procurement program. Eventually, in 2010, after a series of border incidents, India finally started to rectify this neglect. But it had barely taken a couple of decades for Indian culture to forget the shock of 1962 and for leaders to revert to their internally focused personal agendas and blithe neglect of military matters.

Individual Paths

One of our consultants was working with an American team of a company that was acquired by an Indian-owned group. A senior executive from India was sent over to help turn the business's performance around, as it had been threatened with closure unless things improved. The consultant found the Indian executive to be a talented and incisive individual who had a clear, nonnegotiable view of what needed to be done. He regarded the culture in the American subsidiary as soft, overly focused on consensus, and prophesied the collapse of the business unless it changed. However, the executive had built virtually no relationships with other members of the senior team—and as a consequence his strongly held views, while creating ripples of tension and consternation in almost every meeting, gained only modest acceptance and traction within the business. From the outside our consultant thought that the executive must have been lacking in emotional intelligence and an understanding of how to operate in a different cultural context. However, when he started to work with him, he found that he was highly aware of how others saw him and the impact he was having. He refused to accept that his approach needed modification in any way. Delving even deeper, he found that the executive had undergone a profound process of self-reflection in the past that had led him to develop his convictions about how leaders needed to be in business, to which he adhered with religious-like zeal. It was his own individualized journey, rather than anything he had picked up from mentors or the *Harvard Business Review*—and he was going to pursue it come what may.

The above story points to a common observation by our consultants operating in India, which centers on the extent to which there are a cacophony of voices and multiple individual agendas being played out within a business. While Indian business culture is highly hierarchical in many senses, a kind of anarchistic individualism can reign at any given level within a hierarchy. While this can lead to a sense of dynamism and creativity, teamwork can often be skin deep and perfunctory. Departments, subunits, or individuals will frequently pursue their own agendas, blithely ignoring collective goals or the common good. When the Japanese firm Suzuki set up manufacturing plants in India, they were completely taken aback—given their own cultural norms—by how difficult it was to get talented and gifted people to show even a semblance of teamwork. A joke started to go around among the Japanese executives: "India is full of talented people and one Indian on his own can be worth 10 Japanese. However you have to remember 10 Indians together are usually only worth one Japanese." We found in our evaluation of Indian executives that 24 percent had a development need around teamwork and collaboration—a far higher rate than any other region in the world. By contrast, 28 percent of American executives were rated as strong in this area with only 4 percent having a development need.

Many leaders operating in India can get frustrated by the amount of time they are required to spend resolving team disputes that individuals themselves are incapable of working through together. Experienced executives also learn that they need to follow up in detail to ensure that employees implement things as agreed. Otherwise, they run the risk that people simply go through the motions of accepting something before passively and quietly reverting to their original agenda. A survey comparing Indian and American leaders found that 40 percent of Indian executives routinely monitor progress compared with only 17 percent of American executives, and that only 15 percent of Indian executives rarely do so compared to 45 percent of American leaders. Western executives who are used to a more straightforward relationship between collective agreement and action can be caught out by this lack of transparency and follow-through.

India's stance as a country also shows this idiosyncratic tendency. For example, Indian time is not five or six but five and a *half* hours ahead of GMT—a quixotic choice on the part of Indians that causes great confusion and leads to international calls or meetings often being half an hour early or late. Stubbornly, Indians refuse to march in step with the utterly sensible practice of unit-hour differences that just about every other country in the world observes. When much of the world chose to be either in the Western or Communist camps after the Second World War, India frustrated many global powers by forging the nonaligned movement. Even in many international gatherings today, India's stance can be stubbornly independent—sometimes with validity, but at other times to the point of derailing agreements that most of the global community endorses.

A focus on the individual at the expense of the wider group is also apparent in many other areas of life outside of business in India. When the legendary Indian batsman Sachin Tendulkar played his last test match, there was virtually no interest in the country about the Indian team's performance against the West Indies; everyone was solely preoccupied, to the point of irrational fixation, by how many runs Tendulkar might get. When batsmen before him in the order were given out, incongruously and confusingly for the bemused West Indian team, the Indian crowd cheered wildly, as this brought closer the appearance of their idol. The first question an Indian parent will typically ask their cricketing son after a game is, "How did you do?" My Australian wife says it is always, "Did your team win?" in her country. Indian cinemagoers are predominantly drawn by the prospect of seeing their heroes on screen, with the quality of the film often being a secondary consideration. As a consequence, it is not uncommon for Indian movie stars to be involved in dozens of films simultaneously, their mere presence being what is required for box office success. In politics, too, people will often follow individuals, even as they leave parties or undertake radical about-turns in their ideologies.

Yet there is another aspect to this individualistic focus in Indian society. The other side of the coin is a tolerance of diversity. Societies strongly focused on teamwork, such as Japan or Australia, typically exhibit a much lower tolerance of difference and consequently feel much more uniform. India on the other hand is a mind-boggling kaleidoscope of diversity where everyone can have a say and a voice. For example, there are more than 2,000 ethnic groups and over 150 languages spoken. Newspapers in the country are published in close to 100 different languages, and radio programs are broadcast in 70 different tongues. No other major culture in the world, with the exception of Sub-Saharan Africa, has as much ethnic, linguistic, or genetic diversity as India. This diversity is expressed in a multitude of voices on any topic you care to name. Many recent works on India, such as V. S. Naipaul's *India: A Million Mutinies Now*[6] or Amartya Sen's *The Argumentative Indian* focus on this essential theme in Indian culture.[7]

The tolerance of difference, with its associated predilection for individual paths, has deep roots within Indian DNA. One manifestation of this is the obvious point that Hinduism is the only major polytheistic religion in the world. Polytheism is a natural expression of the Indian instinct of letting differences coexist rather than trying to shoehorn things into some common framework of belief. In my experience you don't necessarily even have to be Hindu to show this plurality. My mother, a Sikh, was entirely comfortable putting up pictures of Hindu gods, or random spiritual figures that had caught her attention, without in any way feeling that this contradicted or diluted her commitment to Sikhism, a monotheistic faith.

Psychologically, the core belief that drives this inherent tolerance of different paths is the quintessential Indian view that the same underlying reality can be manifested in many different and potentially contradictory ways. All versions and interpretations of reality are acceptable because there is an underlying unity to all things at the core. Polarities and contradictions are easily acceptable to the Indian mind, and some of the deepest philosophical works in Indian culture play to this sense of contradiction. Such contradictions are not just evident in Indian culture; they also exist within individuals themselves. From experience, this can make Indians somewhat opaque and difficult to read in spite of their surface warmth and enthusiasm. An Indian is able to shed psychological clothing more easily than people from other cultures perhaps because of the underlying tolerance of difference and acceptance of paradox.

This aspect of Indian cultural DNA likely arises from an orientation toward perceiving rather than doing. The benign Indian environment that allowed Indians to move quickly up the Maslow hierarchy meant that the equation between being and doing was tilted more in favor of the former in the Indian environment. The perceiving orientation allows one to accept the world, get underneath it, see basic patterns of unity, and appreciate the potential value of different paths. The doing orientation naturally requires one to simplify the world, to narrow its boundaries, and to make choices rather than to observe. This forces closure of thinking, reduction of paradox, and a desire to enforce some kind of uniformity. While Indian culture is highly regimented in some spheres, there is a much greater tolerance for individual paths in other respects. This leads to opportunities as well as problems in business. When the fear of hierarchical power is removed, Indian executives can be vociferous, creative, and dynamic. However, organizations can only reap these benefits by encouraging leaders to allow this diversity of opinion to emerge. Otherwise, the default tendency within Indian culture for ritual and horizontal hierarchical rigidity—which will be discussed later—can take over.

Indian business culture can be suited to creative industries such as filmmaking, design, publishing, or pharmaceutical research. However, organizations have to adapt in areas that require strong teamwork. It is more important in India than in many other cultures to create a common sense of organizational purpose and to continue reminding people of it. Concerted effort to build teams and alignment across departments is also more necessary in India than some other regions. In the absence of this, individuals can focus inordinately on their own roles or how particular responsibilities will look on their CV at the expense of just doing what is necessary to achieve a collective goal. Incentive schemes that are too focused on the individual can exacerbate this tendency—something that the Indian education system, with its emphasis on rankings, also magnifies. In our experience, companies in India benefit much more from focusing reward on group performance.

This is also true at a national level; without an overarching sense of unifying purpose, activity in India can lapse into disconnected chaos. One governmental department can launch an initiative only to be stymied by another. Political parties can fracture on an individual's whim, and decision making at the national level can become paralyzed by multiple agendas being pursued by a plethora of parties or factions within them. Even bribing officials can be a more arduous and inefficient activity in India. Global executives will often say that at least in China you know you will get what you have illicitly paid for when you bribe someone. In India, even when you think you have got the right person, a multiplicity of minor and major characters can emerge out of nowhere and do their bit to block your path, with each having to be bought off individually. After the collapse of India's nonalignment stance, the failure to create a common and compelling sense of national purpose in the world is the root cause of many problems in the social and political life of the country.

Yet for all these issues, India's tolerance of diversity is one of its greatest potential gifts to world culture. In 2004, after a general election in India, a Muslim president swore a Sikh prime minister into office to head up a predominantly Hindu country because a Catholic woman—Sonia Gandhi, who had won the election—did not want the post. There is no other country in the world in which one could remotely imagine this kind of scenario unfolding. While nations in the West pride themselves on their openness, the idea of a Muslim president anytime soon in a Western democracy is implausible. An inherent tolerance of diversity is a tremendous strength of Indian culture and something that our globalized society needs to learn from and embrace.

Inner Directedness

In 1888, a young Mahatma Gandhi was sent by his family to study law in London. The British Empire was at its height and in many senses London was the center of the world—not just with respect to political power, but also culturally and economically. The young Gandhi must have been overawed by this move from a far-flung, predominantly rural backwater of the empire to the very center of power. Focused and determined, even as a young man, Gandhi's initial instincts were to do everything possible to integrate into and be accepted by British society. He quickly ratcheted up huge expenses by going to the finest tailors and by trying to be seen in the right places. He even went as far as to take elocution lessons and learn ballroom dancing. However, sensing reticence and resistance on the part of the British he met, Gandhi did something that Indians are more prone to do than many others: He flipped to a polar opposite stance and made a conscious decision to drop the gent-about-town image and return to his Indian roots. He writes of his experiences of London in his autobiography *Experiments with Truth*. As has been pointed out by the writer V. S. Naipaul, what is interesting about Gandhi's narrative is a complete absence of any descriptions of the enormous city that stood at the center of the vast empire. There are no references to London's buildings, its cultural life, or people. Rather, Gandhi's account of his life in London revolves primarily around his struggles to keep the promise that he made to his mother about staying vegetarian, details on how his body reacted to the new environment, and musings on his inner life—with virtually no reference to the pulsating, grand city into which he had been catapulted.

Fast-forwarding to modern India, one of the most common criticisms that businessmen and other visitors have about modern India is how appalling the infrastructure is, and the generally poor quality of the environment. Even when it comes to world-class monuments, blithe neglect of the surroundings can cause a jarring experience. Visitors to the Taj Mahal are typically shocked by the dowdiness of Agra and the incongruity of such a breathtaking monument being surrounded by derelict buildings, uncared for fields, and pothole-strewn roads. This neglect seems particularly unfathomable given the importance of the monument to India's tourist industry. People who visit Banaras, a spiritual center for Hinduism on the banks of the Ganges, are often shocked by the dirtiness of the water and the general filth that exists in this sacred city. Indians are blindly able to put up with a lack of quality in their external environment that many other cultures simply would not accept.

Both Gandhi's nonchalance about the London environment and the above observations about India today illustrate a significant theme in Indian cultural DNA that might be termed *inner directedness*. More than any other culture in the world, Indian culture developed early on an emphasis on the inner workings of humans, coupled with an enormous parallel neglect of the external environment. Inner directedness arises fundamentally from deep-seated beliefs about humans' relationship with nature. Compared to other cultures, the Indian instincts around their environment is to accept it for what it is and to withdraw from it as much as the demands for everyday survival might allow.

This orientation has had a strong impact on Indian philosophy. The central task for humans in India's dominant religions is to go into themselves, reach for higher levels of insight and consciousness, and to see beyond the obvious forms with which the external world presents itself. In as much as an individual has to act in the world, it is done with a view to performing one's duties or, as the Bhagavad Gita extols, tempered with a philosophical detachment from the rewards that action might yield. It is this inner directedness that also leads to Hinduism putting Brahmins, the introverted pursuers of intellectual and spiritual values, at the very apex of its social pyramid. Warriors, whether they are kings or ordinary soldiers, those who engage in commercial enterprise, till the fields—or anyone who does something of practical value—are all subservient to those who detach themselves from the world.

This inner directedness also expresses itself significantly in terms of an introverted, intellectual orientation within Indian cultural DNA. There is a predilection for abstract, intellectual enquiry and debate. Indians are also great talkers. Many significant Indian intellectual contributions to the world revolve around abstract ideas or concepts. Indians invented the zero, chess, many areas of esoteric mathematical enquiry, as well as the world's main "becoming" faiths—that is, religions that focus on elevating an individual's consciousness as a route to a higher reality. India's extensive system of Ayurvedic medicine, which goes back tens of thousands of years, and yoga also reflect this inner directedness. By way of illustration, Chinese thought, as we shall see later, is much more externally oriented, practical, and concrete and has in the past enabled China to lead the world with respect to a range of inventive technologies such as the compass, paper, and gunpowder, to name but a few.

This inner directedness also leads to certain particular qualities with respect to Indian intellectual enquiry. When one looks at the pattern of Indian philosophers and thinkers over the ages, one is struck with how little regard there is for collecting systematic data from the world or testing out ideas in practice compared to other cultures. Rather, the focus is on intuitively playing with ideas and concepts. As writer Amaury de Riencourt observes, this gives Indian thought certain clear characteristics.[8]

> *The valuable writings of Indian culture belong either to the realm of startling and brilliant poetry, of oceanic epics such as Ramayana and the Mahabharata, with their colossal jumble of fantastic tales and their appeal to wild imaginations—or to the brief, stinging Sutras, flashes of lightning over which disciples ponder endlessly and which appeal to pure intuition. But, by Greek or Western standards, Indian philosophical rationalism is extremely weak, and often the logical thread in Indian thought is so tenuous as to be non-existent.*

This pattern of thinking explains a paradox that business leaders from other countries experience in India. At one level, Indian leaders are highly analytical and numerate. As I will argue later, this arises from another distinct feature of Indian cultural DNA. However, outside the world of numbers, Indian thought is highly intuitive, broad, and unstructured. Freed from the constraints of being tethered to the external world, Indian thinking has the ability to roam free and wide. When combined with high levels of numeracy, this can be powerful in terms of developing creative strategies that have commercial edge. However, like the Sutras, such strategies can come out of the blue and often with limited reference to external data or a clear chain of logic. Indian leaders can find the process of justifying their thinking to skeptical and data-driven global executives somewhat tedious and unnecessary. Steve Jobs, who traveled to India as a young man and developed a strong attachment to Zen Buddhism as a result, had this to say about how the Indian intellectual tradition had influenced him:

> *The people in the Indian countryside don't use their intellect like we do, they use their intuition instead and their intuition is far more developed than in the rest of the world. Intuition is a very powerful thing, more powerful than intellect, in my view.*

However, as always there is a downside to moving up the Maslow hierarchy and neglecting the realities of the external world to focus on internal, intuitive exploration. As a result of this approach, many practical things in India just do not work. In fact *anything* practical that does not require the application of process or ritualistic thinking—such as effective infrastructure, high-quality buildings, or modern agricultural practices—can be something of a hit or miss affair. The industries in which India excels are often in the thinking spaces, such as IT, pharmaceuticals, or film. China beats India hands down when it comes to manufacturing. Steve Jobs found this lack of practicality to be true as well. While the Indian intellectual tradition pulled him in and gave him a way of looking at the world that he embraced for the rest of his life, the blithe Indian neglect of the fundamentals of life also led him to develop dysentery. He became seriously ill, going down in weight from 160 pounds to 120 in barely a week.[9]

The inner directedness also leads to another feature of Indian psychology: a stubbornness born of a tendency to judge ideas through one's internal belief system rather than with reference to the external world or others' views. Our consultants report that Indian executives are some of the most resistant to feedback when it does not accord with their self-beliefs compared to executives from just about anywhere else. In particular, they can engage in elaborate intellectualization and justification when their self-image is challenged. There is an odd contradiction here: Indian executives are highly concerned about how others see them, but become very self-defensive if presented with a mirror that does not accord with their internal image or how they want to project themselves. In particular, a lack of awareness about how others might see them is not uncommon. In our research, 34 percent of Indian executives had a development need around self-awareness, the highest percentage out of all global regions. This compared with 13 percent for European executives, 19 percent of Americans and 16 percent for Chinese leaders. Even when they accept feedback on a point, many Indian executives can tend to build up an elaborate intellectual facade around why the issues raised are not important or indeed constitute some kind of inverted strength. Persistently questioning any ratings that are even mildly negative is also not uncommon.

This introverted bias toward judgment of things is also present on a wider level in Indian culture. For decades after independence, many Indian leaders, economists, and intellectuals remained self-satisfied and complacent about the economy's performance, oblivious to the strides that Far Eastern and Latin American countries were making with a different model. More positively, while Indians are partial to global brands—as are many people from less developed countries—they are less overawed by them than people are in, say, the Far East. Chinese culture is highly tuned to best practices elsewhere and will copy anything that seems to have merit, sometimes slavishly or unthinkingly. Indians are more inclined to pursue their own path in a proud, but also somewhat complacent, manner.

Horizontal Stratification

If you visit a senior business leader or government official in India, you will be struck by the number of junior officials, drivers, runners, tea makers, and other assorted helpers that hover around that individual, for the most part not doing very much until the very specific task that they are responsible for is invoked. If you ask for a drink, the senior official will more than often ring a bell or shout impatiently for someone to deliver it, even if the act of ordering help involves more effort than simply walking to the fridge a few yards away. Sometimes you will see a complicated chain of command spring into action for even a menial task such as moving a desk or a painting. If you try and do any of these things yourself—or worse, commit the faux pas of asking the wrong person to do it—you will often get the sense that you have ruptured the natural order of the universe. One senior executive who gently tried to tell his driver that he did not have to leap out of the car to open the door for him every time he wanted to get out, was surprised when the driver burst into tears, saying, "But Sir, that is my job." To be sure, many of the extreme manifestations of this cultural phenomenon are now in decline and some executives even complain about the old sense of service, or more accurately servitude, being eroded.

This phenomenon, of course, mirrors the institution of caste in Indian society, something that has been a feature of the Indian landscape from time immemorial. Over its long history, Indian society has developed an elaborate system of trade-guild like structures whose membership is genetically determined. However, unlike ordinary trade guilds, they also specify a bewildering range of other issues— such as how you address people, patterns of ritual and worship, where you are permitted to live and, of course, your marital options. There are literally thousands of hierarchically organized castes and the whole system has been the cornerstone of Indian cultural DNA for thousands of years. Modern, democratic, urban India is for the first time seriously challenging this institution, through national quotas and a myriad of individual battles and acts of rebellion; but it's not so easy to toss the weight of history away. Horizontal stratification still remains an important aspect of Indian cultural DNA.[10]

Speculations as to the origins of caste have suffered from the Indian neglect of recording their history in any great detail—itself an offshoot of the Indian tendency to regard worldly matters as relatively unimportant in the grand scheme of things. As we saw earlier, David Reich and his colleagues established that caste in genetic terms has been fixed in India for thousands of years. More detailed research indicates that while there was more mixing in the population some 4,200 to 1,900 years ago when the ANI and ASI populations mingled, caste became relatively fixed after that period. Indeed, it seems likely that the origins of caste may go back to the spread of settled agriculture in India, which pulled tribes together. While the current caste system was elaborated as Hinduism took hold around 1500 BCE, the architects were almost certainly building upon existing patterns of social segregation in India prior to the invasion.

Why did Indian society, more than any other existing culture, create this highly developed sense of horizontal segregation? The first point to note is that next to Sub-Saharan Africa, India has the highest levels of genetic diversity in the world. This is a reflection of the fact that India was the next staging post for the out-of-Africa exodus. And like Africa, India is also a high-pathogen environment. As argued earlier, this combination in Africa likely led to geographical segregation—with literally thousands and thousands of tribes living in a state of wary distance from each other. In India, the predominantly subtropical environment allowed agriculture to spread more easily and India developed some of the world's earliest settled civilizations. Geographic separation was rendered difficult in such circumstances, so the societies were forced to move to horizontal segregation.

In fact, the whole notion of purity and impurity is central to the edifice associated with caste. Most of the more extreme caste distinctions also relate to activities that are considered polluting in some way—such as jobs involving contact with animal or human waste, dealing with dead carcasses, or various cleaning roles. The whole notion of untouchability involves elaborate limits around where certain castes are allowed to eat and gather, including the banning of any physical contact, as well as elaborate purification rituals that need to be performed if defilement occurs. These strictures seem, at one level, bizarre, but they start to make sense if viewed through the lens of genetic distance and the avoidance of infectious disease in a very high-pathogen environment. I believe these were almost certainly the early forces that uniquely came together in India to set an unusually rigid approach to horizontal stratification in motion. Later, of course, it was built upon and became a social construct that justified and preserved elite domination and economic exploitation.

In any case, whatever the reasons for the origins of caste—or whether it arose during the spread of agriculture or following invasions from ANI-dominant populations—there is little doubt that it has been a feature of Indian cultural DNA for millennia. The thousands of subcastes, or Jatis, that have arisen mean that certain families and communities have perfected specific arts and performed the same roles in society for generations. Many of the incongruities and contradictions of Indian society arise from the fact that the country is a collection of tens of thousands of minicommunities, each with their own predilections, mores, and ways of being.

In business, especially modern multinational companies, the sense of caste that exists within village society is vanishing, and at one level the Indian workplace is rapidly moving to being caste blind. However, Indians cannot so easily shed cultural baggage that has been around for millennia. A keen sense of hierarchy is deeply embedded in Indian culture. You see organizations developing and observing a very finely tuned pecking order, as well as rigidity around duties and roles. Companies quickly develop their own elaborate caste systems, which specify an intricate hierarchical order, tight role definitions, and determine issues such as who can approach or sit with whom and how you are expected to address people. Executives have to work at injecting flexibility and openness into such systems.

Sycophancy and exaggerated outward respect for seniors is also part of the furniture in Indian corporate life and can make it difficult for executives to get a sense of what people are truly thinking or even going to do. This leads to another problem that is perhaps one of the biggest surprises for Western executives—the "yes, sir" surface culture. Executives seeking to explain something or offering instructions on a task will typically get a compliant "yes, sir." However, they find with experience that this does not necessarily denote understanding or agreement—it's just a way of showing hierarchical respect. The underlying independent mindedness of many Indians means that they may happily pursue their own path after saying "yes, sir." Alternatively, people may have no idea what you are talking about but project agreement and understanding as a way of saving face or projecting respect. After a while, many executives learn to check for understanding and put in place more extensive processes for following up on things than they might do in other environments.

Beyond the above considerations, there is also another more substantive point around how the whole notion of business fits into the caste system. The broad caste associated with business, the Bania, is relatively low in the Indian caste hierarchy and certainly lower than the Brahmins, the priests, and thinkers, or the Khastriya, the rulers and warriors. The elite tended to see commerce as an activity to be tolerated rather than a worthy calling in life. Furthermore, there is a tendency to view such revenue-generating activity as an opportunity for other nonproductive castes to extract their cut. This idea—that those who are productive have a duty to sustain the priests and thinkers—goes back a long way in Indian history. The Bhagavad Gita, a sublime and philosophically profound central text within Hinduism, has significant sections that focus on the duty that members of society have to provide material goods for the priestly castes. In these sections, the profundity evaporates and is replaced by admonitions of barely disguised self-interest.

This is one of the deeper reasons for the exceptionally high levels of difficulty associated with doing business in India, as well as the fact that Indian officials have taken corruption to the level of a fine art. Too many of the elite in India feel they have a right to something that it is the duty of productive members of society to provide for them. When combined with an inherent predilection for ritual, this deeply rooted tendency leads to businesses encountering a plethora of bureaucratic obstacles, unfathomable delays, and constant shifting of the goalposts.

However, while the caste system does create issues for businesses in modern India, it also creates certain opportunities. Historians who have examined the institution through Indian history often comment on how much fluidity it has despite surface rigidities. The pecking order and status of castes can change over time, sometimes radically. This seems paradoxical given the evidence cited earlier of virtually no gene flow between castes. However, this contradiction can be resolved by recognizing that, while people are tied by birth to their caste, where that caste stands in society is open to change.

With economic growth, modern India offers huge opportunities for castes to change their status or occupations and this has been seized upon enthusiastically. The tight social bonds and mutual trust that exist within the Jatis creates an environment for disseminating learnings and practices between members and for subcastes to move rapidly into areas of business and corner that segment. Journalist S. Gurumurthy sees castes as operating as "open-air business schools," giving a strong competitive edge to communities. Whole areas of business can be dominated by a subcaste that has moved into an activity, sometimes by accident.[11] The Gounder community in Tamil Nadu has in this way built a formidable presence in the international knitwear business. According to Gurumurthy, there are thousands of subcastes that have created niches in a whole host of areas, ranging from trucking and digging wells to various forms of trading. These communities operate on the basis of high levels of mutual trust and cooperation, sharing of resources, and rapid learning from each other. In his book *India's New Capitalists: Caste, Business, and Industry in a Modern Nation*, author Harish Damodaran describes a myriad of castes that are on a journey from fields, bazaars, and offices to modern industrial enterprises.[12]

This phenomenon is not just an internal affair to India. Subcastes acting as trade guilds can shape global industries as well, as the Hasidic Jews who once dominated the international diamond trade found to their surprise. From a standing start, within a few decades from the 1980s, over 90 percent of the trade they had historically controlled came to be dominated by the Palinpuri Jains and Parsis, both tiny communities from India. These communities were mirroring the strengths that allowed the Jews to become a significant force within the industry in the first place—just more intensely. More recently, the Kathiawaris have also rapidly moved into a prominent position in international diamond trading and polishing—the surprising thing is, they were tilling fields only a few years ago.

Within India, but also within Indian communities outside of the country, whole areas of business can come to be dominated by small, tightly bound groups. Once established, anyone trying to burst into these areas is essentially up against a system whose members have been tied together by blood for generations. Outsiders seeking to do business in this context can often fail to understand the forces that are at play. Investing substantial time in building relationships with key members of such subcastes is essential for any meaningful engagement. Executives also learn that there is no substitute for face-to-face contact in order to break into these established circles. In fact, this is one of the main implications of Indian society being a collection of thousands of tightly bound microcommunities—you have to spend time building relationships and trust through personal contact before you can be let through the door, otherwise India will always feel paradoxically like an unfathomable set of fast changing, but nonetheless closed systems.

Mathematics: The Art of the Hindus

Srinivasa Iyengar Ramanujan was born in 1887 to a poor Brahmin family in the Indian state of Tamil Nadu. In his early schooling, he showed good abilities in mathematics, coupled with a complete lack of discipline with respect to other subjects. In spite of his talent, he avoided school—his family had to enlist help from the local police to make sure he attended. His mathematical skill enabled him to receive a scholarship at a government college. However, once there, he could only focus on mathematics and failed most of his other subjects, which led to a prompt withdrawal of the scholarship. Discouraged, he ran away from home and enrolled in a college in Madras but failed his degree, again because he only focused on mathematics. Ramanujan's life at this point consisted mostly of avoiding starvation and just existing from day to day. He sought clerical work and eventually found a job in a government revenue department. He was encouraged by the deputy collector there to continue his interest in mathematics and did so virtually entirely on his own steam and without any formal training. While working as a clerk, he developed insights and proofs in a range of mathematical areas that he recorded in a characteristically idiosyncratic and unconventional manner.

At the age of 25, Ramanujan drafted letters to three Cambridge University professors—H. F. Baker, E. W. Hobson, and G. H. Hardy—detailing some of his work. They were among the leading mathematicians of the time. The first two returned these unusual looking papers from a clerk in a far-flung corner of the empire without comment, possibly not having read them at all. Luckily for Ramanujan, his letter to G. H. Hardy arrived just as he was having breakfast and, with nothing else to do, he paused momentarily to look at the contents. He was immediately intrigued by the unconventional and creative nature of the theorems and proofs that Ramanujan presented. Perplexed, he asked a colleague to take a look, who also expressed amazement at the depth of the mathematical insights. They concluded that while Ramanujan was in all likelihood a charlatan who had plagiarized someone else's work, they had possibly stumbled upon a man altogether of "exceptional originality and power." Intrigued, they wrote back to Ramanujan and invited him to Cambridge. This invitation, to put it mildly, was a left-field development for Ramanujan's parents, who were disbelieving and thought the whole thing some kind of joke or scam. They forbade him to go but after much argument, he eventually persuaded them that the offer was genuine and set sail for England.

At Cambridge, once people had gotten used to Ramanujan's unusual path into the institution, his genius was quickly recognized—and the self-taught revenue clerk without any significant qualifications to his name became the first Indian to be elected a fellow of Trinity College. In a short space of time, he produced a prodigious volume of work covering mathematical analysis, number theory, infinite series, and continuous fractions. G. H. Hardy, his mentor, considered his work to be in the same league as the best mathematicians in history. His methods were, however, characteristically Indian: highly intuitive and often lacking in systemic written proof or rigor. Sadly, his prodigious output was cut short at the age of 32 after he contracted tuberculosis. He died in 1920, but over the years the depth and profundity of his mathematical thinking has increasingly been recognized and appreciated by mathematicians the world over.

Extraordinary as Ramanujan's story is, it is an expression of an underlying feature of Indian cultural DNA. Mathematics is an area where a certain section of the Indian population has precocious talent; there is a comfort and feel for mental arithmetic and commercial/financial reasoning culturally. This theme has wide and deep implications for how business is conducted in India, how Indian executives operate, as well as the areas of natural strength for the Indian economy. Before discussing these, it is helpful to explore the nature of this attribute.

It's easy to notice the extent to which an interest in mathematical enquiry has endured through the entire period of recorded history in India. This is unlike other cultures, such as the Greeks or the Arabs, where it flourished for defined periods, when the circumstances were right. Ancient Vedic culture, the Jains, and a string of notable mathematicians through the ages right up to the present illustrate this interest. In the recent past, from 1300 to 1632, the Kerala school of mathematics made significant advances with respect to the series expansion of trigonometric functions and anticipated many of the developments in calculus several centuries before it was formally advanced by Isaac Newton and Gottfried Leibniz in Europe. In fact, many scholars feel that it was the infusion of ideas from the Kerala school through the spice-trade routes into Europe that laid the basis for the formal development of calculus in Europe.

We can perhaps gauge the depth of the Indian contribution to mathematics from the fact that the number system the world uses today is of Indian origin. The simplicity of expressing every possible number using 10 symbols including a 0, with each symbol having both an absolute value and a value dependent upon where it is placed, seems obvious now. However, this was an insight that eluded most world cultures, including the Greeks and the Romans. The Greeks may also have borrowed their earliest mathematical ideas from the Indians. Pythagoras is credited with launching this aspect of Greek and Western thought. However, several centuries before Pythagoras, around 800 BCE, the Indian mathematician—and likely priest—Baudhayana notes the following in one of the *Sulba sutras*, appendices to the Vedas, concerned with the construction of religious altars: "The rope which is stretched along the length of diagonal of a rectangle makes an area which the vertical and horizontal sides make together."

Every schoolchild would recognize this as Pythagoras's theorem. To be historically accurate, we should now perhaps start calling it Baudhayana's theorem, as there is also a numerical proof of the result in the *Sulba sutras*. In his work, Baudhayana also enumerates a number of Pythagorean triples, as well as providing the formula for the square root of 2. It is now known that Pythagoras traveled extensively, including to Mesopotamia, where he might have absorbed Indian influences. But following his travels, Pythagoras more or less morphed into being culturally Indian. He started wearing unusual non-Greek white tunics and trousers, embraced the Hindu idea of the transmigration of souls, and became an ardent vegetarian. He created an order focused on philosophical, mathematical, and theological enquiry, as well as the pursuit of ascetic discipline, very similar to countless similar orders in Indian culture at the time. In fact, Pythagoras's views were so out of place with the local values at Croton, where he based his new order, that eventually locals stormed the Pythagorean sanctuary, set fire to the buildings, and killed virtually all of his disciples. Pythagoras may also have perished during this attack, but more likely managed to escape and subsequently died in exile.[13]

However, the Indians were far less systematic than the Greeks in writing down proofs or collating their knowledge. Brilliant and penetrating insights were captured in small and pithy statements and just left there for whoever might want to pick them up. Ultimately, it was the Arabs who were responsible for taking what they called "the Hindu system of reckoning," and a multitude of other Indian mathematical insights, to the rest of the world. The introverted nature of Indian mathematical enquiry is also illustrated by the historical Arab word for mathematics, *Hindisat*, which literally means the art of the Hindus. The other point to note is this strength is only evident in select Indian populations.

The mathematical strength of Indian cultural DNA, however, expresses itself today in some tangible and practical forms. One is struck when doing business in India by the extremely high levels of financial and commercial dexterity that people display. I have found that Indian executives expect a high level of financial fluency in all business leaders and are quietly dismissive of those who do not display these skills. Many Indian executives feel they can run rings around, in particular, Western executives when it comes to financial negotiations. "It's bewildering how fast they can work things out and you find you have given away things that you just didn't realize at the time," one executive said to me. Others can become confused by the complexity of the commercial arrangements that Indians put in place. "You have to be careful you count your fingers when you shake on a deal," a German leader laughingly said to me.

For this reason, Indian DNA was always going to be well-suited to something like the IT industry, in which the country is now a recognized global leader. In Tamil Nadu, the birthday of Ramunjan is celebrated on December 22 as IT day. Bill Gates once remarked that south Indians were perhaps the sharpest people that he had encountered with respect to intrinsic IT capabilities. Microsoft now has an Indian CEO. It is easy to see why underlying mathematical capability, when coupled with the Indian propensity for memorization and ritualistic thinking discussed later, would combine to give the country a natural advantage in a sector such as IT. You do not need high levels of industrial infrastructure, investment, or even reliable supplies of energy—all traditional areas of weakness in India—to succeed. You just need a laptop and a mathematical mind. There was a tendency initially to see India's success in IT as purely down to cost advantage and focus on the activities at the lower value chain within IT. However, global companies are increasingly finding that Indian workers are adept at the highest and most cutting-edge areas within IT. Something like one third of the people who work within the IT sector in Silicon Valley are of Indian origin, and a very high proportion of Silicon Valley firms owe their origins to Indian founders.

More generally in international business, Indian executives gravitate toward roles in finance or IT. Business strategy firms also have a large number of Indians and a number have led such companies, including McKinsey. The combination of deep numerical skills with a natural facility for conceptual thinking is well-suited to strategic consulting. The banking industry also is a place where one sees many Indians, as well as people from other cultures with strong trading and commercial skills, such as the Middle East. A number of global banking institutions, such as Citibank and Deutsche Bank, have had Indian CEOs. "Quants" inhabit the most esoteric areas of investment banking; applying arcane and complex mathematical models to investment and pricing decisions. This is an area of banking where Indians are massively overrepresented.

Ritualistic Thinking

The American documentary film *Spellbound* popularized the Scripps Spelling Bee contest. The contest involves contestants being asked to accurately spell a bewildering range of rarefied words from the English language. One of my American colleagues recently asked me, "What's going on with Indians and the National Spelling Bee competition?" Apparently since 1999, 11 of the 15 winners of the contest have been Indian-Americans. In the 2013 final, out of the top 10 places, Indian-Americans took eight. This is a vast overrepresentation given that the community constitutes barely 1 percent of the American population. The obvious explanations for this center on the high educational levels of Indian-Americans, as well as Indian versions of Tiger Mums pushing their kids relentlessly. But Chinese-Americans, with real Tiger Mums, show no such overrepresentation on the Spelling Bee, so something else must also be going on here.

The answer to this puzzle lies in the oral tradition of religious transmission in Indian culture. The Vedas, the sacred texts of Hinduism, comprise a vast encyclopedic series of hymns, chants, epic poems, as well as profound philosophical treatises. Just to get a sense of scale, the Mahabarat, an oceanic epic poem, which constitutes a fraction of just one section, is, at 1.8 million words, 10 times the length of the *Iliad* and *Odyssey* combined. It is commonly accepted that the Vedas started to be compiled around 1500 BCE, but some scholars suggest an even earlier date. The ancient Indians, faced with the challenge of submitting this dense body of work to the next generation, decided that oral transmission was the only viable method—in part because the melodic hymn-like nature of many sections could not be faithfully conveyed in writing. While there are written records of the Vedas dating from 500 BCE, the culturally preferred method was, until a few hundred years ago, oral transmission. You might wonder how this kind of transmission worked across thousands of years and with text as frighteningly complicated as the Vedas. The ancient Indians were aware of the problem of textual corruption and assigned certain groups the task of transmission from generation to generation. Those involved in this gargantuan exercise developed elaborate mnemonic methods to ensure that the sacred verses were never ever corrupted. For example, over 10 different styles of recitation were developed. The Pada method was the most straightforward and involved learning the texts in their natural order. Another method was the Jata where one learned the words paired together, but then also recited the paired words in reverse order. Other recitation methods were even more complex. Families across the subcontinent were given texts that became their religious duty to transmit without fault or error.

What is extraordinary about this whole endeavor is that when the British arrived in India and heard about this characteristically unpragmatic Indian tradition, they assumed that over such an expanse of time the text must have become highly corrupted. This was not an unnatural assumption given the elaborate game of Chinese whispers that the Indians had played with the Vedas across thousands of years. To their astonishment, however, across the whole of India, they found the Vedas had been faithfully transmitted with barely a handful of errors. Furthermore, they found that written reproduction had corrupted the text much more than the near faultless oral tradition. Huge swaths of the Indian population throughout the ages were involved in this task. In 2003, UNESCO proclaimed that this extraordinary cultural feat represented "a masterpiece of the oral and intangible heritage of humanity."

Indian cultural DNA is strong on disciplined memorization and learning. The Spelling Bee as a task pales into insignificance when one considers the feat achieved with the Vedas. When one sees the Indian education system in operation, one is struck by the emphasis on rote learning—sadly, at the expense sometimes of critical thinking. When I arrived in the UK as a seven-year-old, I was unable to speak a word of English. However, I surprised my teachers considerably by my power to recite multiplication tables all the way up to the 15 times table. I had only spent a year or so at an Indian school but quickly learned that unless you wanted to risk disgrace—which at my school entailed being forced to squat on your desk in a humiliating posture while holding your ears—you knuckled under and learned what was put before you. The intense effort and application that Indian students put into rote learning for exams is stupefying. If anything, things have gotten worse as the competition to get into elite institutions has intensified. A whole industry consisting of cramming colleges, study aids, and cheating practices has arisen to cope with the intense race of getting into the top subjects and colleges.

There is another point to be made about the history of oral transmission associated with the Vedas. While there are many parts of the Vedas that contain searing philosophical insights or fantastically imaginative allegorical tales, large sections are devoted to complex hymns and chants, as well as intricate rules of ritual. Much of the cultural effort associated with preserving the Vedas was oriented toward rigidly transmitting these strictures for ritual and worship. The idea was that individuals should absorb these rules uncritically and enact them with precision and fidelity. The recitation of verses was and is today primarily an exercise in recapitulation; virtually no attention is given to the verses' meaning. Certainly it is anathema to critique or question what is being uttered.

This essential element likely leads to two facets of Indian cultural DNA that color organizational culture and the way business operates—one of which is a lack of critical thinking. Students are taught to memorize and recapitulate rather than question and interrogate. While India produces 5 million graduates every year, less than 5 percent are deemed to be employable in international organizations, and only 50 percent employable anywhere because of this gap in critical thinking.[14] In spite of the effort that Indian students put into their studies, Indian pupils are virtually at the bottom of the league in international comparisons of critical thinking.[15] These results also illustrate the picture of excellence at the top, tailing off sharply as one gets to other levels. Following a procedure in business life is psychologically akin to following a religious ritual. The casualty in this is the practical relevance of the procedure to the achievement of end goals. Rather the ritual or behavior is seen as an end in itself. One does one's piece and it is left to others to ensure that everything fits together. The other side of the intellectual ingenuity and argumentation that occur at senior levels in Indian business is the equally strong desire for clear processes and a slavish adherence to rules, which gets more accentuated the lower one goes. The level of direction people expect and require in India can disorient Western managers or Indians who have been educated in environments that encourage initiative more. Even in areas of strength for India, such as programming, the penchant for procedure means that while replication is near faultless, international customers often complain of poor work because of a narrow or literal interpretation of the brief rather than people thinking more broadly about the purpose of the request.

This lack of critical thinking also means that many Indian executives are less good at questioning or developing new ways of working, or changing a system, as opposed to operating within one. Change in the way things are done can take time and there can be psychological resistance in Indians to altering established procedures once they are put into place. Indian executives need to be trained to develop the muscle for driving and envisaging change at a broad level. This also applies to the country more broadly. Indians can be highly successful minorities in other countries' systems, but find it harder to create a framework for national success. The default is always to fall back on what is in place already as opposed to critically examining its relevance to current realities.

The penchant for ritualistic thinking and pedantic detail is also the psychological building block for another very obvious part of Indian cultural DNA, which is the mind-numbingly high levels of procedural delay and bureaucracy anyone conducting business in the country encounters. Something as simple as buying a train ticket in an Indian train station can quickly become a Kafkaesque exercise, requiring the negotiation of various arcane layers of bureaucracy. Doing anything official in India typically involves dealing with frustratingly rigid and unerringly unempathetic officials who pass you around from one desk to the other. Tasks like opening a bank account or retrieving a birth certificate can take months, often requiring several visits and endless reserves of patience. Bureaucracy is a trait in many high power, distant environments in Asia and Africa, but it reaches its own very distinctive levels in India. A recent survey found that India was by far the most bureaucratic across a number of Asian countries, getting a score of 9.41 out of 10 for the level of hurdles put in the way of people.[16]

The extreme slowness with which certain things happen in India—particularly anything involving the government—also arises in part from this ritualistic mindset. Indian courts set the world record for the slowness with which cases are processed. For example, there were 31 million cases pending in 2013, which would require over 300 years to clear at current rates.[17] It can take decades to hear a simple case of property ownership in an Indian court. In many walks of life, Indians operate as if time is of no consequence. The process for military procurement, for example, can take decades as detailed rules and protocols are laid down and then slavishly followed. Negotiations can all too frequently get bogged down in mysterious detail and often fail, even when a deal has been agreed upon, due to procedural wrangling.

Unless India addresses these issues around critical thinking and the efficiency of its systems and processes, it will always be competing with one hand tied behind its back. Oddly, some things such as decision making in business can happen fast, and the country is changing rapidly on many dimensions. However, in areas where the ritualistic mindset takes hold, the drag is palpable and exacts a severe economic price.[18]

Looking Ahead

The Indian psychological orientation toward thinking, talking, and perceiving, as well as for internal focus, is something that is of increasing relevance as other parts of the world also move up the Maslow hierarchy. It is not a coincidence that Buddhism, yoga, and vegetarianism find fertile ground in some of the most forward looking and advanced areas of the world. India's inherent instincts around diversity and nonviolence also represent themes that other cultures could learn and build upon. In business, India's strengths in IT, pharmaceutical research, and finance could enable the country to do to these high-value sectors in the global marketplace what China has done to manufacturing.

However, many of the weaknesses in the Indian psychological tradition mean that the country will always walk on feet of clay, neglecting the practical realities that are necessary for a strong foundation for success, whether in business or society. Looking outward rather than inward, developing the capacity for critical thinking, and controlling the Indian instinct for ritual and bureaucracy will be necessary in a faster-moving world. Many of these issues have served in the recent past to bring India's natural rate of growth down when it should really be leaping ahead of China's. Frustrated, many Indian businesses often choose to seek their fortunes abroad.

Critical to India moving forward is the need for people to look at themselves and the society around them in an open and honest manner. The Indian instinct to sweep uncomfortable truths under the carpet means that problems are only ever addressed when they get serious. Once a partial fix has been achieved, there is a tendency to revert to an inward-looking complacency. Overcoming this tendency will be necessary if the country is to move forward on a consistent basis rather than the more usual pattern of fits and starts.

Fortunately, the open and vociferous democratic culture of India means that many of these issues are increasingly being surfaced and confronted. State and national governments are being judged much more on performance than ever before. The idea of caste-based parties simply banking votes from their members is also fast changing. The cultural handbrakes that have held the country back are slowly but surely being released. There is a renewed emphasis on cleaning up the environment, tackling corruption, addressing India's appalling infrastructure issues, and making it a hub for manufacturing. These initiatives are rightly challenging many aspects of India's cultural DNA that need to be tackled. Going against the grain in this way will not be easy and will require persistence. However, if this process continues, the country has every chance of becoming what it has been for much of world history—one of the dominant economic powers on the planet.

Chapter 4

The Middle East: Ambivalence and Uncertainty in the Modern Age

I f most external observers with limited experience of the Middle East were prompted to apply a psychological lens to the region, they would likely come up with perspectives formed through knowledge of recent global events or the image of Islam as a religion. Western observers, in particular, if asked for their authentic rather than politically correct observations, would in all likelihood produce a generally negatively tinged list: intellectual and emotional rigidity, intolerance of different value systems, excessive emotionality, propensity for empty posturing, and underlying hostility to the outside world. Worrying stories of seemingly sophisticated and well-educated young, middle-class men transforming overnight into Jihadists, or the rise out of nowhere of groups such as ISIL, all add to a sense of a world in which psychologically regressive, unpredictable, and potentially troublesome themes are at play.

However, if you were a time traveler and could go back a few hundred years, your views might be very different. Between the ninth and the thirteenth centuries the Muslim world was at the center of a vast global commercial hub with deep trading connections to China, India, Africa, and Europe. Only the New World was outside of this trading and commercial Pax Islamica, renowned for its openness, tolerance, and receptivity to learning from other cultures. The Muslim world at that point was far ahead of Europe with respect to accounting, commercial activities, and the application of fair and balanced rules of trade.

Adjectives like forward looking, commercially sophisticated, inquisitive, open-minded, and protective of other cultures' intellectual traditions might spring to mind. Sure enough, our time traveler would also see non-Muslim populations treated very differently, the uncomfortable reality of Arab-driven slavery, and perhaps have been reminded by many non-Muslim subjects of the brutal conquests that predated this period. Nevertheless, the picture of Middle Eastern psychology and culture formed would have been very different from some of the images that are at play today.

In my experience both sides of the coin are apparent in the views of people who actually know the Middle East, as opposed to judging it from a distance. Business leaders, for example, will often comment positively on the openness to learning, the desire to be cutting edge, as well as the sheer multiplicity of nationalities that come together in many Middle Eastern organizations. Many are also struck by the warmth of the culture and even more so by the polite gentleness of people's day-to-day behavior. Yet most would also say that there are complex and retrogressive psychological forces at play as well.

The reality is that many of the above themes are evident in the psychology of the Middle East and for very tangible and powerful reasons are deeply rooted in the cultural DNA of the region. Furthermore, these themes are at play and, at times, in conflict with each other at numerous levels—within individuals, subgroups, and nations within the Middle East. Perhaps more than any other part of the world there is more evidence of powerful and contradictory impulses pulling people and societies in different directions. In order to understand this more deeply, we need to first explore who moved there, why, and the dominant environmental conditions the early settlers faced, in response to which the particularities of Middle Eastern culture and psychology were formed.

How Modern Humans Populated the Middle East

It is commonly accepted that the first modern human incursion into the Levant 125,000 years ago proved to be a dead end. The Saharan gate that had opened and lured the first modern humans out of Africa proved to be something of a lethal trap as the new human inhabitants were caught between the advancing Arabian and Saharan deserts caused by a much colder climatic spell. It is now clear, both from archaeological and DNA evidence, that the Middle East was populated in substantial measure some 65,000 years later by a movement of people from the early colonies to the west of India. The mitochondrial data indicates the dominance of the *N* offshoot of the original *L3* out-of-Africa line, and the virtual absence of the other ancient offshoot, *M*. If humans had occupied the Middle East directly from the first out-of-Africa colony, one would see both *N* and *M* haplogroups in that region. The evidence from sites such as Skhul and Kafzeh are also consistent with this picture, as it suggests that large parts of the Middle East were, and remained, settled by Neanderthals for a full 20,000 years or so after the out-of-Africa exodus, some 70,000 years ago.[1] It seems that modern humans wisely stuck to the coast, penned in by the extreme desert to the north, as well as wisely avoiding the Neanderthals who had recolonized the area.

The *Y*-chromosome evidence backs up this picture of a movement into the Middle East from the west of India and then south into the Middle East. Of the three sons of the out-of-Africa Adam, it is haplogroup *F* that dominates this area. One of *F*'s descendants, *J*, is responsible for close to 50 percent of modern male populations in the Middle East. It is estimated that *J* first arose in Iraq as the modern humans made their way into the Levant from the west of India. Stephen Oppenheimer believes that this movement probably happened during a series of warm spells that occurred 50,000 years ago, opening up a route through Iran, into Iraq, and then south into the Arabian Desert, as well as northwest into Kurdistan and Anatolia.[2]

It is likely that the initial movement into the Middle East involved relatively small groups of people. Substantial settlement of the region required changes from the hunter-gatherer lifestyle. The *Y*-chromosome evidence indicates that out of the *J* haplogroup, two offshoots, *J1* and *J2*, rapidly became common in the region. *J2* is more common in the north of the Middle East, including modern-day Iran, Kurdistan, parts of Iraq, and Anatolia. It reaches some of its highest concentrations in Mesopotamia and is thought to have originated some 30,000 years ago. Its explosion much later on is widely regarded as being related to the spread of agriculture. Interestingly, *J2* is also found at rates close to 30 percent in parts of Greece, Italy, Sicily, Corsica, and Crete. The pattern indicates a maritime dispersal at some point, perhaps involving Phoenician or Greek colonies.

J1, a subtype of *J*, is much more common in the Arabian Desert and in North Africa. It closely parallels the presence of Semitic languages. It is believed that *J1* arose perhaps 15,000 years ago in the Anatolian region and that it is closely related to the spread of nomadic animal husbandry. There was a migration south some 10,000 years ago, driven in part by the spread of herding to the Arabian Desert. Interestingly, *J1* rates, while consistently high in the Middle East—nearly 50 percent in Saudi Arabia and even 65 percent in Bedouin tribes—also crop up in isolated pockets in certain parts of Europe. *J1* was then further spread out of the Arabian Desert with the Islamic armies that swept into the surrounding regions in the seventh and eighth centuries.

Even people of Middle Eastern origin who left the region some time ago show a strong pattern of *J1* and *J2* haplogroups. Ashkenazi, Sephardic, and Kurdish Jewish groups all have high representation of both—in the region of 40 percent—with the northern Middle Eastern group being more common. All three Jewish groups are closely related to each other, indicating that they have preserved their genetic identity despite thousands of years of separation. Intriguingly, one difference is that there is a relatively high representation of two central Asian and east European haplogroups (*R1A1* and *Q1B1*) in Ashkenazi Jews. The rates of 5 to 10 percent for each suggest that these haplogroups were not just a minor intrusion from living in the relevant territories, and their presence possibly represents the signature of the conversion of many Khazars from the central Asian region to Judaism in the eighth century, as popularized by Arthur Koestler.[3] Apart from this difference, and in spite of the virulent current antagonism between the two communities, Jews and Palestinians are closely related, indicating common origins only a few thousand years ago, probably in pre-Judaic times.

Deserts and Civilization: The Twin Drivers of Middle Eastern Cultural DNA

The conditions that early human settlers faced in the Middle East and North Africa were a far cry from those that their forebearers left behind in Sub-Saharan Africa. These challenging climactic conditions had caused earlier communities of humans from Africa to perish without trace about 90,000 years ago. The humans who moved there some 40,000 years later subsequently also faced major climactic challenges, but this time managed to adapt and hang on in some way. To have lived, survived, and eventually thrived in this new and unusual ecological niche required ingenuity, resilience, and new forms of behavior and patterns of social organization, leading to the rise of a very particular psychological and cultural DNA. It appears that there have been two main drivers of this DNA within the region, associated with the two main Y-chromosome haplogroups, *J1* and *J2*. These are respectively related to the existence of desert herding on the one hand, and the spread of settled agriculture and urban living on the other.

Many people in the Middle East today live in or close to the two largest, driest, and hottest deserts in the world; the Arabian and the Saharan. It would be an understatement to say that humans and most other species of animals or plants are not naturally adapted for life in the desert. The reality is that short of going to the North or South Poles, those early modern humans who ended up in the desert could not have picked a more challenging or aversive environment. The Jews joke that Moses could perhaps have walked a bit further before deciding his people had arrived in the Promised Land.

The need to maintain our body temperature through sweating means humans can lose as much as 12 liters of fluid a day in the extreme heat of the desert. The loss of salt is also a severe problem. This is necessary in order to maintain energy production in the absence of which painful muscle cramps can set in. Extreme daytime temperatures in the desert (the highest ever recorded is 58 degrees Celsius (136 F) in the Sahara) can also quickly cause heat stroke. The night does not offer much respite either, as temperatures can plummet without too much of an intervening milder phase. Humans are barely able to survive on their own for more than a day or two under these conditions, unless they take great care to seek shelter, preserve water, and very carefully marshal the meager resources of animal and plant life that are available. In short, the desert is not an environment where one can go off and do one's own thing in a carefree, exuberant South Seas island type of way. These simple and obvious facts of desert survival have had a profound impact on cultural attitudes toward a whole array of areas, including power, social order, individual autonomy, and religious beliefs.

Humans have learned to survive in deserts by binding themselves into small, tightly knit nomadic groups with strict rules for governing their behavior. Members are typically tied to these groups for life unless they marry into another tribe. Because plant life is scarce, most desert tribes have to move as one, regularly in search of water and food. People rarely go off in all directions on a whim or because of a surge of independence. The mobility required by desert life also means that inhabitants typically carry everything that they own. The biggest investment here is in livestock, which is carefully nurtured, looked after, and defended as a matter, literally, of life and death. While there are advantages to carrying all one's worldly possessions, there are also some obvious risks that ensue from this portability. It can be all too easy for someone else to come along and relieve you of your burdens.

The raid on other tribes is therefore an integral part of life for most nomadic desert communities. The warfare inherent in raids is different from the kinds of conflicts in which more settled communities engage. The raid involves lightning fast strikes seemingly out of nowhere, where the main objective is to cart away as much of the other tribe's possessions and womenfolk as humanly possible. The alliances involved in raiding are also typically different from normal warfare. They involve short-term, opportunistic groupings when an opportunity presents itself, then moving apart once the project has been executed. All too often, partners in a raid at one time may become adversaries the next time they cross paths. Alliances in raiding communities are therefore fluid and skin deep, combining surface solidarity with the constant underlying threat of betrayal. These pressures create strong, emotionally rooted tribal identities, but also require psychological agility and flexibility with respect to one's emotional orientation to other groups—sworn brothers in arms at one moment, mortal enemies at another.

However, the desert is rarely just a never-ending expanse of rock and sand with no respite for humans. Frequently, it is dotted with oases, marshes, small lakes or rivers, which create the opportunity for more settled living. Transitory regions where populations are partly settled and partly nomadic are also common. In part because the surrounding environment is so hostile, areas that offer the opportunity for more settled and permanent existence can became densely populated centers of human existence. It is no coincidence that many of the world's first civilizations, such as the Sumerian, Indus Valley, and Egyptian, all arose clustered around rivers passing through desert or near desert landscapes.

In the Middle East, this process of enforced concentration led to both settled agriculture and then some of world's earliest settled civilizations arising in the region, with the Sumerians coming first, followed by Babylonians and then the Egyptians. This new form of living represented a quantum shift in human organization. Once humans develop a form of social organization, powerful forces that drive new psychological attributes come into play. Settled civilizations move quickly to tame people, give them differentiated roles, and provide a powerful impetus for the development of trading, financial skills, and new forms of intellectual inquiry and learning. Individuals who are able to respond to these challenges rise upward in such societies—before economic advances and the rise of contraceptives equalized things, there is plenty of evidence to suggest that high status also conferred considerable advantages in terms of reproductive success. The capacity of societies to punish deviance and exile or execute people who do not fit the new norms also creates a new selection force. Though these forces have come into play everywhere, parts of the Middle East have been traveling down this road longer.

The behavioral and cultural patterns driven by nomadic desert life—as well as those arising from the requirements of settled agriculture and urban civilization—are the building blocks of the Middle East's psychological and cultural DNA. Sometimes these very different forms of existence, all driven at root cause by the conditions of the desert, reinforce each other, but at other times they pull in different directions. This creates potentially contradictory impulses and sharp polarities, whether at the level of national culture, the social group, or within individuals. For these reasons the psychological and cultural DNA of the Middle East world is more complex and prone to contradictory and constantly shifting psychological impulses than that of other global cultures.

The Rules of Life

Frank Herbert's *Dune* is one of the best-selling science fiction books of all time. It is set on the planet Arrakis, a daunting and inhospitable desert world virtually devoid of water. Humans, however, live on this planet despite its hostility to any form of life. The Fremen, as they are called, have evolved extremely strong codes of behavior that are rigidly applied to all members. Water is so important for the Fremen that they conserve it with ferocious intent. All Fremen are required to wear clothing that extracts and stores moisture that they might otherwise lose through sweating and breathing. While they are free to roam the desert, tight rituals and rules that circumscribe the Fremen are necessary for them to survive the hostile ecosystem of Arrakis. The Fremen also have a strong warrior tradition and live in tribes whose leaders are selected through combat. They are bound by a strong sense of honor and depicted as courageous, noble, and purer in intent than many of the other communities of humans who are attracted to Arrakis because of its valuable, life-enhancing spice.

It is clear that Frank Herbert based much of his description of Fremen society on the cultural norms of Bedouin Arabs. The interesting point about the work is the very obvious fact that desert living requires the formation of tight groups, all members of whom must obey the rules for living that are necessary in order to survive the extreme conditions of the desert. The group must impose its will on the individual and the individual must submit to the laws of the desert. If you reside in temperate or tropical lands and you don't like the rules of the group you have the option of setting forth on your own. You may not have a great time of it, but you have at least some chance of survival. No such possibility exists for the individual in the desert. You cooperate and submit to the rules of group survival or you die. This also leads to another feature of tribal life in the desert; the need for strong, decisive, and unambiguous leadership. Even if a tribe opts not to rely on a strong leader, but instead on more democratic principles, it's still necessary to ensure that everybody follows the agreed line to ensure group cohesion.

Does the stringent environment of the desert inevitably lend itself to societies oriented toward the exercise of clear authority and the imposition of tight rules for living one's life? Anthropologist Janet Bennion thinks so, based on her study of Mormon and Mennonite communities in the Chihuahua Valley in the high desert plateaus of northern Mexico.[4] Bennion, herself from a Mormon background, was interested in observing at close quarters the social and cultural norms that evolved in these isolated desert communities. She coined the phrase *desert patriarchy* to describe the principles around male supremacy, rigid social norms, and a rejection of many aspects of modern global culture, to describe the ethos that evolved in these disparate and isolated communities. She observed these communities at close hand, and while a lot of what she finds fits in with the image that the term *desert patriarchy* conjures up, there is more going on underneath the surface. For example, even though women in these communities live under the shadow of male authority, they find many creative ways of achieving self-expression and accessing power. They form intricate, and to some extent autonomous, networks for meeting their needs within an overtly patriarchal system. Bennion's view is that the isolated conditions of these tribes and the harshness of the desert environment create a community where individual freedom is necessarily, and in many cases voluntarily, relinquished. Could the processes that Janet Bennion describes for these communities in the north Mexican desert have also taken place 40,000 years ago and led to the same cultural forms arising in the Arabian and north African deserts?

Certainly the term *desert patriarch* seems to capture many of the features of Middle Eastern culture seen today. Here perhaps more than most other parts of the world, a myriad of caveats and frequently conservative rules seem to be vigorously applied to provide clear guidance on how one is to live one's life. Furthermore, all these characteristics seem to increase the deeper one goes into the desert. Throughout the Muslim world, conservative clerics dictate what people can and cannot do in ways that just would not be acceptable in many other cultures. Critically, people for the most part want to obey these rules, impose them on others, and can react with great emotion to efforts to renegotiate or modernize the interpretation of these rules.

Of course, a simple and more proximal explanation for these tendencies is that they arise from the natural instincts and rhythm of Islam. But this naturally leads to the question: Why is Islam the religion that it is, and why does it express itself differently in different parts of the world? It is interesting that most of the world's major religions have arisen in two tightly defined triangles in the world. Judaism, Christianity, and Islam all arose within a stone's throw of each other in the Arabian and Judean deserts. A few thousand miles away in North India is another small patch of the world in which Hinduism, Buddhism, Jainism, and Sikhism all arose. The three major monotheistic religions of the world all arose in the desert. A single, all-knowing God who sets the rules for life would seem to be a natural extension of the concept of desert patriarchy.

It is interesting also that in all three of these religions the major founders traveled into the desert where they experience some form of spiritual conversion. Although this is less true of Christianity, certainly Judaism and Islam also differ from other religions in prescribing clear rules for life. By contrast, the Indian-centric religions, while placing strong emphasis on how society should be ordered, seem to orient themselves to a hunt for philosophical truths on the one hand or the prescription of everyday religious rituals on the other.

That Islam itself means *submission* reinforces the sense that it plays to a psychological desire for the clarity and order that arises from people being held to a universal code. It is also noteworthy that the desert seems to put some boundaries on Islam. In Africa, for example, Islam is triumphant in the north, but its hold over people seems to wane as the desert gives way to other types of terrain. It is dominant in Somalia, the Sudan, and to some extent Ethiopia, but becomes patchier once one gets into the African savannah proper. When one looks west of Arabia, Islam's hold extends all the way up to the deserts of Pakistan, but it then fades. To be sure, it crops up in the jungles of east Bengal, Malaysia, and Indonesia; perhaps because the dominant form of social organization in this type of terrain is small, mobile tribal units rather than large scale, more settled communities. In these nondesert locations, however, there tends to be a more flexible and tolerant form of Islam. By contrast, the strictness of Islam increases the deeper one goes into the desert.

There is plenty of concrete evidence for the presence of a psychological theme around the imposition of tight rules in Middle Eastern populations. A relevant set of findings concerns Geert Hofstedes' dimension of uncertainty avoidance, which refers to the extent to which individuals want to live their lives within clear boundaries, and conversely, the level of psychological tolerance for ambiguity and greyness in their outlook. Middle Eastern societies score extremely highly on this dimension. Interestingly, high uncertainty scores are also evident in the Catholic cultures of southern Europe, a fact not unrelated to how this part of Europe was populated in ancient times. The highest recorded scores globally for uncertainty avoidance have been found in Australian Aboriginal populations.[5] In his analysis of Middle Eastern societies, Michael Minkov, finds them among the highest in the world on monumentalism, a dimension associated with pride in observing clear rules, as well as exclusionism, which measures the prioritization of close relationships over wider societal commitments.[6]

The trumping of business values by religion is a ubiquitous feature of corporate life in the Middle East. In no other global culture does this happen to the same extent. A workshop organizer described how a member of a group he was working with simply stood up and without a word left in the middle of an important part of a discussion. He had gone to pray and there was no question of any flexibility with respect to this need. Breaks for prayer are mandatory in businesses in the Middle East, as are appropriate arrangements for workers around Islamic festivals or the Haj. In fact, many businesses that know the region well see the Haj as a tremendous opportunity to boost sales and market themselves to over 1 billion Muslims. Some achieve close to half their sales during the period. A simple thing such as understanding that the Islamic world operates on a lunar calendar is helpful, as otherwise plans made according to the Western calendar can quickly get out of sync with the rhythm of the region.

Faith and family trump business obligations or civic responsibilities for most people. Threats to this faith can arise from seemingly innocuous acts such as FIFA's move to put the Saudi-Arabian flag on match balls. The flag is inscribed with the Sahada, the Islamic declaration of faith, and the idea of this being kicked around a football field raised real and deep emotions. When a Danish magazine published controversial cartoons depicting Mohammed, the boycott of Danish products was swift and dramatic across the region. The reaction was even more extreme when the French magazine, Charlie Hebdo, did the same. The politician Geert Wilders' anti-Islamic rant similarly caused Dutch companies to be ostracized from Saudi Arabia. More generally, people in the region also want to know your faith and are comforted if you are a believer in something, especially if it is also a monotheistic faith. Americans in this regard can be more acceptable than Europeans, whose overt atheism can land discordantly with locals.

Hierarchy of a patriarchal type is also a strong feature of many Middle Eastern organizations. Decision making on even relatively minor matters is frequently referred upward. In our analysis of leaders only 7 percent in the Middle East were seen to have a strength around inclusive two-way leadership. Although scores were low on this dimension globally, this was the lowest score except for leaders from Sub-Saharan Africa. Furthermore, a full 40 percent of Middle Eastern leaders were assessed to have a development need with respect to stepping back and empowering others, by far the highest ratings globally. Power distance scores also are very high in the Middle East, in both the Hofstede and Globe surveys. The patriarchs often employ relatives or members of their community who also exercise referred power, without always necessarily being particularly visibly productive themselves. There is often a hierarchy in which professional, employed managers sit alongside such individuals in a subtle and complicated pattern of relationships. At the bottom sit ordinary workers, many from Africa or south Asia, who are not always treated with respect.

While these arrangements can appear anachronistic, they do confer some benefits. If you are dealing with a person in authority, decision making can be both rapid and bold. An ambitious plan that would take months of analysis in Western organizations can be embraced in the course of a conversation. I remember being both surprised and impressed when a Middle Eastern leader—after talking to us only briefly about our findings on the leadership and culture in a major part of his business—decided seemingly on the spot to sell the business. His advisors looked a bit taken aback as he left the room with the instruction to execute the decision promptly. I expected perhaps a period of reflection given that the business was valued in the billions, but when I returned three months later, the sale was all done and dusted.

Below the top, one also sees a penchant for setting clear rules and values in Middle Eastern companies. In YSC's global database, 39 percent of Middle Eastern leaders had strengths around organized and structured approach to leadership, by far the highest score out of all global regions. This compared with 13 percent of American leaders, 15 percent of Latin Americans, and figures in the 20 to 30 percent range for Chinese, Indian, and European leaders. African leaders were much more free flowing and flexible, with only 6 percent being seen as strong in this area. These perceptions are confirmed by research using instruments that look at core emotional drivers. In our consulting practice, we commonly use a psychometric instrument based on transactional analysis that measures the extent to which people adopt a parental, adult, or child orientation in their dealings with the world. Parent refers to the extent to which people have absorbed clear rules and frameworks, which they impose in a paternalistically caring or more rigidly demanding way on others. Leaders from the Middle East score very highly on this dimension and have the highest scores of all regions globally.[7]

However, there is a paradox here. Leaders may want to impose clear rules and structures, but the emotional pull of people is much more toward strictures that spring from deeper, religious roots. The more recent behavioral requirements, whether of a political state or a corporation, may be observed if there are strong sanctions, but sit psychologically more lightly and can easily be bent or subtly undermined if the opportunity presents. The day-to-day experience of Middle Eastern business may therefore be less clear cut and structured, with variable timekeeping and considerable delays not being uncommon experiences. Nevertheless, rooting one's personal leadership practices in clear and uncompromising values is helpful for creating true followership.

Understanding that the emotional drive to impose clear and immutable rules that people cannot opt out from arises fundamentally from an orientation that was necessary in the fight for survival in the desert can help Westerners make sense of the resistance to modern values they sometimes experience when dealing with Middle Eastern societies. It also helps to explain why something like the Arab Spring morphed so easily into the return of old authoritarian patterns or the rise of religious fundamentalism.

In the Middle East today, tensions between the impulses for continuity, order, and observance of rules laid down in the distant past versus the demands of modernity are to be seen in just about every country, including Israel. There is no society in that part of the world that does not experience ever-growing tensions between the forces of conservatism and change, or between the secular and the religious orientation toward life. This, of course, occurs in every society; but in the Middle East, there is an emotional intensity and virulence to the manner in which this tension is played out both in society but also internally, within individuals themselves. The tendency for people who seem modern minded and forward looking to revert seemingly overnight into Jihadists illustrates how alive this tension is for people. The sudden rise of ISIL and many other extremist movements, sometimes out of nowhere, is also only explicable if one understands the powerful emotional drivers for the certainties they offer to the people of the region.

The Commercial Instinct

About 25 years ago most of what constitutes Dubai today was simply a sleepy stretch of desert, populated by cacti and scorpions. The town itself was named after a locally occurring locust, the Daba, which regularly visited the area, annoying the local population. An unremarkable village on the edge of the desert where the chief occupation for people was diving for pearls was transformed, in the space of a few years, into a major global financial, business, and tourist hub. Until the ignominious financial crash of 2008–2009, Dubai was a global byword for glitz and excessive consumption. A huge proportion of the world's cranes were employed there, fueled by a property boom that, to give a sense of perspective, created several hundred five-star hotels in close proximity. Within the space of a few decades, Dubai became the shopping capital of the Middle East, and in 2007 was the eighth most-visited city in the world. It rated seventh in the world for the volume of container traffic passing through its busy ports. It became officially one of the world's richest cities, although the glitz and the glamor disguise the fact that it is propped up by a life of servitude for the mostly south Asian workers who built and run many of the services in the city.

It is natural to assume when one sees the glamor and glitz of Dubai that it has all happened because of oil money. However, the surprising fact is that Dubai itself has virtually no oil. While the creation of a world leading megacity in an area formally only notable for its voracious hoard of locusts is intriguing, it is less surprising when one does a little bit of research into the cultural DNA of the area. Data from over 5,000 years ago from the Sumerian civilization, widely regarded as the earliest civilization, provides some relevant clues. The Sumerians were quite meticulous in keeping records of their history, important astronomical events, and most importantly of all, their patterns of trade. The Sumerian civilization was wealthy but, according to their records, their wealth was dwarfed by a place called Dilmun.

The city of Dilmun sat on an island close to modern-day Bahrain. Extensive excavation of the area indicates that a huge city lay there, which by 2000 BC covered an area that equaled the size of the largest Mesopotamian cities. Since there is very little agricultural land around Dilmun, the city existed purely on the basis of its trade. Texts reveal that this consisted mostly of copper from Oman, as well as a large amount of trade with the Indus Valley civilization. Stone seals similar to those found in Gujarat, designed to show that goods were sealed after packing, have been found in Dilmun. Similarly, animal-head Mesopotamian pins have been found in the Indus Valley. Dilmun's wealth, like modern-day Dubai's, was based principally on the financial, business, and trading acumen of its people.

The Sumerian civilization was the earliest in the Tigris–Euphrates River system. Countless others followed and for over 2,500 years, up to 500 BC, this part of the world was the site of the world's biggest urban centers, including the cities of Ur, Uruk, Lagash, Kush, and Babylon. However, while these cities benefited from being located in relatively fertile alluvial plains, and were therefore rich in agricultural production, they were almost completely dependent on trade in order to secure vital minerals, timber, precious metals, and stone. The Sumerian shekel barley and shekel silver represent the earliest recorded units of money. Trade also requires records to be kept, and the Sumerians developed the world's first recorded writing system, cuneiform. Hundreds of thousands of cuneiform tablets capture the religion, customs, legends, poetry, and also the trading activities of the Sumerian people. William Bernstein, in his book *A Splendid Exchange,* also says that this led to the development of the world's first financial markets.[8] He quotes the following financial record from a cuneiform tablet that details a loan from a wealthy man (U) to two trading partners, L and N, involving:

> *Two mina (120 Shekels) of silver, (which is the value of) five gur of oil*
> *and 30 garments for an expedition to Dilmun to buy there copper for*
> *the partnership of L and N ... After safe termination of the voyage, you*
> *will not recognize commercial losses; the debtors have agreed to satisfy*
> *you with four mina of copper for each shekel of silver as a just price.*

On first inspection this seems like a typically opaque contract that an investment banker today might foist on an unsuspecting client. Summarizing, it appears that U has lent L and N two mina of silver to fund an expedition to Dilmun, for which he expects to be paid back a thumping 480 mina of copper on L and N's return. Like any good banker, he has also indemnified himself against all risks, as the responsibility for any commercial losses due to the expedition failing has to be borne by poor L and N. On the basis of current relative prices of copper and silver, this would seem like a pretty good deal for U, with a very healthy, low-risk bonus element built in. Sound familiar?

Once humans invent a way of living, there is an impetus for both biological and cultural evolution to drive adaptations to the new way of being. It is no accident that cultures that are renowned for commercial and mathematical skills—such as the Chinese, Indian, and to that one might also add certain, but not all, peoples of the Middle East—are places where some of the world's earliest civilizations and hence trading activities occurred. It is interesting that the trading ships that went from Sumer through Dilmun and on to India would have docked in Gujarat. Gujaratis are considered to have some of the most finely developed commercial and trading instincts in the Indian subcontinent. Similarly, the settled and coastal communities of the Middle East have developed in their people deep commercial instincts and skills.

The drumbeat of ancient trading DNA did not just find expression in ancient times. Mohammed himself was a trader and Mecca was a vibrant and important commercial center in the sixth century. It is not surprising therefore that the Koran—as well as the Hadith, which captures stories about Mohammed's life—are infused with advice and ground rules around the conduct of trade and commerce. In Islamic teachings, trading and commerce are praised as worthy and noble activities. The existence of Islamic financial institutions today is testament to the very clear codes prescribed by Islam for the financing and conduct of commerce and trade. Barely 100 years after the death of Mohammed, the all-conquering Muslim armies moved rapidly to create in the Middle East an elaborate, sophisticated, and wide-ranging system of trade with long tentacles reaching into China, India, Africa, and Europe. William Bernstein describes a Pax Islamica that existed for over 400 years and under which the vast bulk of the world's trade and commerce was conducted.

Within a few centuries of the prophet's death, his followers had knitted almost the entirety of the known world into a vast emporium in which African gold, ivory and ostrich feathers could be exchanged for Scandinavian furs, Baltic amber, Chinese silks, Indian pepper and Persian metal crafts.

This commerciality is evident in many aspects of business life in the Middle East. In our analysis, 50 percent of Middle Eastern leaders exhibited strength in commercial thinking. Only American executives came close to this with a score of 40 percent. Commerciality was the strongest area for Middle Eastern executives in the thinking sphere, indicating that the commercial lens is their primary way of looking at business. People working in the Middle East are inclined to comment on the skill, acumen, and sheer pleasure that Middle Eastern executives show in commercial negotiation. A desire not to accept the first set of terms and a broad-brush approach to assessing fairness is also evident. Seeing the wealth of many Middle Eastern companies, some Western firms in particular can think they are able to drive highly favorable terms. However, there is a high level of sensitivity to the terms upon which business is conducted, and firms that get caught taking advantage or seeming to be unfair can quickly get blacklisted.

However, while Middle Eastern executives were strong on commerciality and on a par with most other groups of executives on an analytical approach to business, they were much weaker with respect to strategic thinking. Only 10 percent showed strength in this area and 40 percent had a weakness—the weakest scores globally, with the exception of Sub-Saharan Africa. Commerciality, therefore, appears to be about deal making and achieving the best terms in a negotiation rather than the pursuit of long-term strategic objectives.

Apart from the modern temples to this commercial DNA, exemplified by cities such as Dubai, Bahrain, and Jeddah, this commercial element of Middle Eastern cultural DNA finds expression in a large number of successful trading communities, such as the Syrian and Lebanese communities operating in Africa, the Caribbean, and the Far East. In Brazil, communities from the Middle East are considered to have highly developed commercial skills. The relatively large numbers of people of Middle Eastern origin working in the world's great financial centers, such as London, New York, and Frankfurt, is also reflective of this DNA.

The centrality of the Middle East to commercial trade has been a fact for much of known history. In ancient times, commercial centers such as Dilmun lost their edge as the center of gravity moved up the Tigris and Euphrates Rivers, following the collapse of the Indus Valley civilization, one of its main partners. Similarly, the trading hub created by the Pax Islamica collapsed in the Middle Ages following the gradual rise of Europe and the victory of the European navies, first in the Mediterranean and then in the Indian Ocean. The Middle East lost its role as a connector commercial hub. However, all that is about to change. The rise of China and India, as well as the largely neglected but nevertheless real economic boom that is occurring in Sub-Saharan Africa, are starting to put the Middle East back in the picture. The region has been strongest when it has looked east and south and not just to the west and could again become a commercial hub for the world again.

The Best Ideas in the World

In 2010, the Victoria and Albert Museum in London held an exhibition called 1001 Inventions to remind the world of the Arab contribution to science, technology, and intellectual discourse. The centerpiece of the exhibition was a 20-foot-high timekeeping machine called the Elephant Clock, considered to be one of the world's first mechanical clocks, built around the thirteenth century. The whole edifice sits on a statue of an Indian elephant. It is decorated with Chinese dragons and an Egyptian phoenix. Perhaps in recognition of where it was invented, it also features wooden robots dressed in Arabic clothes. However, the timing mechanism for the clock, which is water-based, was borrowed from ancient Greece. The Elephant Clock demonstrates a preparedness—at least in that period of Arab history—to absorb, learn, and build on ideas from all parts of the world.

Just up the road from the Victoria and Albert Museum stands the British Museum, with a section called the Abdul Latif Jameel wing, funded by one of Saudi Arabia's most significant companies outside of the oil sector. It is a modern and progressive company whose business roots lie in the motor retail industry, but which has expanded into a range of other areas including property, electrical retailing, and through ancillary companies, scientific and technical research, as well as a range of social enterprises, including agriculture in northwest Africa. It is an iconic and highly regarded company, both in the Middle East and more widely, because of its success and forward-looking values.

Our work with the ALJ company over the years has given us a good understanding of its historical roots and DNA. Its founder, Abdul Latif Jameel, gave the company an edge in the 1950s by hiring a large number of British executives who set the tone for ALJ with respect to process and a meritocratic approach to the treatment of people. For a long time they used to call them the Britishers. However, one day the company owners decided that many of the executives had become complacent expats and that they had learned all they could from them. Many of the Britishers were edged out. The owners then turned to China and hired a number of senior Chinese leaders from Hong Kong to take their business to the next phase—since the East was rising and the owners were keen to absorb new ideas. I remember visiting the firm's headquarters in Jeddah for the first time in the late 1980s and was surprised to see that the CEO and other senior executives did not have their own offices, but sat with all their staff in a large cavernous room bubbling with noise and interaction. At the time ALJ was way ahead of Western companies with respect to open-plan working. "We learned this from the Japanese," I was told.

ALJ then went through a phase of really valuing and wanting to attract Indian leaders into its business. However, overlaying all these different phases was a strong drive to get whoever at the time was good from whatever part of the world. Indeed I believe it was this drive that made ALJ one of our earliest clients when psychological consulting was considered a new trend and something of a minority taste in the West. When the Soviet Union collapsed, ALJ made a concerted effort to recruit scientists and technologists who had suddenly lost their State jobs. Today the company is strongly invested in building local Saudi talent.

The Elephant Clock of the thirteenth century and the modern-day culture of ALJ 700 years later are not unrelated phenomena, and neither are they one-offs. Rather, they represent a strong underlying theme in Middle Eastern cultural DNA around intellectual openness. This absorptive learning orientation seems natural to us today, surrounded as we are by the interconnected world of international research publications, conferences, and of course the Internet. However, you do not have to go too far back to appreciate the extent to which the intellectual traditions in Western Europe, China, or India existed predominantly in worlds created by themselves, with a small amount of recognition of the advances made elsewhere.

There are numerous references to the importance of seeking knowledge in Mohammed's writings and sayings, particularly, as recorded in the Hadith. "Seek knowledge from the cradle to the grave," "The ink of the scholar is more sacred than the blood of the martyr," "Seek knowledge even if you have to go to China," are some examples. The early followers of Islam went far and wide to search out the best ideas in the world, including keeping alive the Western classical tradition and sourcing Indian mathematics and Chinese printing technology.

However, the region did not just absorb these influences passively. While the mathematician Al-Khwarizmi was free in acknowledging his debt to Indian mathematicians, he made considerable advances himself in several fields. The term *algorithm* is derived from his name and *algebra* is derived from the Arabic *al-jebr* meaning "reunion of broken parts." Critical advances in trigonometry also occurred in this period. The Arab world was also the center of medical advances. Acknowledging and building on Greek, Roman, Indian, and Persian insights, the famous philosopher and physician Ibn Sina in the eleventh century combined known medical knowledge with his own insights to produce numerous textbooks, one of the most important of which was a series of volumes called *The Canon of Medicine*. For the best part of 500 years this work constituted the bible for physicians everywhere—including in the West where his name was Latinized to Avicenna. The Arab world also made significant advances in astronomy and navigation. The famous Chinese admiral Cheng Ho made extensive use of Arab charts for his groundbreaking Chinese voyages of discovery and was himself a Muslim.

The long history of agricultural innovation in the Middle East was also carried forward in this period. Crop rotation and cash cropping were first invented in this part of the world. Coffee was a Yemeni creation used initially to help Sufis stay awake. Its use gradually percolated, both literally and metaphorically, through the Arab world until Venetian traders in Cairo picked it up. From time immemorial the environment of the Middle East has demanded agricultural innovation, and even in modern times one sees countries like Israel leading the way with respect to a range of agricultural technologies, such as drip irrigation and computerized monitoring of soils and plant development.

The extent to which this still runs through Middle Eastern culture is illustrated by how far afield students go to learn. Perhaps more than any other region, the Middle East also invites people from all over the world to teach in its centers of higher learning. The same DNA also can be seen echoing through the business world. Executives comment on how important it is for customers in the region to feel that they have the best, even at times when they do not even need it. There is a desire within businesses to be at the cutting edge and to source practices, people, and products from anywhere in the world to make this happen. This orientation also creates a positive attitude to change in areas that do not touch upon traditional social values. In our research, 32 percent of Middle Eastern leaders had strength in improvement and change orientation, a figure near the top end of global scores despite the perceived conservatism with which the region is sometimes associated.

The receptivity to ideas also makes Middle Eastern people highly entrepreneurial. There is a spirit of trying something new across the region, which is in part driven by the skew of many populations toward youth. The American venture capitalist Christopher Schroeder had this to say following his trip to the region:[9]

> *I saw unbelievable entrepreneurs and innovators in Egypt ... Amman,* Jordan, *because I think the government and the young are really focusing on it. And at the same time, I have seen them in Beirut and other places as well.*

In fact, he was so impressed by what he saw that he wrote a book: *Startup Rising—The Entrepreneurial Revolution Remaking the Middle East.*[10] This spirit finds expression in the number of world-leading conferences that are held in the region, the active use of the Internet, and the openness to academics from all corners of the world. More broadly, the Arab Spring was an expression of this desire to 'look outward and learn' mindset.

However, a question that many in the region ask—and one that's also relevant to the future—is: "Why did our intellectual contributions to the world fade so much over the past few centuries to the point where people can hardly remember them?" One possible explanation is that intellectual openness to other cultures can only occur when you feel confident and secure in your own. This is exactly the psychological frame that the Middle East world was in at the height of the Arab conquests. A number of historians have suggested that it was the impact of the Crusades and the Mongol invasions that caused Arab culture to start acting more defensively and looking inward rather than outward. If your dominant intellectual style is to absorb and build, then one can see how the process of closing off positive interactions with other parts of the world could have stymied Arab intellectual efforts.

The same process seems to be occurring today in parts of the region, while other parts reach out. In response to real and perceived aggression from the West, a natural reaction is to become defensive and protective. Thus, while there is openness flourishing in parts, we also see the rise of traditonal Madrassa schools across the Middle East and beyond. In response to perceived attacks, one is forced back to core traditional definitions of self, which in the Middle East are essentially religious. The battle between intellectual openness and rigidity will be played out in a dynamic and expressive way in the Middle East; but if the right conditions of security can be created for people, the power of the former is likely to prevail, because for centuries it has been the embedded psychological tradition of the region.

The Honor–Modesty System

A client in the Gulf told me a story about one of his key customers that illustrates a core theme about the psychological DNA of the region. Two business partners who were on an equal footing managed the company that distributed his products. The partners got on well but inevitably, as happens in such duopolies, there were tensions in the relationship. My client had nervously watched these tensions build up over time. Then one day he learned from another senior member of the company that one of the partners had gone to the other partner's office and, in a fit of rage seemingly out of nowhere, had smashed up the whole office, including destroying some valuable vases and works of art. The client had a meeting scheduled with the partners later on in the week and thought it would be canceled or at least postponed. When this did not happen, he attended—intrigued but expecting a somewhat awkward and tense dinner. To his surprise both partners turned up in good humor and much more together and aligned than he had seen in the recent past. He later learned that the partner who had smashed up the office felt he had been disrespected and dishonored by the other partner at a senior social gathering. After the incident, which the company kept a tight lid on, the partners apologized for their lack of respect toward each other and, mutual honor restored, reset their relationship. "I am not going to leave either of them alone in my office, though" my client mused.

Much psychological commentary on Middle Eastern culture focuses on the importance of honor and its corollary, the avoidance of shame. Honor appears to be one of the most important currencies at play in the Middle East. The way in which honor is played out, however, can be subtler than many accounts suggest. Honor has different psychological qualities than, for example, face in Far Eastern cultures, which arise from the different factors that drive each orientation. In addition, if one takes a close look at how honor is played out in the Middle East, pride is only one side of the polarity. There is also a strong emphasis on modesty, which is not always evident in honor cultures in other parts of the world.

Why are Middle Eastern societies more prone to the currency of honor than others? The answer lies in the research cited earlier regarding the link between pastoral agriculture and honor cultures. The essential point is that your possessions are mobile in pastoral societies and can easily be taken in a way that is not possible in more settled societies. Males have to puff themselves up and project a sense of power that may or may not be real in order to protect what they have from simply being taken off them. The Wild West, characterized by an every man for himself ethos and a reliance on individual machismo and personal projection of strength to protect oneself, is illustrative of the type of honor culture that can develop in societies where the chief livelihood is cattle rearing or animal husbandry.

Honor cultures exist all over the world and are not restricted to the Middle East. Parts of Southern Europe also have tendencies toward honor cultures driven partly by pastoralism—but also by the fact that, as the DNA evidence shows, southern Europe was significantly occupied by people originating from the Middle East. People also moved up the coast of Spain and into Ireland and the west of Scotland, where there is also a strong tradition of honor cultures. Most writers on the honor culture in the Appalachians in the United States ascribe it to the traditions of the Scottish/Irish settlements there. This makes the Middle East an important fountainhead for honor cultures in many other parts of the world.

There is an important difference, however, between the honor cultures that exist in Western society. Here the notion of honor exists in a fundamentally individualistic form—that is, it accrues or is taken away from specific individuals or families. In the Middle East, while clearly the distinction cannot be made in a black and white manner, the collective honor of a clan, tribe, or nation is more important. The likely explanation for this is that in the desert environments of the Middle East, pastoralism has been predominantly practiced in a collective, tribal, and nomadic form.

The sensitivity to personal slights, displays of emotion, and aggression when crossed, and preoccupation with one's personal image of strength, is therefore only one side of the coin of how honor operates in Middle Eastern cultures. There is also an exaggerated modesty, politeness, and low-key interactional style in other situations. Collectivist honor cultures emphasize modesty, especially in upward hierarchical dealings or with potential partners or allies. Modesty and humility are emphasized again and again in Islamic teaching, and not just with reference to women and their dress.

How does an honor–modesty culture express itself on a day-to-day basis in business? On an obvious level, it drives a strong sense of leaders needing to look both strong and pious to others. Cultures strong on honor can be inclined to showiness, whether with respect to material manifestations of success or a certain theatricality and posturing in everyday interactions. One sees this, particularly, in downward dealings by leaders or when relatively junior or powerless partners are being engaged. In such situations, the other party has to be careful to go along with the show and not do anything that might ruffle the peacock display.

However, the modesty system can also be activated in situations where the distribution of power is less certain. It can be easy to misread the signals in such situations and lose sense of the underlying pride that is still the currency at play. Actions that dishonor the other party will be remembered, however meek the party might seem on the surface. Job titles are also important signals of honor and can evoke strong emotions if they do not accord the required level of status. Public criticism or overt disagreement is also generally frowned upon in Middle Eastern business culture, especially if the targets are senior, high status individuals. Such cultures also require a high level of tolerance for emotional displays, which are common when the honor of another party is at stake. People from less expressive cultures—as the example cited earlier of rapprochement following the office being smashed up illustrates—can misread the depth or longevity of the feelings on display. Outsiders must also be sensitive to situations where overt displays of honor and modesty are required for acceptance or credibility.

Those who come from societies where honor is less bred into the cultural DNA may perceive some of these attributes slightly negatively, or with gentle amusement. However, there are many positive aspects of an honor culture. Most humans strive to the ideal of my word is my bond, but this concept translates more obviously into everyday life in honor cultures. When you shake on a deal—however loose the details are—you can be generally sure that the other party will carry out their part of the transaction. I remember once when the Arab owner of a business, whose finance department had been tardy in paying one of our invoices, found out about the delay. A check was dispatched within minutes in a black cab across London, despite our protestations that it was not necessary—because the owner felt that his honor was at stake. The natural Western instinct to translate agreements into detailed legalistic commitments can also backfire: "Is my word not enough?"

The honor culture also influences one's approach to negotiations. Soroush Aslani and Jean Brett at the Kellog School of Management were interested in exploring American and Middle Eastern differences in business negotiation. They set up a task requiring 63 pairs at an American university and 68 pairs at a top Qatari University to reach an understanding with another business leader on both commercial and people-related issues and found a number of significant differences. The Qataris displayed a prouder, competitive, and aspirational approach. They were also more emotionally charged, being quicker to show sympathy, anger, and frustration, whereas the Americans were more focused on information exchange. Qataris tended to be more guarded in sharing information and took time to develop trust. They were also much more emotionally committed in the negotiation to hiring a brother into the business. The researchers attributed all these differences to the impact of an honor culture, where negotiation with an unfamiliar third party activates pride and a competitive emotional set.

The honor system also produces some clear trends, when it comes to consumer psychology. Having the right prestigious brands is important for consumers in the region, as it is in China where the concept of face leads to a similar pull. However, a concern for image taken too far can be detrimental. A number of overseas executives I have dealt with in the Middle East complain of the difference between highly public, declared achievements versus the prosaic reality on the ground in their companies. The gap between declared intention and execution, an issue in all organizations, can be particularly wide in Middle Eastern companies. Steven Royston, who runs a site collecting posts on the Middle East, quotes one

Middle Eastern executive: "One thing you have to understand about our company is that no project we undertake makes any sense unless it is preceded by three words: The appearance of."[11]

This gap between appearance and reality also shows up in how people present themselves. A 2013 investigation into the CVs of Saudi Arabian senior government workers, many of them at very senior levels, found that 620 employees had fake degrees. Interestingly, 234 of these illusory degrees were doctorates, another 230 were masters, and only 56 were ordinary degrees. Clearly, a judgment had been made; if you are going to make something up, do it big. The honor culture can also lead people to make promises that, on reflection, they regret or change their minds about. Trust can, therefore, be an issue. However good a relationship is, there is the ever-present fear of being let down or double-crossed, just as has happened for so long in the fluid, ever-changing world of raiding alliances.

More widely, the psychological drive for honor can be an issue. Theodore Roosevelt is famous for his advice "Speak softly and carry a big stick." In honor cultures the principle seems to be—make sure others think you have a big stick regardless of the size of stick that you possess, or whether you actually possess a stick at all. The history of the Middle East after World War II is full of instances where leaders exaggerated the capabilities of their country, often just before incurring humiliating defeats. Saddam Hussein promised "the mother of all battles," and there was great expectation in the Arab world about how his battle-trained army might fare against the West—but it just melted away after a few days fighting.

These and many other examples illustrate a predictable and disappointing pattern for many Middle Eastern nations. An exaggerated notion of capability is projected, which causes a heightened sense of threat for other parties, who then latch on to it—either because they are genuinely afraid or because it gives them a justifying excuse—to take appropriate "preventative" action. All too often this ends up with perplexed Middle Eastern populations, led to expect sweeping victories, having to cope with abject defeat. The emotional gymnastics that such disorienting experiences require is perhaps more natural in Middle Eastern cultures than in many others; however, the process is nevertheless not an easy one psychologically.[12]

The Other Sex

The first thing that you will notice if you visit a business in one of the conservative countries of the Middle East is the virtual complete absence of women—not just at the top of organizations, but extending all the way through to the most junior of roles. The only exception occurs in businesses or institutions that cater to women clients, such as female shops, hospitals, or schools. Here the pattern is reversed and there are no men in frontline jobs. Women working for foreign firms need to follow precise rules of engagement. For example, it can be a faux pas to try to shake the hand of a male executive. There is also extreme sensitivity to female executives challenging male colleagues. Nothing causes more tension and disquiet in the relationship between the West and the Middle East than the perceived treatment of women in the area.

For people from the region, the picture is more complicated. While at one level there is a rejection of the immorality of other cultures, many from the Middle East are not immune to the temptations afforded by the more liberal states in the region. For Middle Eastern women, too, the surface picture of piety seems to coexist with many private acts of freedom, which include wearing designer Western outfits underneath traditional dress or leading a double life when outside of the Middle East. On one occasion, as I had just boarded a British Airways flight from Jeddah back to London, I noticed two Saudi Arabian women dressed in Burkhas disappear into the toilets immediately upon boarding the plane. Some kind of magical transformation occurred inside the cubicles and a few minutes later out stepped two model-like women, decked out in designer tops and vanishingly small miniskirts, which would have raised an eyebrow even in the more adventurous nightclubs of New York or Paris.

Certainly, on the surface there is plenty of evidence for retrogressive attitudes toward women in some parts of the Middle East. If you take Saudi Arabia, the quintessential Islamic desert state, local women are required to wear the Niqab, which allows a slit for the eyes, or the Burkha, which has a veil over the whole face, at all times in public life. Women are not allowed to drive or go anywhere without being chaperoned by a man. Women are discouraged from working and constitute only 5 percent of the workforce. The consent of a male is required for a Saudi woman to be treated by a doctor. Of course, many other states in the Middle East are more liberal than Saudi Arabia. In the Gulf States, the position of women appears to be much more in keeping with the norms in other societies, but nevertheless underlying conservative attitudes still dominate.

Seeking to understand why a certain attitude toward women is deeply embedded within some populations in the Middle East, it is important in the first instance to point out that women suffer second class status in many societies. However, it is in the Middle East where traditional attitudes toward the place of women in society seem to particularly hold sway. I believe the strength of these emotions stems from the confluence of the DNA strands discussed earlier with respect to the imposition of rigid rules for life, high uncertainty avoidance, male patriarchy, and the honor–modesty system. Together, these strands form a powerful and explosive cocktail of emotional instincts that become activated by the prospect of any change in the traditional position of women.

In another sense women have been, for tens of thousands of years in nomadic pastoral societies, the equivalent of livestock—like goats and sheep, valuable possessions that can be taken by others. Even today, in certain parts of Somalia and Ethiopia, men obtain their wives through stealing them on raids. Rather than losing a valuable asset to an enemy, it is better to destroy it yourself, if you feel the risk of loss is high. Churchill's decision to sink the French fleet in Marseille before the Germans could get to it did not make him popular in France, but did have a cold logic that makes sense in times of back-to-the-wall, zero-sum conflict. The instinct to kill one's women rather than losing them to external parties makes a kind of barbaric sense in the raiding world of a pastoral society and has for tens of thousands of years been ingrained in such societies. This I believe is one of the root causes of the honor-killing culture in the Middle East today.

These attitudes toward women create particular issues for businesses operating in the region. Beyond the obvious fact that the workplace can seem weirdly unrepresentative of normal human society, businesses face the choice of how much to compromise and fit in with restrictions that are alien to their corporate cultures. Those that chose to send female executives have to school them carefully in the cultural mores of the region. These can vary tremendously from country to country and, indeed, between cities in the same country. In many ways Dubai feels like the West. You can get away with a bit more in Jeddah, a trading outpost in Saudi Arabia, than in Riyadh, which is deep in the desert. Judging what is appropriate in different places is hard. This can be made harder by the fact that locals are often mindful of the differences in values and can internally take offense but be reluctant to show this openly when a person has stepped over the line.

Another complexity arises from the fact that many attitudes are driven by public perception. If one is careful, people may turn a blind eye in some places. However, people can risk being caught out by someone who capriciously decides to implement the full letter of the law. A female American executive, for example, was arrested and faced the prospect of a few years in prison for the seemingly innocuous act of meeting a male colleague in a Starbucks café; this technically violated the restrictions on any contact with a male who is not your husband. A highly attuned sense of what is allowed in what situations—what is not allowed but will be overlooked and what will get you into deep trouble needs to be developed and constantly refined as one moves around the region.

Another consequence of the attitude toward women is that while people's private lives and work are frequently intermingled in the Middle East, areas to do with one's wife or daughters are often off limits. Attempting to enquire about a male executive's wife—a normal act of politeness in most parts of the world—can evoke discomfort in the Middle East. The lack of gender balance in the workplace also means that work social activities are often rather stale, formulaic affairs. Work can be seen as an alien environment, separate from one's real life by Middle Eastern executives, which can affect levels of true engagement.

Many Middle Eastern societies pay a real economic price for relegating women to less than full status. Retrogressive attitudes toward women also act as a psychological anchor holding back potentially progressive ideas in other areas. Broader democratic sentiments, social openness, and lowering of the distance from power between people are all ideas that cannot be taken seriously when certain attitudes toward half the population prevail. Understanding the underlying forces that create these emotional impulses is a prerequisite psychologically for eradicating them. Interestingly this is not just a task for men—women in the Middle East also have absorbed these impulses and often are resistant to changes that would help their sex. For example, large proportions of women in Arab countries do not think that women should have the vote. Many women are also complicit in honor killings. Until these societies formulate ways of giving women more of a role in their economic, social, and political lives, they are trying to succeed in the modern world with one hand tied behind their back.

Concentric Circles of Belonging

Life in the Middle East is relational. You deal with the person—not their role or position. There may be ups and downs once you've established trust in a relationship—but nobody can take away the fact that you do have a relationship. Western observers are often bemused when Middle Eastern governments lavish time and attention on minor members of a Royal family from places such as Britain, or on the relatives of people who hold political power in the West. This attention seems misplaced since these individuals frequently do not formally hold any significant position within their countries. But for many in the Middle East, this is a means of building relationships with the family as a whole. What counts is not what a person does but to whom they are connected. The primacy of a relationship is also illustrated by the fact that even when notable figures in the West have moved on from their positions and become virtual non-entities in their own land, they can experience a strong afterglow of respect when they visit the Middle East.

Being part of a family and community is therefore a deeply ingrained aspect of Middle Eastern psychology. In part, this tendency is explicable in terms of the tight relationships that are needed and formed in nomadic or semi-nomadic tribal cultures. Once you are in the club, you are in—even though the status or sense of honor you are afforded may go up and down. However, another feature of desert life is the shifting alliances between tribes. Frequently, a group of tribes will get together to raid another tribe or settled area. Once the task has been accomplished, the different tribes can go their own way. In some ways, the extraordinary military successes achieved early on in the history of Islam arose simply because Mohammed had effectively united a series of desperate and warring tribes together under the banner of a new and fresh religious order that treated all male members as equal. The new identity that emerged from out of the blue was one of the factors that made the Arab armies virtually unstoppable for the best part of 200 years.

So while a sense of belonging is an extremely important part of Middle Eastern culture, it exists on a variety of psychologically fluid planes. A person feels a sense of belonging to their family, their network of relationships, their tribe, their ethnic group, their religious group, then above this, to the Arab family, all Islamic people, and ultimately, to humanity as a whole. To some extent, all people share this layered sense of identification and loyalty. However, these identities carry more emotional weight in the relational world of the Middle East and there is also more fluid movement between them. At one time, for example, a person may identify with their company, but at another time with their religious group, or tribal background, or the Islamic world as a whole. The ease of these shifts can be confusing for people who come from societies that have a narrower range of identities, with less movement between them.

This focus on relationships and the fluidity of identification leads to a number of consequences in business. First, you don't get anywhere unless you have built a relationship with the other party. This can make business meetings seem extremely unstructured and unfocused to outsiders, particularly in the early stages. Even when relationships have been formed, meetings ostensibly with a clear focus can seem more like a social gathering with an occasional lapse into business relevance occurring almost as an afterthought. It takes time to develop trust—but once this occurs you are on the inside and can start to do business. However, unlike other relational cultures where such loyalty can last a lifetime, in Middle Eastern cultures you can fall in and out of favor in short succession.

Many family-owned businesses in the region will employ members of the extended family, often in senior roles. Such connected individuals know it is close to impossible to remove them, which can at times lead to a highly relaxed approach to their performance. The task of managing politics and achieving change in such contexts for professionally employed outsiders can also be bewilderingly complex. You have to work out who is related to the owning family and who is part of the wider community or untouchable because of their nationality. A pecking order also exists for employees from different parts of the world that conditions levels of respect and power. More so than in any other culture, the organizational chart will tell you only a fraction of what you need to know about the way things work.

More broadly, these influences from the past create a strong sense of tribal identity that is never far from the surface with respect to people's psychological identity. All conflicts in the region have a strong sense of tribalism, where there is limited empathy for the other side and an emotional taking of sides, regardless of the rights and wrongs of the situation. Even seemingly rational, well-educated people can be surprised by the vehemence and emotional intensity that surfaces when these tribal identities are activated. This was necessary in the past where your fortunes waxed and waned with that of your tribe, but now such depth of sentiment seems out of place, at least when viewed from a distance.

The capacity to shift identifications also influences politics in the region. Alliances can arise and be broken in a bewildering merry-go-round like manner. In this context, one of the weakest and least historically embedded psychological layers of identification is with the nation state. With the exception of Egypt, the only people who have a strong sense of identifying with their national state are the ruling elites of the said states. When a state's authority fractures, or cannot be imposed by force, as has happened in Iraq or Afghanistan, a wide range of other ethnic, sectarian, and tribal identifications—which are more real for people—come to the fore. Today, the turmoil in the region, the fracturing of national states, and the challenge to authoritarian governments are all creating a dynamic, not to say confusing, kaleidoscope of shifting factions that mirror, in a new context, the ever changing and fluid alliances that have characterized nomadic, tribal societies for millennia.

Managing Contradictions and Tensions

Middle Eastern culture displays more polarities and contradictions than perhaps all other cultures considered in this book, and these are likely to play out in complex ways as the future unfolds. In part, this stems from the very different psychological impulses that nomadic desert tribalism versus settled agriculture and urban civilization has given rise to in the region. The tensions between staying within a well-ordered world versus embracing the uncertainties of change, accepting authoritarianism versus driving for a say in things, or being narrowly tribal versus empathizing with other groups are arguably all at play within individuals, families, tribal groups, and national states within the Middle East. At every level, there is a dynamic tension between these different psychological pulls, resulting in creativity and energy but also, perhaps less positively, in sudden and rapid movements between different emotional modes that perplex outsiders. Deep feelings drive many of these impulses and this is perhaps why emotionality in many varied forms runs high in the region.

The world of business in the Middle East also shows these contradictions. Stephen Royston writes of his experience of Middle Eastern organizations as follows:[13]

> *When I look at enterprises in the Middle East and their leaders, I can't help lapsing into a metaphor. Sometimes I imagine a chimera—a hybrid beast made up of bits of lots of animals. The leader is a jockey riding a giant chimera whose many legs point in different directions. The jockey has no idea which part of the animal to whip to make it go forward. Bits fall off the beast periodically, and it frequently changes direction because the jockey keeps changing his mind.*

This captures to my mind the cultural complexity of many organizations in the region with their multiple facets and polarities.

More broadly, in embracing their position within the modern global world, Middle Eastern people will find, like all regions, that some elements of their cultural DNA are more helpful than others. Specifically, embracing the intellectualism, openness to learning, and respect for knowledge that is a core part of the cultural heritage of the Middle East is likely to be helpful. The region also has the opportunity to become a great connecting culture commercially between many of the world's significant trading blocks, because of its position and also because of the strong commercial DNA that lies at the heart of many Middle Eastern societies.

As a new world buffets traditional societies, Middle Eastern people will need to relinquish the idea that tight and rigid norms are required for survival and that any concessions to modernity will lead to a collapse of society. This was true for a long time in the deserts of the Middle East, but it is no longer remotely true. Yet the psychological attractiveness and emotional pull for the old simplicity and order are still there. The ever-present threat of defaulting to narrow family, clan, or tribal identities that characterized life in the region for millennia will also need to be resisted if the region is not to collapse even more into internecine conflict and warfare. The siren call of ISIL, firebrand Mullahs, authoritarian leaders, and narrow tribal loyalty may be psychologically appealing to many caught up in the injustices and complexity of life in the region, but the solutions they offer are likely to prove a dead end. All people in the region need to understand and manage the emotional impulses that drive them toward such answers.

There are lessons, too, for external parties. People are much more likely to embrace the new when they feel secure. It is interesting that Islamic culture was at its most vibrant, expressive, and open minded when the religion was all conquering and had no rivals. Many speculate that it was the reversals the region suffered at the hands of the Mongols—and to a lesser extent the Europeans—that pushed people into a narrower and more defensive embrace of Islam's conservative side. In this context, the West's instincts to meddle may be the last thing that Middle Eastern societies need if they are to evolve in the right direction. In fact, there is something about Western cultural DNA, with its ever-present impulse for interfering and imposing its will on others, that seems to bring out the more negative aspects of people's psychology in the Middle East. Leaving well enough alone, or intervening only when there is popular and widespread support internally and internationally, may be the better long-term path for Western countries to take.

Chapter 5

China: The Seekers of Harmony

China is fast emerging as a major player of the twenty-first century. The palpable shift of power can be seen in the delicacy with which American leaders handle sensitive issues for China, the increasing weight given to the country in various global forums, and the anxiety with which both Americans and Europeans pursue Chinese investment to support their indebted economies. More prosaically, if you visit Harrods or Selfridges in London or Bloomingdales in New York, you will be surprised at the sheer number of Chinese people buying Western luxury brands. The quintessential English boarding school, Roedean—renowned in the past for turning out well-heeled English ladies for the upper echelons of British society—now has a substantial student body from China.

Outside the country, the prospect of China's rise elicits emotions that are at best ambivalent but, if you scratch the surface, shade into anxiety and concern. This motivates people to look for weaknesses in the China story. This is partially because Chinese people and the country appear more opaque and unpredictable than a lot of other major global cultures. Historically, China has been an introverted country that set itself apart and held an internal image of superiority over other nations. Even when they do go abroad, Chinese students at university tend to keep to themselves. There is often a Chinatown in many major cities of the world that sets the community apart. This sense of separation will inevitably be eroded as China engages the world, and other countries will need to develop a deeper and more nuanced appreciation of Chinese cultural DNA.

The Chinese themselves, so defined by their internal points of reference, will be challenged in terms of engaging and developing relationships with members of other cultures that go beyond the transactional. Historically, the Chinese have been quite willing to reach out to other countries for trade and commercial reasons. However, they have tended to keep *psychologically* distant from these populations. Chinese authorities are acutely aware of this and recently have sought to address the issue by setting up a variety of soft-power initiatives, such as Confucian institutes abroad or creating scholarship schemes for Third World students. But it will take more than these relatively pragmatic fixes to connect genuinely with other cultures.

The business challenges of engaging the Chinese market or working with Chinese companies have become more apparent over time. The theoretically massive opportunities of the Chinese market for global companies have materialized for some but have stayed theoretical for many others. It is difficult to operate in China without a local partner and many have found such relationships problematic or at best difficult to read. Behind a seemingly market-based economy sits the Chinese state with its capacity for opaque, ad hoc decision making. Companies often find that their partners, products, or business operations have suddenly been ruled offside by the State, as happens with a capricious and dodgy linesman in football. There's a pervasive feeling that global companies are being used for access to their brand or intellectual capital. "We want the Western hens to come here so we can then get them to leave their eggs behind" is a phrase that hangs in the air for overseas executives. Understanding how to manage talent in a promiscuous market or how to read an organizational culture, let alone create the one you desire, is a constant challenge for overseas firms. Many global companies wonder just where their China story is going.

In a relatively short space of time, the world will need to understand and come to terms with the fundamental psychological DNA of Chinese culture. However, for China to assume dominance in the world, its people will also need to understand elements of their cultural DNA that will help or hinder them as the country reaches out to more deeply touch a range of other global cultures for virtually the first time in its history.

The Peopling of China

Jin Li, Professor at the National Human Genome Centre in Shanghai and at the Institute of Genetics of Sudan University, initiated a research project aimed at proving a long-held Chinese view that people in that part of the world evolved from local *Homo erectus* species, through Peking Man, and into the modern Mongoloid population. Official Chinese views have vehemently opposed the African origin of their population. Jin Li collected DNA samples from over 10,000 men across China and the surrounding regions. He identified a genetic marker on the Y chromosome that had undergone mutation about 80,000 years ago in Africa. If the Chinese population had evolved from earlier local human species, this would be proven by the absence of the genetic marker in large numbers of the men studied. To his astonishment, Jin Li found that *every single person* possessed the African-based mutation. Professor Jin Li was allowed to publish his study, but in other respects his results were quietly buried. Just like everyone else, the Chinese come from the original out-of-Africa movement[1].

But just what route did humans take in populating the Far East? Again, it is genetic evidence that casts the sharpest light on a field that was earlier dominated by speculation and extrapolation. In terms of mitochondrial analysis, it is haplogroups A-G, X, and Z that are present in Far Eastern populations. All these haplogroups are descendants of the major haplogroups M and N that are seen relatively early on in the coastal train out of Africa. The mitochondrial diversity is much greater in the south of China than in the north, which suggests that at least in part there was a south to north colonization process that occurred. However, three of the haplogroups, C, X, and Z are only found in the north. Clearly, these could not have originated from a southern thrust and must have come from elsewhere. However, C and Z are found in India and Tibet, as well as parts of Mongolia.

In his analysis of the mitochondrial evidence, Stephen Oppenheimer provides compelling evidence to suggest that the haplogroups C, X, and Z—which reach their highest rates in Siberia and northeast Asia—arose from a completely different route to the south-to-north colonization that appears to have been the case in the other Asian haplogroups. It is likely these groups arrived in the Far East through the same northerly exodus that moved up the Indus valley, to the west of the Himalayas, and which moved into the Asian Steppe between 40,000 and 50,000 years ago. Elements of this group then split off westward to populate the Middle East and Europe through two movements. However, there was also an eastern splinter, which was responsible for populating Siberia, Mongolia, and northern China, and ultimately also the movement of the first peoples into the North American continent, when it became possible to make the crossing from Siberia to Alaska.[2]

The *Y*-chromosome evidence supports this picture. As noted earlier, all Chinese males are descended from the original out-of-Africa line. Again, we find evidence in China of populations that are an offshoot from those following the coastal beachcombing trail around the coast of southeast Asia. Branches of this group moved west in a variety of movements, predominantly along the rivers that run into the Pacific and Indian oceans, such as the Brahmaputra, Yangtze, and Irrawaddy. However, the distribution of the descendants of other groups illustrates another pattern, which is consistent with the mitochondrial evidence of the colonization process from India through central Asia, and then east into northern China and Mongolia.

Pulling all this together, a clear picture emerges of China being colonized 40,000 to 50,000 years ago through three essential movements by modern humans. One consisted of the beachcombing trail, going around the coast of southeast Asia and up the pacific coast of China. Initially, offshoot populations from this group colonized southern China through a northward movement out of southeast Asia and a westward movement out of southern China, principally along some of the major river valleys. This second thrust was responsible for getting deep into China, including up to the Tibetan plateau. However, the third movement came from the other side of the Himalayas, up through the Indus, into western Siberia. This movement split into two parts, with one group moving westward to populate the northern areas of Europe and another group eastward to populate northern China, Mongolia, and the eastern parts of Russian Siberia. Thus, as with India, we have evidence for a north-to-south divide in the Chinese population.

This was the early story of settlement. However, whether they took the northern route or had edged up westward and northward from the southerly route, all inhabitants of the region experienced a severe ice age about 25,000 years ago. This lasted 10,000 years and, at its height, led to vast swaths of Siberia and northern and central China being enveloped in even more extreme, ice-cold, tundra-like conditions. Modern humans were pushed south and east toward the sea, as well as in the west toward the Lake Baikal region of central Asia. When the ice started to retreat, human beings again started the process of nomadic hunting and herding in the north. However, this period led to a substantial infusion of populations from Siberia and northern China into the south.

Since then, the pattern has tended to be migration of northern people to the south rather than the other way round. The most notable of these incursions involved the Han people who trace their ancestry to the ancient Huaxia peoples who lived in the Huang He (Yellow) river area in the prehistory era. The name later became associated with the famous Han Dynasty that united much of China between 206 BC and 220 AD, following the Warring States era. Genetic analysis shows that these Han populations infused much of the populations in other areas of China, particularly, on the male side. The *Y*-chromosome haplogroup *O3* is considered one of the main Han markers and is found in 50 percent of Chinese males. Mitochondrial analysis indicates that female diversity was preserved more, indicating perhaps elite dominance by the Han males from the north as they moved south.

While there have been repeated incursions on the margin over history—and wholesale occupation of China by nomadic tribes from the north on occasion—the underlying dominance of the Han still exists. So while there are today technically 56 ethnic nationalities in China, they are numerically dwarfed by the Han, who number 1.2 billion, by far the largest ethnic group in the world. Since this early pattern of settlement, regular incursions have occurred from the north, chiefly from Mongolia and Manchuria. These invaders frequently settled in China, but the impact on population structures, while evident, did not replace the earlier established Han dominance.

The Forces That have Shaped China's DNA

As we saw before, the environmental factors that shaped African, Indian, and Middle Eastern DNA have all been quite different and embodied certain unique features. The same is true of China; the challenges that modern humans faced in settling and thriving in this region were also unique and have led to a very distinctive psychological DNA in this part of the world. There are four essential factors to consider.

The first point relates to the challenges and opportunities that the people who went along the three routes into China faced. The most straightforward route that modern humans followed was the coastal beachcombing path around South East Asia and around the coast of China. The environments modern humans confronted in pursuing this path would have been comfortingly familiar, as they essentially resembled the early out-of-Africa environment that modern humans faced. However, unlike the beachcomber populations on the edge of the Middle Eastern desert, the Chinese environment offered the possibility of inland progression.

The same was true of the modern humans who pursued the coastal path in India. However, there are two central differences that the Chinese adventurers into the hinterland faced that earlier humans going into India did not. The first was that they would have had to encounter substantial colonies of earlier human species because, unlike their Indian cousins, they did not have the double-edged consequences of the Toba event, which for a significant part of the Indian subcontinent wiped out all traces of human, animal, and substantial plant life. Rather, the Chinese inland adventurers faced the challenges in the south of tropical and subtropical forests that they were forced to tame. In his analysis of Chinese history, French philosopher Amaury de Riencourt identifies the distinctively high levels of intensity and energy with which historic Chinese populations attacked their environment and settled these easterly and southeast lands.[3] Jungles and woodlands were cleared with voracious intensity and came to be densely settled by human populations over time.

Needless to say, the environmental challenges posed for the northern population that colonized China from the Asian Steppe were both unfamiliar and extremely testing. This was a forbidding environment, suffering from icy, subzero temperatures, as well as dry, windy conditions. The region was also teeming with wildlife, and the sheer challenge of surviving these conditions required new ways of thinking. The humans who opted for settled agriculture in areas to the south of the steppe were also required to work out ways of surviving extremely cold climates for prolonged parts of the year. An important factor that has influenced the DNA of Chinese culture is, therefore, the psychological orientation required to survive in conditions of extreme challenge, as well as environments requiring an intensive process of clearing and control. This necessitated practical inventiveness, planning, and sheer physical energy and endurance to survive. The luxury of going off into the jungles to reflect upon life was never an option.

The geography of eastern and southeastern China is complex, ranging from broad alluvial flood plains, through temperate grass-lands, down into subtropical coasts indented by vast rivers running through hilly terrains. To the west, the environment is much less hospitable and consists of high, desert-like plateaus with lunar-like characteristics at times. An essential point is that while the west and northwest of China is now an environment that can only sustain relatively sparse population loads, the alluvial plains of the north, the temperate grasslands, and the subtropical riverbed environment of southeast China are all ideal for settled populations. Today, these parts of China are some of the most densely populated parts of the world and have been so for some time. In fact, as will be argued later, many aspects of Chinese cultural DNA stem from the psychological orientation required to thrive in densely populated human environments. This developed a focus on what it takes to live in harmony with each other in Chinese culture. This process has naturally driven discipline, impulse control, respect for law, relational focus, commerciality, and a multitude of other psychological traits. To some extent all human societies have been heading in this direction, but it is a road that the Chinese have traveled along for longer and much further.

However, there is a third factor in the preceding account that has also had a powerful impact on Chinese cultural DNA. More than any other population in the world, the extensive and densely populated settled regions of China faced the pervasive and regular threats of the nomadic tribes roaming the Asian Steppe. In some sense all settled civilizations face this threat from the barbarians outside of the orbit of their civilization. However, the Middle Eastern civilizations did not have to contend with densely populated outer regions of nomadic hunter tribes. For different reasons, the settled populations of India found themselves protected—on the one hand by the world's highest mountain range, as well as vast desert regions on their western borders, and reasonably impenetrable rain forest to the east. The Chinese-settled populations had no such protection. Throughout history, they have been exposed to recurrent and incessant attacks from less-settled populations.

Europe experienced a version of this when, in Roman times, the Huns suddenly appeared from the east to terrorize vast swaths of what are now Russia, Eastern Europe, and Southern Europe. This was repeated in the thirteenth century, when Genghis Khan and his descendants swept out of their Mongolian homes to create a far-flung, if somewhat brief, empire. The Europeans, with the exception of the Russians, have at least had a degree of distance protecting them from regular incursions of nomadic raiders from the Asian Steppe—not so for the Chinese. This is the reason that the settled populations there, over thousands of years, built and extended the Great Wall, one of the most significant structures in terms of sheer scale and ambition in human history.

It seems that a critical consequence of such consistent, persistent, and aggressive pressure from their outer borders has led to one of the most notable aspects of Chinese culture—the willingness of people to accept authority and highly centralized unified states for much longer stretches of time than just about anywhere else in the world. China's vast alluvial plains also facilitated the creation of such states. Therefore, from the time of the Shang Dynasty, which arose in 1766 BC, to the Ching Dynasty that fell in 1913, China has had strong centralized governments for most of its known history. While periods of turmoil have occurred as dynasties changed and invaders came and went, the norm has been for settled, unified states ruling until they lost their "mandate from heaven." The names of periods of more extensive fragmentation, such as the Warring States period, which lasted from about 450 to 221 BC, themselves suggest that such episodes were the exception rather than the norm, an aberration from the natural state of affairs. This constant external threat facilitated the existence of these universal states and has led to a particularly distinctive set of attitudes to authority. Exactly the same attitudes were fostered in Russia, albeit less strongly, but for the same reasons.

Densely settled civilizations oriented to reducing external threats and maintaining internal harmony inevitably create a fourth factor: a sense of distance from the rest of the world, coupled with a certain level of in-group homogeneity. The Chinese have always regarded themselves as somehow separate and apart from others. Though the population descended from the out-of-Africa movement like everyone else, a certain in-group homogeneity and out-group distance developed in China—both physically and psychologically. The high proportion of the Chinese population that is Han is illustrative of this homogeneity. As J. Philippe Rushton observes, Chinese people are outliers on many physical and psychological indices—with Sub-Saharan Africans at one end of a continuum and the Chinese on the other, with Europeans in between.[4] This applies to physical size, the distinctiveness of Mongoloid features, the incidence of twins, different rates of infant maturation, and legions of other attributes. Recent data on genes determining key neurotransmitters, including dopamine, serotonin, monoamine oxidase or oxytocin, reinforces the idea that people in the Far East are frequently on one end of a dimension for particular alleles. As will be discussed later, this is almost certainly because genes and cultural coevolution has created a distinct pattern in China by virtue of the length of time that populations have been subjected to the selective pressures of continuous civilizational living. In a sense, the deeply held view of the Chinese as a people apart has some validity, although not necessarily on the dimensions that have hitherto been posited.

A final point is that buried deep in the early history of how China was populated, there is a sense of a deep north-and-south divide. Over time, this has been accentuated by the fact that ecologically the south developed rice cultivation and the north, wheat. The infusion of invaders from outside has also tended to be from the north. There is a widespread and pervasive perception in China of deep north and south cultural differences, the evidence for which will be explored later.

The Drive for Harmony

American psychologist Richard Nisbett and his colleagues from the University of Michigan performed a large number of studies on the differences between how East Asians and Westerners look at the world.[5] They presented people from both cultures with a diverse range of tasks and examined their responses, patterns of eye gaze, reaction times, and explanations for their behavior. More recently, neuropsychologists have looked at patterns of neural activation in response to different types of tasks. These investigations show significant differences with respect to key aspects of psychological functioning between Western and Far Eastern people and, on the whole, greater variation than found in differences between other global cultures. These studies in themselves confirm the earlier point that Chinese culture developed in a separate and distinctive way from many other regions of the world.

One set of experiments found significant differences simply in how people look at things. When given images of objects embedded in a surrounding field, there was an overwhelming difference in eye-gaze patterns, as well as what people described as happening in the pictures. For example, when Westerners looked at a fish in water against a background of rocks and water plants, they were much more likely to focus purely on the central object and describe the picture as a fish swimming in a lake. East Asians showed quite different patterns of eye gaze. They looked at the whole picture and moved rapidly between the central object and peripheral features, seeking connections and the context. East Asians tended to make many more statements about the background and the whole scene, as opposed to just describing the central object.

In another set of studies, Westerners responded to potentially contradictory information by polarizing their beliefs and by choosing between contrasting, relatively clear-cut options. East Asians, on the other hand, were much more inclined to moderate their beliefs when presented with contradictory information and to seek some sort of harmonious, synthetic resolution. Researchers found that Western people also had a highly developed rhetoric of argumentation, while East Asians often sought in discussion to find an agreeable middle way that resolved contradictions. Relatedly, Westerners tended to see events as flowing forward, and to think that an established pattern is likely to continue. East Asians' implicit sense of balance about the world means they feel that a pattern that develops is likely to reverse itself, in order to maintain a sense of harmony between different elements. As a consequence, people from the West see events unfolding predominantly in a linear direction, while those from the Far East are inclined to see cycles arising and fading.

These differences in outlook also led to very different mindsets for explaining events or people's sense of agency in the world. The researchers found that East Asians were much more likely to look at the context and provide situational explanations for peoples' behavior, whereas Westerners were more inclined to make attributions to the individual. East Asians were also much more inclined to see the world as a complex set of relationships, which made prediction and control of events difficult. Westerners had a much greater sense of personal agency, preferring simpler, more focal explanations for events.

The researchers summarized their conclusions across an array of different fields by hypothesizing that East Asians are much more inclined toward holistic, synthetic thinking and for both seeing and wanting to achieve interconnectedness and harmony between different elements. By comparison, Westerners are more analytical, particular, and reductionist in their approach. Writing in the 1950s, long before these experiments were conducted, Amaury de Reincourt had come to just about the same conclusion:

> *(As far as Chinese thought is concerned) there is never a succession of phenomena in nature, but a mere alteration of complimentary aspects. This concept of "mutation" largely destroys causality as the West has always conceded. Instead of an effect springing out of a cause, we now have related elements that are "matched" and instead of the succession we have interdependence.*

Culturally, there is also plenty of evidence for this proposition. Once the Han people settled in East Asia, they focused more intensely than just about any other civilization on establishing principles for the smooth functioning of society. This is the central focus of Confucianism.

Although the Tao is in some senses quite a separate philosophical tradition, here too one can see the preoccupation with the relationship between things and the concept of harmony. Tao literally means the way or path, and heavily influenced both Confucianism and Zen Buddhism, when the latter was incorporated into Chinese culture from across the Himalayas. Tao refers to the underlying natural order of the universe and the relationship between all inanimate and living things. A key objective in life is to harmonize oneself with nature. The concept of the Tao is intuitive and metaphysical, but in essence it refers to a notion of the underlying flow of events and the patterns in the universe that keep things balanced and ordered. Central to the notion of Yin and Yang is the idea that every action, sense, or taste has its counterpart and that one should look for an alignment and balance rather than dominance of any one attribute.

These patterns of thinking have deep roots in the culture of Chinese society. East Asians—who have a much longer history of densely populated agricultural settlement, followed by continuous civilizational society—are inevitably oriented toward seeing relationships and connections between objects, events, and people, simply because they have lived in a more interconnected world longer. In this sense, the Chinese are highly collectivist—or as Shalom Schwartz would term, highly embedded cultures.[6] Sure enough, we find on the Hofstede individualism–collectivism dimension that China scores as one of the most collectivist societies in the world.

However, this is a relatively simplistic way of understanding Chinese culture, as Chinese collectivism is very different from Indian, Sub-Saharan, or Middle Eastern collectivism. In the latter societies, it exists at the caste, tribal, or familial levels. Collectivism in China exists on a completely different scale. The Globe dimensions of institutional and personal collectivism are relevant here. The former refers to the kind of interpersonal collectivism seen in these other cultures, while the latter refers to the existence and observance of tight institutional rules and regulations at a wider societal level. China is the only major society that is exceptionally high on both.[7] However, collectivism—or the mindset associated with it—runs deeper than this in Chinese culture. It also encompasses a profound level of a sense of interconnectedness to all things and events.

Recent findings in behavioral genetics suggest that there may be an emotionally hardwired aspect to this preference for interdependence and harmony. East Asians are at an extreme with respect to particular mutations for genes that regulate key neurotransmitters that influence emotional patterns. Serotonin is significant in this regard; the drug Prozac impacts mood by influencing the uptake of this neurotransmitter. One gene that influences the level of this neuro-transmitter is the serotonin transporter gene. There is a short allele on this gene, which is associated with greater sensitivity to negative emotional events and rejection. This version is present in only 40 to 45 percent of Westerners, but appears in a full 80 percent of East Asians. Other cultures lie in between these two ranges. Similarly, genes that modulate the enzyme monoamine oxidase also show a difference. One allele, associated with sensitivity to social rejection, varies significantly by culture. East Asians again have the highest frequency, 65 percent, of the version associated with greater sensitivity to social conflict, compared with other global cultures. This compares with figures in the 20 to 40 percent range for populations from Western countries.[8]

Researchers J. J. Chiao, Katherine Blizinsky, Baldwin May, and others argue that this pattern of genes in East Asia has arisen from a process of culture–gene coevolution.[9] In essence, the creation of a collectivist culture with an emphasis on harmony has led to the selection of genes associated with greater sensitivity to negative emotional and social stress, which in turn has helped to further embed a cultural focus on harmony. This gene–culture coevolution has driven a tight sense of in-group cohesion needed for managing stress and anxiety. When these conditions are present, Chinese populations show lower levels of anxiety and mood disorders. However, outside of such supportive structures, these very same genes can make East Asians more prone to anxiety and extremely sensitive to slights or disharmony in relationships.

Interestingly, there is evidence that all these tendencies may be particularly hardwired into southern Chinese culture. The psychologist Thomas Talhelm and his colleagues have suggested that the Yangtze River is a psychological dividing line in China.[10] Wheat is the dominant crop north of the line, where people are more individualistic, direct, and less emotionally sensitive. Rice cultivation, Talhelm argues, requires much more collectivist endeavor—thereby resulting in greater psychological interdependence in the south. The journal *Science* reported a variety of studies across six Chinese cities that show northern Chinese to be more analytical, less holistic, and less interdependent than those in the south. Greater commerciality is also often reported in the south and perhaps stems from the greater interconnectivity of life that rice cultivation drives. However, these comparisons do not change the overall differences between Chinese culture and other regions of the world.

In the world of business, this focus on harmony finds expression in the lengths that Chinese leaders will go to preserve smooth and balanced relationships in their dealings both with each other and outsiders. They will frequently paper over or indirectly address disagreements and tensions. Etiquette and politeness dominate formal relationships—although as we will see later, there can also be a distinct lack of empathy that borders on rudeness when people are going about their day-to-day business in the midst of strangers. The concept of *face*—which essentially represents the personal currency with which one relates to society—also reflects this notion. Loss of face occurs when someone deals in an overly assertive way, criticizes you publicly, shows insufficient respect, or acts in a way that dents your pride. There is extreme sensitivity around this—and actions that would not give a Westerner pause for thought can cause near lifelong resentment.

As noted above, there is a neuropsychological basis to this sensitivity. Chinese drama and films are full of retributive stories that unfold when face has been lost. Giving face is the other side of the coin and involves paying compliments and otherwise acting in a way that increases someone's self-esteem. While face is similar in some ways to the Middle Eastern concept of honor, it has different qualities. Face is less showy, subtler, and involves a much more emotionally controlled and sensitive style of operating.

The notion of *guanxi*, which represents the relationship networks that are obligatory for doing business in China, also stems from this underlying preoccupation with interconnectedness. You remain a disconnected outsider until you are integrated into these networks or—as is more universally the requirement—partner up with somebody who is plugged into them. The need for such intermediaries often frustrates global businesses; they feel that they represent a rip-off tax, without appreciating the cultural forces that drive this requirement. In the absence of a minder who connects you into the web of social relationships, you're not just a nonentity—you are a potentially disruptive influence who may clumsily upset the web of delicate relationships that have been built up over time. Worse, if you're an outsider, you may not care about preserving face—which renders your future behavior beyond social sanction and therefore highly unpredictable. *Guanxi* is something that all people in China seek to build and it is regarded as almost as important as one's educational qualifications.

The drive for harmony also influences attitudes toward negotiations. There is always a desire to find a middle ground, and anyone who is perceived to be using their power to drive an unfair result evokes strong internal reactions within Chinese culture. The Chinese concept of *Zhong Yong*—which literally means the doctrine of the mean—is deeply embedded culturally, and refers to the constant drive to find the middle path in negotiations. As one executive said to me, "If you don't show flexibility and some give, the Chinese form the view that you are immature and do not understand the middle way concept; conversely, sticking to your guns is regarded as a sign of strength in the United States."

A sense of fairness rather than the letter of the law also regulates the attitude toward contracts. Chinese leaders will feel it is entirely fair to renegotiate a minerals contract, for example, when the global price drops. This can lead to acrimonious arguments with Western firms used to a more legalistic interpretation of an agreement that has been signed. As will be argued later, this difference arises from the fact that a drive for prediction and control is fundamentally hardwired into north European cultures, whereas fairness and harmony are prioritized in China.

This attitude also shows itself in the Chinese view of organizations, which is to see them predominantly as a living, harmonious set of interdependent relationships. The research by Fons Trompenaars and Charles Hampden-Turner cited earlier shows that while Americans overwhelmingly see organizations as systems for efficiently driving goals, the dominant view in East Asia is that they are a complex set of relationships that need to be cherished and nurtured.[11] In fact, there are powerful committees in many organizations in China, many with communist party sympathizers, that concern themselves with preserving the right cultural values. The interdependent view of organizations also shows up in leadership behavior. In our analysis, 30 percent of Chinese leaders were strong in teamwork and collaboration, one of the highest scores globally. The average for other global regions was just over half this figure at 17 percent.

The powerful drive to see connectedness everywhere can also lead to seemingly irrational beliefs—particularly to Western observers. Historically, the Chinese have shown an obsession for the rituals that their leaders had to observe in order not to disrupt the flow of the universe. These included precise instructions on how they were required to move around their kingdom and elaborate statements of the duties and ceremonies they were required to conduct. All this was predicated on the belief that disorder and chaos would ensue if these harmonious cycles were disturbed in any way.

Feng shui—with its elaborate rules for how different elements of an environment should fit with each other—also illustrates this point. I remember being surprised when visiting our Hong Kong office by the office manager politely, but firmly, requesting that I sanction a red horse to be put in our lobby, as this was necessary to counteract malign forces that were being channeled toward our office from nearby buildings. Interconnectedness taken to a high level also leads to superstition. The number 8, for example, is considered lucky in Chinese culture, while 4 is considered a harbinger of bad outcomes.

This sense of the unity of things and the importance of order and harmony is one of the great gifts of Chinese civilization to the world. In many ways it represents a more evolved and sophisticated notion of how to live with one's environment and other people than that established in any other culture. This applies also, to some extent, to China's relationship with nature—although by virtue of its astronomic economic growth, China has quickly become one of the largest carbon dioxide emitters and severe environmental consequences have emanated from its breakneck industrialization; global environmental campaigners frequently comment on how much easier it is to have a fruitful dialogue with Chinese leaders about the environment than with leaders, for example, from India or Brazil.

Certainly a focus on these kinds of things will be essential as the interdependencies that govern our globalized world multiply exponentially. The Chinese instinct of thinking about whole systems and how a myriad set of interconnecting cogs need to work together for the mutual benefit of all will be increasingly necessary.

The Authoritarian Compact

DRD4 is one of the genes that control dopamine receptors in the human brain. There are a variety of alleles of this gene, but one called the seven repeat has been particularly closely studied. A range of investigations has indicated that this particular allele is associated with independent-minded behavior, impulsivity, and risk taking, particularly in young adults. The presence of this allele is related to novelty seeking, as well as being mildly linked to attention deficit disorder. An association is also widely recognized between *DRD4-7R* and the history of migration; this version is sometimes referred to as the migration gene. This makes sense in that some immigrants are likely to self-select because of a drive for novelty and new experiences.

DRD4-7R has a different level of prevalence in different populations. In Caucasians, some 15 percent of Europeans have the *7R* allele, compared to close to 20 percent of Americans. The rates are highest in South Americans, where various studies put prevalence at close to 50 percent. However, *DRD4-7R* rates are close to zero in Chinese or Japanese samples. This is at first sight a mystery, given that East Asia lies quite far along the migratory train out of Africa. The differences could reflect the random process of genetic drift. However, it appears that some distinctive may factors have led to the *DRD4-7R* allele being selected against in East Asia.

The complete absence of a gene associated with risk taking, sensation seeking, and a liking for novel environments is likely not unrelated to another fact about China. The country has the highest per head—for want of a better word—rate of capital punishment in the world. This reflects a historical abhorrence of crime or disorder, which has always been severely punished throughout Chinese history. Some might wonder whether this high rate is simply because China is still a relatively poor country; however, the second highest per capita rate of capital punishment is in Singapore, one of the wealthiest countries in the world. The fact that Singapore is a predominantly Chinese outpost on the tip of the Malaysian peninsula is probably not unrelated to its China-like high rates of execution. Century after century of this kind of response to antisocial behavior, including strict penalties in places like Singapore simply for chewing gum, helps perhaps explain why anyone with *DRD4-7R* would have packed their bags very quickly, been socially ostracized, or, more tragically, jailed or executed.

There are virtually no accounts of the psychological culture of China that do not refer to the central importance of obedience within the society. Whether it is studies using the Asch conformity experiment or scores on the Hofstede dimension of power distance, the pattern is clear: Chinese people place a high value on obedience and conformity. It is almost impossible to get people to criticize their bosses or government officials or to dissent in any way from the sanctioned views of things. Efforts to elicit such opinions make people visibly uncomfortable and invite fairly rapid social distancing. However, this acceptance of authority is conditional and has some associated subtleties. While China is high on power distance on the Globe values survey, it is lower than many African and Latin American countries. Acceptance of authority is very different psychologically in each of these cultures. There is a paradox in China: In the midst of a culture of seeming obedience, there are countless acts of collective rebellion—both in firms and in the wider society—on a daily basis.

In order to illustrate the power of obedience first, one only has to look at recent events in Chinese history. During the Cultural Revolution in the 1960s—prompted by Mao Tse Tung's paranoid belief that the bourgeois intelligentsia was undermining socialist values—the government sent large numbers of suspect middle-class people into the countryside or penal colonies to undertake personal reform. It was an arduous and painful experience from which many did not return. Mao and the communists also requested that children report their parents to the authorities if they felt that their attitudes and behaviors opposed any key tenets of communist ideology. Thousands and thousands of children reported their parents, despite the severe consequences this entailed. Though Chinese culture is highly family focused, obedience to a higher authority trumped such loyalties on this occasion. It is inconceivable to imagine something like this happening in India, the Middle East, or even Europe.

This central thrust of the Chinese character emanates from the distant past and from the strong sense of historical continuity that Chinese civilization has had literally over tens of thousands of years. The settled populations of China faced two pressures that were discussed earlier. One was that they were an incredibly driven, energetic, and proactive people who cleared their initial environment with intensity and focus. As social structures were established, there was—and still is—a fear of this underlying intensity surfacing and becoming disruptive. Second, the settled societies existed under constant threat from attack by the aggressive, nomadic pastoralists that existed in relatively large numbers on the edges of settled society. Over the ages, the Chinese population made an implicit pact with their authorities: Keep us safe and we will accept the collective authority that is imposed upon us. Historically, authoritarianism has always been an attractive proposition for people who feel under threat.

We can see this authoritarian compact in many business settings. Young Chinese managers often freeze in the presence of their superiors. Something like 360-degree feedback, even when it is clearly anonymous, can create uneasiness and discomfort—not for the individual receiving the feedback, but for the person required to give it. In our assessments, only 4 percent of Chinese leaders had a strength around inclusive leadership through others. This was the lowest rate in the world, with the exception of Latin American leaders. The figure for Western leaders was low, but was still treble the rate for their Chinese counterparts.

Hierarchy and protocol abound in dealings with Chinese businesses. People invest a huge amount of effort upfront to determine an individual's status so Chinese firms can provide an appropriate match from their side. Incongruities that occur by accident can cause embarrassment and discomfort. With respect to education and training, it is rare for Chinese students to question or second guess what they are told, even though they preserve a high level of independent mindedness and thinking at an internal level. Nondirective forms of learning, where a teacher and a student work together to develop insights, typically create discomfort.

I remember running a development program for the high-potential leaders in a global company. The program had very little by way of didactic teaching and consisted exclusively of exercises and tasks designed to help leaders develop better insight into their strengths and weaknesses. I noticed two Chinese participants looking progressively more and more uncomfortable as the program proceeded. The only moment that they looked vaguely happy was when one of our consultants put up a model of feedback. The Chinese students enthusiastically began taking notes at this point. Later on, as I was talking to them at dinner, I discovered that their general manager had told them that the whole company would be waiting for them on their return, at a specially prepared conference, to hear what they had learned. Since the program itself was highly individually focused, this was inevitably going to be a meaningless exercise. However, the Chinese participants were terrified of telling their general manager this and were at a loss about what to do when they returned to China to face this expectant gathering. They rightly sensed that one meager model on feedback skills was not going to meet the expectations of the proposed audience.

However, outsiders can make the mistake of assuming that Chinese executives are intellectually passive on the basis of the above behaviors. In fact , in my experience this is far from the case, as internally there is a constant process of questioning and evaluating ideas. A number of studies support this view. Professor Francesco Sofo, of the University of Canberra, for example, using a questionnaire on thinking styles, found that Chinese executives had a high preference for independent and exploring styles of thinking and were low on conditional thinking, which referred more to obediently absorbing ideas.[12] Sensitivity about preserving face means that open displays of such critical thinking are highly repressed. If, however, one creates the conditions for this to be put to one side, Chinese executives can be highly vociferous and challenging. Many of the younger generation have understood that Western companies in particular want this and can surprise leaders from outside by their capacity to air disagreement when permission is given.

At the wider societal level, the obedience gene on the surface—with a more questioning stance underneath—is also relatively easily observable. This arises from the fact that while power is respected in China as it is in other places, there is an important difference: Obedience is a social contract in China and is only a valid expectation if rulers or leaders deliver on their part of the bargain. Although it is rarely mentioned, at any one point in time, Chinese life is punctuated by continuous mini-riots and rebellions when this compact between the leader and the led breaks down. This occurs at a societal level, but also within firms—where workers can be quite vociferous in demanding their rights. In this sense, Chinese society moves in a fluid way between obedience and conformity to energetic and vociferous rebellion when a perceived compact is felt to have been violated. The rise of communism was exactly an example of this type of rebellion against a violated social order. Underpinning this dynamic is a constant question in people's minds: "Are our leaders showing the wisdom and judgment that means we are prepared to go along with their authority?"

In China today, one sees the rise of the sentiment that the rulers—whether on a micro scale in cities and firms or in the nation at large—are in danger of violating their compact with heaven. Chinese authorities are not wrong to assume that their society teeters on the brink of rebellion if this sentiment takes hold. Political authorities display an almost paranoid terror about loss of control and, Canute-like, employ vast armies of people to sift and delete material from the Internet that could threaten order and structure in society—"The Great Fire Wall of China." There is also a very real fear that the ruling classes may have taken corruption too far. These fears may seem paradoxical in a society with such low levels of the disobedience gene, but the fears are founded on a valid reading of Chinese psychology.

Another point arises from the factors hypothesized to drive this authoritarian compact in the first place. There has been a lack of interest in Chinese culture in imposing themselves on others outside the Middle Kingdom. However, this benign attitude exists alongside an extreme, emotionally intense set of attitudes around defending what is seen to be China's natural territory. Chinese attitudes toward Taiwan, the Senkaku/Diaoyu islands, and its border with India are the opposite of flexible. These emotions are driven by an age-old paranoia about protecting the civilization from external intrusion, which is not easily going to dissipate even in today's more secure world.

Concrete and Practical Inventiveness

A senior figure in the research arm of a global American pharmaceutical company was once invited to visit a newly created research center in China. The Chinese were interested in showing their facilities to a world authority and learning about what they could improve. The scientist went around the facilities, which he found to be more pristine and advanced than he had seen anywhere. The Chinese had done their homework and created state-of-the-art laboratories stocked with the latest equipment. The scientist complimented them, and then asked, "But where does the thinking take place?" He had seen lots of well-qualified people going about their tasks; but nowhere had he witnessed huddles of people engaged in intellectual exploration, debate, or creative theorizing. This question flummoxed his Chinese hosts, who were eager to learn how they could create a more thinking culture. The scientist invited the Chinese to come visit his firm's research headquarters, an offer they eagerly accepted. He expected perhaps two to three people to come over, but was surprised many months later when over 30 turned up, notebooks at the ready, to learn about thinking.

There is both a lack of historical perspective, as well as a degree of wishful stereotyping, implicit in this view that the Chinese are not innovative. One could even argue that until a few hundred years ago, China was responsible for more innovation than just about any other culture in the world—with the most obvious examples being gunpowder, the compass, paper money, and, as Marco Polo found, noodles/pasta. However, this represents only the tip of the iceberg when it comes to Chinese inventiveness. More detailed and less ethnocentric investigation of Chinese history has revealed that legions of lifting and motion machines, complex pulley systems, the paddle wheel, locks and other mechanisms for channeling water, as well as a range of aeronautical inventions such as the kite and the parachute, existed in China often hundreds of years—sometimes over a thousand—before they appeared in the West. Indeed, in his work *1434: The Year a Magnificent Chinese Fleet Sailed to Italy and Ignited the Renaissance,* author Gavin Menzies provides compelling evidence to suggest that many of the practical inventions that supposedly originated with the likes of Leonardo da Vinci and others during the Renaissance had their source in Chinese texts that had made their way to Italy.[13]

However, one thing becomes clear when comparing Chinese thought with the West. In spite of the extraordinarily high levels of practical creativity, the Chinese did not, like the Greeks, invent a theory of science or abstract systems of knowledge. Comparison with both India and the West illustrates a profound feature of Chinese thinking: It is practical and concrete rather than having an abstract or conceptual focus. In part, this practicality also explains another unique feature of Chinese thought compared to all other cultures in the world—the absence of strong, indigenously grown religious sentiments. These generally arise from a concern with the world beyond the here and now and from a fundamental drive to answer deep questions about existence. Abstract scientific thought also comes from a desire to answer fundamental questions about why the world is the way it is. The practical and concrete-minded instincts within Chinese culture meant that such philosophical enquiry always had a real world or social focus.

Nothing illustrates this concrete rather than abstract intellectual orientation more than the Chinese language itself. Distinctively, it is the only major written language in the world that is based on pictographs, which then morphed into more complex phonographs (symbols denoting both meaning and sound). In Indo-European languages the elements are divorced from their meaning and only a small number are needed to describe everything. Chinese written language has thousands of characters, each an amalgam of different concrete or phonic elements. This drives and is reflective of a precise and concrete chunking up of the world rather than a concern for deeper abstract principles. Incidentally, it is also reflective of a detailed sense of visual acuity, another feature of Chinese intellect.

In terms of reasons for this fundamental difference, the divergence with India is easier to explain than that with Europe. As mentioned earlier, a very particular confluence of benign conditions that modern humans had to contend with in India allowed for a retreat from the practical world and into a search for self-improvement and a quest for the fundamental nature of human existence. The harsh and challenging environments, particularly of northern China, afforded the early modern humans in that part of the world no such luxuries. The practical problems of surviving in extreme conditions could not be treated as an afterthought, as it tended to be in Indian culture. The reasons why European thought is more conceptually oriented will be explored later in the European chapter, but essentially boils down to Middle Eastern influences and a greater tolerance for individual exploration of ideas.

There is another reason why thinking in Chinese culture has been focused on incremental and practical innovation rather than deeper theoretical advances. The latter requires one to act somewhat individualistically, challenge the authority of accepted giants, and put one's head above the parapets in a way that creates waves and invites ridicule or loss of face. This kind of risk taking just goes against the cultural grain in China. The authorities in China have also historically had an ambivalent attitude toward intellectuals. While disciplined study of accepted societal wisdom has been always encouraged, broader intellectual exploration has generated suspicion. The first Chin emperor, Chin Shih Huang Ti, who provided the enduring legacy of the name China to the country he unified in 226 BC, set the pattern early on. His dynasty was so opposed to intellectuals that he had the majority of them put to death or sent into exile. All books, except for those related to practical and technical matters, were burnt. Thousands of years later, Mao instituted a similar vendetta against intellectuals, through the quixotically named Cultural Revolution.

The practical and concrete orientation of the Chinese intellect perhaps also explains another puzzle. Why, after literally thousands and thousands of years of trailblazing inventiveness, did Chinese scientific creativity dry up in the last three or four centuries? While the West surged forward, China—which had led the world in so many areas of inventiveness—simply stagnated. Nobel Prize winners since 1901 include 349 for America, 101 for Germany, 116 for Britain, 9 for India, but only 8 for China—of which only 4 were for science. Yet China has had a far bigger population than any of these countries over this period of time. One hypothesis is that innovation in today's world involves going beyond the obvious and concrete parameters of the world. It requires, more than in the past, abstract and theoretical innovation first. For example, the theories of relativity and quantum mechanics were areas of abstract exploration for decades. Yet over time they led to the development of nuclear energy, the atom bomb, the microwave, lasers, and in the near future super-fast quantum computers.

These differences in thought patterns find expression in business in other ways. The concrete and practical inventiveness theme is evident in the fact that China overtook the United States in the number of patents filed in 2012, 2 million, of which 1.25 million were granted. The vast majority of these were, however, for small, incremental, practical advances prompted in part by the government's stated ambition of driving innovation. This kind of pragmatic innovation is deeply embedded in Chinese cultural DNA; more transformational or abstract leaps are less common. This sense is also supported in our data. A full 47 percent of Chinese leaders scored as being strong in analytical thinking, the highest score globally with other cultures scoring on average in the 30 percent range. However, Chinese executives were relatively weak with respect to broader strategic thinking, scoring well below American, European, and Indian executives. Analytical thinking requires concrete intellectual qualities whereas strategic thinking requires an orientation that is more conceptual.

More generally, China's rise to become the manufacturer to the world has surprised many, not least the slow-moving competitors in the West who were caught off guard by the speed of this challenge. Yet in some ways this is just a reversion to the way China has always been—that is, until recently, one of the most industrialized and technologically innovative societies in the world. The underlying strength of Chinese cultural DNA in this respect should not be underestimated. The West will find only cold comfort in the idea that the Chinese will not be able to go beyond just reproducing or copying Western inventions. Nor should one assume that the Chinese lack of interest in abstraction is likely to hold the country back. Practical as ever, once people in China have appreciated the importance of abstract theorizing, one should not underestimate their capacity to embrace new ways of thinking. There is an overwhelming over-representation of Chinese students with respect to the highest levels of attainment in scientific subjects in leading-edge scientific universities in both America and Europe. However, to really move forward in this area, Chinese companies and institutions will need to encourage abstract intellectual play more and give people the permission to challenge orthodoxy at a broad level.

Fast Slow

My family visited China in the mid-1990s. Our American expatriate hosts, working for a U.S. subsidiary, advised us on the penultimate day of our trip to get some clothes made. We laughed and said we had clearly left it too late. "No," they insisted, "Things happen fast here." Sure enough, within half an hour of us skeptically agreeing to the idea, three women tailors arrived at the house and proceeded to measure up the whole family for what seemed like a bewildering array of clothes. The whole process was such a frenzied blur that it was difficult to remember what we had ordered or in what quantities. Amazingly, the Chinese women appeared to be taking no notes and simply barked staccato instructions to each other as they whizzed around us. How could they remember any of this, we wondered? Amazingly, when they appeared as promised next morning, everything was just so, perfectly stitched and right in every respect. The price for all this tailor-made clothing was also amazingly cheap.

I wondered then whether this unique combination of intensity, pace, high standards, and low prices could be replicated at scale. If so, it would be transformative for the global clothing industry. What I didn't realize at the time was that China was well on its way to producing almost half the clothes that are sold in both Europe and the United States. The amazing success of fast fashion, and the reduction to barely two weeks from seeing something on the catwalk to copying it at industrial scale, is not in small measure due to the pace with which Chinese factories operate. Even today, as countries with lower wages become more attractive, the speed of Chinese factories still helps to preserve their edge. Pablo Isler, chief executive of Identitechs (the group that owns Zara), commented in 2011 that the sheer pace and flexibility shown by Chinese firms will make it hard for other countries to compete, even as wage levels rise in the country.

There is evidence of pace everywhere in China. In 2011, the Chinese firm Broad Group set a record by putting up a 30-story building from a standing start in as few as 15 days—a feat that could take 15 years in some parts of the world. The frenzied activity of workers buzzing around the site like gnats, goaded by their leaders issuing instructions and signing papers at a frantic pace, quickly went viral. Now, some people might be reluctant to stay in a 30-story hotel put up in just over two weeks. However, the Ark Hotel is five times more quake-resistant than ordinary buildings and is truly advanced in terms of energy use, environmental standards, and general workmanship. The major reason for the speed of construction was that many of the hotel's components and building structures were engineered offsite and were put into place on site. Nevertheless, it is hard to imagine anything happening at this sort of speed in other parts of the world.

In London, it can tax the local authorities' ingenuity to fill in a simple pothole in a fortnight, let alone put up a 30-story building.

The lightning building speed shown by Broad Group is not an exception. Anyone who regularly visited China over the past few decades will comment on the sheer intensity and pace with which the urban landscape of the country has changed. The Polish writer Ryszard Kapuściński, once witnessed the astonishment of some African leaders visiting China, a couple of decades after communist control of the economy had been relaxed. The China that they had visited in the past had been a third-world country, not that different from their African homelands. "How did this happen?" the Africans gasped, upon seeing the transformation that had taken place in Beijing or Shanghai, or the gleaming multilane highways that had mushroomed across the country. Some of them may be bridges and roads to nowhere—and there may be a huge overhang in the banking system as a result—but at least they exist.

A while back, researchers made a systematic effort to look at the pace at which things happen in different cities and cultures across the world. The idea was that different places would have a different attitude or sense of urgency around time. Researcher Robert Levine looked at three indicators: walking speed at a set time of day in the absence of rain in the middle of a city, the speed with which one was able to perform a simple transaction such as buying a stamp at a Post Office, and the accuracy of public clocks. These three dimensions were integrated into a pace of life index. The researchers duly went round the world measuring this in different cultures.

In the initial study in 1999, Japan had the fastest pace of life and many Western countries were also high. Less-developed countries were relatively slow paced.[14] The measures relating to clocks and buying stamps probably confounded other influences. When the study was repeated in 2006, by Richard Wiseman, looking just at walking speed, Singapore was rated the fastest city and the only Chinese city studied, Guanzhou, was rated fourth.[15]

One long-standing theory is that population density is a key variable for driving pace of life in different parts of the world. The high prices, scarcity, and competition for resources that this creates compel people to use their time efficiently. GDP per capita of the city has been found to correlate with its pace of life. This makes intuitive sense; in a rich city, the adage "time is money" assumes even more importance. City size is also a key determinant of pace of life; the bigger the city, the more people rush around, even in the same cultures. Climate has also been found to be a significant variable; the warmer a city is, the slower the pace.

Given the above relationships, it is not surprising to find that China has moved sharply up the pace-of-life indices as it has developed and its GDP per head leapt ahead. Even Chinese-dominated cities in relatively warm climates, such as Singapore and Hong Kong, are close to the global records on such indicators. Is this intensity a recent phenomenon or is it something more deeply embedded in Chinese cultural DNA?

It's likely that the long continuous history of civilizational settlement, and its associated high density of population, has meant that the prevailing context for thousands of years in China has been scarcity and intense competition for resources. Just like in a modern metropolis, this has driven an acute consciousness around efficient use of one's time. The pragmatic and concrete focus within Chinese culture, discussed earlier, also leads to a similar attitude toward time. And China's rapid economic development has simply aggravated an underlying tendency within the culture—which is why many places in China are fast shooting up in the pace-of-life league.

What does this intensity and pace—which is increasing as China develops—mean on a daily level in business? One is hit with a sense of urgency and energy when you enter any Chinese businesses. Interactions outside of one's networks of relationships are typically crisp and functional. If you sit in a restaurant you will be surprised how quickly you are served. The Chinese also value punctuality and—unlike other emerging economies, such as India where I personally once waited for a train that was two days late—things in China run on time. Indeed in many parts of Africa, India, and the Middle East, endless waiting in line is commonplace even for relatively trivial tasks. This is not the case in China, where things typically happen with a restless efficiency that is rare even in the West.

However, many Western companies have found getting established and doing business in China to be a much slower process. When there is a need to build relationships or negotiations are taking place, Chinese culture shifts into a much lower gear. In fact, anything that requires social acceptance or the development of trust evolves much more slowly. It takes time to accept outsiders or for people to embrace new ways of doing things. However, once a deal is struck or relationships are on a sound footing, execution can move at a lightning pace. Recognizing when to be patient and when to really put one's foot on the accelerator is important. Chinese executives abroad need to rebalance the other way—that is, move more quickly in the early stages of relationship formation and then slow down a bit to enable things to be executed in a balanced way that continues to maintain relationships.

Bounded Sociability and Empathy

Any of the big cities in the world that have a strong Chinese population—London, San Francisco, New York, Sydney, or Kuala Lumpur—tend to have a section called Chinatown. While all minorities congregate together, the use of the term Chinatown is an expression of something different; the creation of a little version of your home country, the near total exclusion of others from the enclave, as well as social, but not commercial, distancing from those who lie outside one's group.

This pattern of traits helps to make sense of the paradox that outsiders experience in managing relationships within China. At one level, people are incredibly courteous, polite, sensitive, and work hard to create harmony in an interaction. They pay attention to nuance and manage subtlety in a way that one rarely sees in other cultures. However, the experience is completely different when you step out on the street. People push and elbow past you in queues. If you ask for help you may find yourself being completely ignored in a way that seems rude and offensive. The needs of the young and elderly on the street are ignored in the intensity with which life is pursued in China. Pedestrians or cyclists may be casually and routinely run over. People do things like park in front of roads or gates with a complete indifference to the likely impact on other road users.

This bifurcated approach to relationships is a clear theme in Chinese cultural DNA, which can be termed "bounded sociability and empathy." It leads to an intense focus on managing relationships considered to be important, coupled with a tuning out of the wider social environment. A consequence of this approach is that Western social behavior is seen as strangely inverted from a Chinese point of view. As a popular Chinese saying goes: "Westerners treat strangers like their family and their families like strangers."

This deeply ingrained pattern within Chinese culture is a characteristic that people typically develop when living in dense, urban environments over a prolonged period. They form tight relationships with some, but the world of people is just so overwhelming that one simply ignores and shuts out those with whom one does not have any day-to-day business. This process happens in big cities the world over. In China, centuries of living in densely populated contexts has created a similar process and leads to an approach to relationships that juxtaposes considerable effort and attention to the management of one's special networks, alongside a capacity to shut out—almost at a neurological level—those who are not relevant to the pursuit of one's goals.

This selective approach to interpersonal attention is illustrated in a variety of ways in psychological research. In a study called "Disregard for Outsiders," Romin Tafarodi and others looked at differences among how people remembered things about people who are either similar to or different from themselves, using Canadian, Hong Kong, and Japanese participants. When told that it was important to learn about the students who were similar to themselves, researchers found the Chinese concentrated virtually exclusively on the person of interest and showed limited memory for others compared to either the Canadians or the Japanese.[16] This difference disappeared when the participants were not given a particular reason for directing their attention to anyone. The authors concluded that Chinese participants required a task-based reason to attend to somebody and when this happened they concentrated on that person and were inclined to ignore other parts of their social environment.

The theme is also illustrated in studies on the levels of empathy shown toward strangers. Steven Myler, who is a Western-based psychotherapist with considerable experience working in China, undertook a qualitative study of empathy in Western and Chinese observers. His researchers interviewed people about recent tragedies such as accidents, fires, and deaths and tested for the participants' emotional reactions toward the victims. Myler found that his Chinese respondents reacted in a somewhat different way to the stories compared to people from the West. In almost all the interviews, the majority of Chinese respondents conveyed a lack of empathy and an inability to understand distress in other people, except in a very superficial manner.[17] For example, after a story about a recent road death caused by a taxi passenger opening a door and killing a cyclist who was trying to pass the taxi, most of the Chinese respondents said that the cyclist should have been more careful. When asked how the passenger might have felt about killing the cyclist most replied, "I have no idea." When Westerners were asked the same question, they tended to say the passenger would feel scared, guilty, fearful of consequences, or sorry about the victim. Even when these possibilities were pointed out to the Chinese respondents, they often shrugged their shoulders and replied, "How would you know?"

In case you are wondering if this just represents theoretical studies, pause to consider the case of a two-year-old child, Yue Yue, who was run over when she had wandered away from her parents' attention on a busy Chinese street. The helpless child lay on the side of the road clearly in pain and needing attention—but as video reconstructions show, was completely ignored by over 18 passersby, as well as the many shopkeepers. Cyclists and rickshaws also steered past her. Horrifically, seven minutes later she was run over a second time by a lorry. She was finally noticed by an elderly lady and taken to a hospital, where she unfortunately died of her injuries.

Recordings of the incident elicited a degree of soul searching in China. A variety of reasons were put forward as to why little Yue Yue was ignored. Some attributed it to Chinese lack of empathy for strangers, others to the busy and frantic pace of life, and yet others to the fear that one might lose out financially from helping someone and having to pay for an ambulance.

Since this incident, a number of equally graphic examples of lack of empathy to strangers have emerged. Interestingly, similar observations about Chinese neglect of strangers in trouble were noted by the British centuries ago as they engaged China. For example, in 1792, the British diplomat John Barrows describes a number of incidents in his book *Travels in China*, which illustrate "a want of fellow-feeling."[18]

He describes with incredulity how not a single boat out of multitudes available came to the rescue of a group of people who had fallen into the water after a collapse of an old wreck on the side of a grand canal. Even worse, he witnessed a man in a boat trying to recover a man's hat from the water, seemingly oblivious to the fact that man himself was drowning and needed help.

The Chinese government has described these kinds of incidents as "violating traditional Chinese values"—which has some truth to it. The Chinese manage their close relationships with sensitivity, empathy, and high levels of mutual responsibility. However, current historical and psychological evidence indicates that this seems to break down when one is in the company of strangers. As well as deeper cultural traits, the tribulations that people went through under communism might, paradoxically, have accentuated this focus on one's own interests.

Both sides of the coin are visible in how the Chinese conduct themselves socially within business. There is an essential sociability and sensitivity that Chinese leaders show in managing relationships within known circles and boundaries in organizations. One sees a high level of social skill in such circumstances. Our assessments found that a full 34 percent of Chinese leaders were seen as having strength around building relationships easily, and 30 percent showed a strength around teamwork and collaboration. With the exception of Latin America, the figures for these attributes were the highest of all regions in the world, and a surprise to those who judge the Chinese approach to relationships from a distance. In addition, one sees high levels of sensitivity and respect in managing valued relationships and in negotiations.

However, social distance and lack of empathy is also evident in organizational life. While there's evidence of team orientation and a drive to develop teams among Chinese leaders, this does not necessarily translate into empathy for those outside one's circle. Only 10 percent of Chinese leaders had a strength around empathy for others, compared with a global average in the 20 percent range. In addition, business practices toward competitors can be ruthless, with an anything goes attitude. Chinese leaders operating abroad can have some adjustment issues on this dimension. One leader described to me how, after moving to manage an operation in southeast Asia, his team eventually told him, "Your style is too Chinese." He asked what this meant, and found that it essentially boiled down to not being sufficiently sensitive toward the people he managed.

These issues of bonding also arise in business and academic settings outside of China—and outside of familiar settings. Over the years, there has been a tremendous increase in the number of Chinese students going abroad, with the United States alone now receiving 200,000 students from China annually. However, a number of surveys indicate that Chinese students find the social aspects of U.S. college life to be a real problem, even compared to other overseas nationalities.[19] A pervasive feeling of not knowing how to connect with American students, despite initial intentions to do so, followed by a retreat into exclusively Chinese networks seems to be the norm. I have seen similar issues arise when people move from China into Western organizations. Outsiders must try to understand the genuine level of emotional uncertainty and sense of dislocation that the Chinese are almost hardwired to experience in such situations. Otherwise, there is a tendency to simply label their behavioral retreats as reflecting arrogance or a sense of exclusivity.

A sense of social separation can also be evident at a macro level. The approach the Chinese have taken in dealing with the outside world through the ages is mirrored today by the quality of the Chinese presence in Africa. Over years, China has built a strong presence in many African countries, driven by its interest in African resources and the opportunities of an emerging market. Large numbers of Chinese workers have traveled to both work in and trade with African countries. However, the overwhelming experience of the Africans is that the Chinese have kept very much to themselves, in their own compounds, eating their own food, and employing Chinese staff to look after their needs.

The Art of Copying

A few years back, I heard an unusual anecdote in our Hong Kong office about an American multinational's experience in China. The company was desperate to bring into its Chinese business high-potential, young talent. They reasoned that offering some scholarships for selected students to enable them to study in the

United States would help them attract talent. This proved to be right, as there was ferocious competition for the small number of places available. In one interview, a young Chinese man impressed his American hosts by recounting a story, involving a series of detailed trials and tribulations, including the suffering his family had experienced in the Cultural Revolution. The story helped powerfully position his case for the bursary. The American interviewers were impressed and duly made him an offer.

Then something unusual happened. As they carried on the interviews the following week, they noticed more and more people coming to them with stories eerily similar to the original one. At first they thought it was a coincidence—but when nearly everyone began saying the same kind of thing, the authenticity of the stories, to put it mildly, came under question. Word had clearly got around about the original story's effectiveness, and others had simply taken the pragmatic decision to copy a recipe that had worked for someone else. What bemused the American interviewers was the thought that a lot of the interviewees must have known that others were also copying the story, yet they nevertheless persisted in recounting their own near identical version of it. In their eyes, they were fitting into a schema that the Americans interviewers were seeking and to which they had already responded positively. It did not occur to the Chinese interviewees that the Americans had been looking for individuality and distinctiveness. Rather they assumed that the Americans would respond positively to the same story because it was the *right answer*. The irony was that many of the bursaries eventually went to the few people who did not shoot themselves in the foot by repeating the much-copied mantra.

It seems that a number of the psychological traits outlined earlier combine to create a powerful drive toward a copying instinct in Chinese culture. The concrete and pragmatic intellectual orientation means that if something works there is a powerful urge to recapitulate the recipe of success. The intense Chinese cultural preoccupation with efficient use of time also fuels this tendency; after all, it is far quicker to copy something that has worked than to figure out your own path in the situation. However, perhaps the bigger driver of copying is that in a culture that values cohesion and harmony there is a positive abhorrence of doing something that sets one apart from the whole in a disjunctive way. In a deep sense, a person in Chinese culture can take pride from copying something whereas someone from the more individualistic West would feel diminished and embarrassed by the thought of simply recapitulating a recipe that has worked for someone else.

The copying instinct exhibits itself in a number of tangible and obvious ways within Chinese culture. For example, plagiarism, as defined by Western standards, is rife in many Chinese academic institutions, both by students but also more worryingly respected academics. In July 2010, Centenary College in New Jersey shut down its satellite business schools in both China and Taiwan after uncovering widespread plagiarism. After an investigation, the school decided to withhold degrees from all 400 students involved in its MBA programs in Beijing, Shanghai, and Taipei. Plagiarism is also a massive problem for papers submitted to academic journals, where some studies indicate that close to a third contain significant amounts of plagiarized material.[20]

However, it is important to recognize that plagiarism is much more of an emotive issue in individualistic cultures where the attribution of everything to a person matters. In a more collectivist culture, intellectual property is a collective good. For thousands of years, Chinese scholars have been required to faithfully learn and recapitulate the work of the masters. When Chinese students produce an essay, they are trying to show they have mastered knowledge in of an area. The arrogance of a spotty undergraduate trying to put their own stamp on years and years of work by notable experts is anathema to people brought up in such a tradition, perhaps rightly so.

Many global-branded companies are aware of the speed with which Chinese factories dissect and rip off their products. When one sees the standards achieved in this copying, one has to admit that there is an art to being able to reproduce things with such high levels of fidelity. From unerring similarities of Chinese military hardware to Russian and American versions, down to fake iPhones, one sees copying prevalent at all levels of Chinese business life.

This instinct is not just evident with respect to obvious and tangible products. As Amaury de Riencourt has noted, there seems to be a strong desire within the Chinese population for "magic keys" that allow one to operate in life. Witnessing that communism had apparently worked in the Soviet Union, the Chinese had no compunction absorbing the recipe and making it their own. When the recipe failed to deliver, it was dropped just as fast as it had been taken up—but with face saving external justifications that involved labeling the red-tooth capitalism of the new era "communism with Chinese characteristics."

Chinese written language also undoubtedly expresses and reinforces this copying tendency. With most other written languages in the world, you can get by learning 30 or so symbols from which you can then phonetically construct tens of thousands of words. In China, there are literally tens of thousands of characters that one might learn—although for most people functional literacy requires knowledge of about 3,000 or so. Nevertheless, this is still 2,774 more or over 100 times what one needs to learn as an English speaker. In order to get started in China, you must therefore be able to recognize and faithfully recapitulate with a high level of fidelity a much larger number of characters than that required in most other languages. It is easy to see why this process drives disciplined learning and finely attuned reproduction skills.

When one sees the detail and quality with which factory brands are reproduced at ridiculously knocked-down prices, one can only admire the ability to reproduce with such fidelity, at scale, and with efficient use of resources. It is not an easy thing to deconstruct and reverse engineer something as complex as, for example, a stealth fighter; yet the Chinese have shown an ability to do this in tight time frames. The idea that copying can *never* be a route to innovation is also open to question. There are many ways to break new ground—and wholly dismissing the process of incrementally building on things that have worked before is simplistic. As outlined earlier, Chinese history has an unparalleled history of technological inventiveness and innovation about which other cultures should not be complacent when evaluating the country's future prospects.

However, Chinese leaders will also need to recognize some of the shortcomings that a strong predilection for copying might create for China in the long term. The first and most obvious of these is the collision with cultures that value much greater respect for ownership of intellectual property and observance of patents and copyrights. Behaviors that in part seem efficient, commonsensical, and pragmatic to the Chinese will be increasingly seen as dishonest and undermining of both individual rights and international law.

Future Considerations

China's rise and integration into the global economy provokes issues for business leaders and society. The Chinese will increasingly be required to engage the wider world in a manner that is deeper than the functional and transactional default setting that has governed external relationships historically for them. This requires deploying the soft skills that are strong within defined social circles in Chinese society on a much wider scale across multiple nationalities and global settings. Such challenges also require Chinese leaders to be more comfortable with ambiguity and to resist the tendency to withdraw into culturally comfortable Chinatowns, whether literally or metaphorically. Engaging the unfamiliar in an open-minded manner and managing the anxiety that this creates will be necessary.

At home, Chinese leaders need to be able to tolerate much more chaos and lack of control than they have ever historically had to bear. You cannot have your cake and eat it, too. If you want to be truly world leading, you have to let go, give people freedom, release creativity, and accept that messiness is the price. Chinese leaders want the country to be more innovative and to have more soft power in the world; however, they do not fully understand the price they need to pay in terms of their own power and authority. They need to put pragmatism and a paranoid fear of disorder to one side and let people breathe. Unleashing the creative potential of the country also requires letting people explore the world for its own sake and creating an environment where it is comfortable for people to stand out in ways that are not always socially positive. People also need to feel it is okay to court failure and be happy with things not working out some of the time. The mindset that resources are precious and that society involves a ferociously competitive race in which you cannot relax goes against this sense of play.

It's equally important for outsiders to replace the wariness with which they engage the country and its people with a genuine sense of respect for what China has to offer the world. The journey that much of the world is on is a path that the Chinese have traveled further down than all others. A striving for balance and harmony are China's great gifts to the world that Western peoples could, in particular, learn from. External businesses operating in China that do not develop genuine respect and empathy for its people and culture will always just be tolerated outsiders whose ideas and practices local firms will learn from and then leave behind. Without a mindset change, external firms—unless they have luxury brands or cutting-edge technology that China needs—will always feel disappointed by the gap between the promise and the actual results that their China operations deliver.

Chapter 6

Europe: The Equal Society

L ike many other regions in the world, Europe illustrates contradictions and tensions as the world globalizes. Visitors are struck
by the continent's history, aesthetic beauty, and cultural depth. You
also experience a relaxed openness and tolerance that is absent from
many other parts of the world. Europeans appear to live comfortable
lives, with a balanced approach to many areas—work and leisure,
the public and private sectors, personal freedom and social responsibility. Europe also feels like the future in many respects, as other
cultures move toward the kind of permissiveness and openness that
are apparent in many countries on the continent.

Yet increasingly one can sense insecurities and tensions. Long
ago, Europeans ceded the role of global leadership to the Americans
but now other cultures such as India and China are catching up
fast, which leads to a sense that the best years of the continent
are behind it rather than ahead. As economic tensions mount, sentiments that challenge the openness of European culture increase
and attitudes toward migrant communities and the outside world
harden. Strains among European nations—a long-standing feature of
the continent's cultural DNA—have started to rise again. Compared to
many other cultures, Europe has always tended toward segmentation,
division, and infighting. This has ebbed away over the past century or so, but fear of such sentiments resurfacing haunts European
political leaders.

In business, European firms have had a long history of engaging other parts of the world. Less parochial and inward looking than

businesses from many other regions, European companies are often highly international and derive much more of their revenues from overseas operations than do firms from the United States, India, or China. The European Union is the top trading partner for 80 countries in the world, compared to only 20 for the United States. In addition, it is the largest trader of manufactured goods and services in the world. It is also a more open economy for others. Excluding fuel, the EU imports more from developing countries than the United States, Canada, Japan, and China put together.[1] All this makes many European business cultures highly internationally minded and flexible in the way they engage the outside world. In this sense, there is a lot others can learn from the European approach to global business.

However, there are also significant issues emerging. Red tape, slowness to change, and lack of agility make many European business cultures feel cumbersome compared to companies from hungrier emerging economies, as well as many U.S. firms. Having achieved comfortable lives with ample leisure time and social benefits compared to most other global cultures, there is insecurity as to how these living standards can be maintained in a fiercely competitive global economy.

Psychologically, Europeans exhibit a complex and layered set of attributes. Intellectual openness, balance, and comfort with life coexist with insecurities about the future and Europe's place in the world. Deeper still one cannot dismiss the possibility of some of Europe's bad psychological habits—such as a tendency toward out-group aggression—resurfacing if economic pressures and challenges continue to restrict people's prospects. Identifying dimensions in their cultural DNA that have run out of road and those that will help them to lead rather than follow—or be defensive about the new emerging multipolar world—is essential for the future prospects of the continent.

The Forces that have Shaped European Cultural DNA

The story of how modern humans inhabited Europe and the challenges they faced on the continent is, as with all groups, critical to our discussion. Surprisingly, it was only 45,000 years ago that modern humans gingerly made their way into the continent. This was much later than the settling of the Indian subcontinent, and 20,000 years later than the oceanic island hopping that took humans to Australasia.

There are a variety of reasons for this delay. First, the barriers of the Sahara and Arabian Desert prevented an easy movement of people out of Africa via the most direct route, through the Levant, into Anatolia, and then Europe. As we have seen, modern humans had to take a beachcombing route virtually all the way around to India before they were able to double back and move north and westward again.

The second, and perhaps more important, reason was that Europe was already densely populated by an earlier version of humans—the Neanderthals. Muscular, strong, and possessing a brain size comparable to modern humans, Neanderthals had been in Europe for the best part of 400,000 years and presented a formidable challenge to other humans entering the continent. As a consequence, modern humans were cautious and slow in moving into the continent. There was at least a 5,000-year war—or if you want to be polite, 'standoff'—for the ecological space in Europe. Neanderthals were gradually and surely pushed back to their final enclave in the south of Spain, which some believe was where the remnants of their species made their last stand, 30,000 years ago. If this latter date is right, the overlap between the two species could have been even longer than 5,000 years.

Just how and why modern humans triumphed over Neanderthals has significant implications for European cultural DNA, given that this was for thousands of years one of the most important challenges facing new entrants. The simple view that modern humans were smarter and had bigger brains does not suffice—because the inconvenient truth is that Neanderthals, in fact, had slightly larger brains. A second view is that a quantum leap in speech capability, associated with the *FOXP2* gene, gave modern humans the edge. This view has, however, been discredited by the recent finding that Neanderthals also possessed this particular speech gene.

The most persuasive theory is one advanced by the likes of evolutionary psychologist Robin Dunbar, who argue that it was modern humans' superior social organization that gave them the edge.[2] The uniformity and relatively widespread nature of the paintings, drawings, and cultural artifacts—which appear to have exploded in quantity and variety around the time that modern humans entered

Europe—suggest that the early groups were communicating extensively between themselves across relatively vast swaths of territory. It is likely that better communication and cooperation beyond the traditional size of hunter-gatherer populations of around 200 to 300 people would have given modern humans in Europe an edge with respect to both technological inventiveness and warfare. Many elements of European cultural DNA—including an openness toward innovation, in-group cooperation, out-group aggression, as well as Europeans' physical size—most likely arise at least in part from the fact that for a significant period of the time that modern humans have been in Europe, they were in a life and death struggle for supremacy against a powerful competitor species.

But just *how* Europe was populated also has profound implications for understanding its cultural DNA. It is necessary here to piece together the archaeological, climatic, and genetic evidence to shed light on the story. It appears that there were two very distinct paths through which Europe was colonized. One migratory trail came from the west of India around Pakistan, through Mesopotamia and the Zagros mountains, into Anatolia, and then into the Balkans and southern Europe. This represents an extension of the same path that modern humans took into the Middle East. While one splinter group went south to the Middle East proper, other groups moved across Anatolia into Europe. A more northerly route again originated in the west of India—but this time up through Kashmir into the Ural, and then west into northern Europe and Scandinavia.

As noted earlier, these two paths seem correlated with the appearance of Aurignacian and Gravettian cultures. The former seems to track the southern migration and entered Europe earlier, some 45,000 years ago. There is a close relationship between artifacts associated with Aurignacian culture and skeletal remains of modern human beings from a variety of locations across Europe, which suggests that this culture was associated with the first arrival of a new version of human rather than the original Neanderthal inhabitants. The earliest evidence of Aurignacian culture is in places in the Balkans near Turkey. Evidence of Aurignacian culture is also found in the Levantine and Turkey. One can see Aurignacian culture flowing across to southern Europe over a 10,000-year period, before eventually hitting the Portuguese and Spanish Atlantic coasts about 35,000 years ago.

Stephen Oppenheimer believes that there is a strong genetic trail that correlates with the spread of Aurignacian culture from the Middle East and into Europe.[3]

In addition to Aurignacian culture, historical records appear in Europe from about 35,000 years ago that indicate another distinct cultural intrusion. This has been named the Gravettian culture, after the site of La Gravatt in the Dordogne, where some artifacts associated with this culture were first discovered. Unlike the Aurignacian culture, the Gravettian culture seems to enter Europe through a northeastern route. Again, there is a clear genetic trail that tracks this possible route into Europe. Innovations in Gravettian culture include the use of semisubterranean dwellings, stone lamps, and the presence of distinct burial customs. One clear difference between the Gravettian and the Aurignacian culture was the use of new technologies for hunting, including woven nets, boomerangs, narrower and lighter blades, and possibly the first use of the bow and arrow. There is widespread agreement that many aspects of Gravettian culture were designed to help humans adapt to the bitterly cold conditions of their new northerly home.

However, after settling the continent and triumphing over the Neanderthals, an unfortunate conjunction of climatic cycles resulted in such a rapid deterioration in conditions that modern humans must have wondered if they shouldn't have left the continent to the Neanderthals after all. About 20,000 years ago, over a relatively brief period of 2,000 years or so, temperatures plummeted, sea levels fell by over 120 meters, and ice caps several miles thick moved down through Scandinavia and into northern Europe. Much of central Europe below the ice caps was rendered steppe tundra—a cold, dry, and treeless landscape with only patches of the land being able to sustain any form of grass or plant life. Modern humans were forced south—but unlike in China where there was woodland and some rain forest to retreat to, humans in Europe were trapped. The population diminished rapidly and survived only by clinging, it would appear, to four clearly defined areas of refuge. One straddled the mountains between northern Spain and France, another was in Italy, a third in parts of the Balkans, and a final refuge was in the Ukraine.

Humans shivered in these small enclaves for 4,000 years before the weather gods relented and the ice sheets started to shrink.

The repopulation of Europe following this warming scrambled up the genetic picture somewhat. So while the genetic trail outside of Europe before the ice age suggests two clear and distinct routes into Europe, the actual pattern of both male and female haplogroups on the continent is now quite complex, because of the bottlenecks and subsequent repopulation that took place. In general, it appears that this led to a greater presence of people across the continent associated with the northerly route.

This repopulation also led to an east-to-west divide in Europe. On the male side, for example, the most dominant haplogroup in Europe is *R1*, a son of haplogroup F, which is associated with the northerly route. *R* has two distinct groups associated with it; *R1A* and *R1B*. There is considerable evidence that *R1B* was prevalent in the Spain/France refuge, as rates of its presence in the Basque population are extremely high, near 85 percent. It appears that the repopulation of Western Europe from this refuge initially followed an Atlantic coastal trail upward. Sure enough, we find extremely high frequencies of *R1B* in Ireland (80 percent), as well as eastern Scotland. Percentages of *R1B*, decrease steadily as one moves eastward across Europe.[4] A contrary pattern is seen for the *R1A* haplogroup, the prevalence of which follows the original path up from northwest India, through western Siberia, and into Eastern Europe. Interestingly, in England, there is something of a divide separating the eastern, Celtic populations of Ireland, Cornwall, and Scotland, who share genetic similarities with coastal areas of Spain and France, versus eastern England where there is much greater prevalence of other groups associated with eastern and northern Europe.[5]

Therefore, those settling in Europe had to get used to a cold, forbidding, and inhospitable environment that required new cultural adaptations. However, Europe suffered much more severely from the ice sheets that swept down than did China. It is also clear from European genetic history that the haplogroups associated with the northerly migration into Europe—such as *H* and *V* on the mitochondrial side and *R* on the *Y* chromosome side—are much more spread out in Europe, in part, because of the movements and repopulations induced by the ice ages. As a result of these factors, while parts of Europe (especially in the south) are relatively benign environments for humans, a substantial aspect of European DNA has been shaped by people who needed to adapt and survive in more challenging contexts.

Strong seasonal variations, bitterly cold nights, and the challenges caused by well over half a year of limited daylight, as well as a dearth of plant life, meant Europe was certainly not an environment where one could just go with the flow. One had to plan, make proverbial hay while the sun shone, as well as store food and fuel for the future. Human groups who did not do that in Europe would quite simply not have survived. In addition, the context required strong mastery of the environment. People had to build shelters, make clothing, and create all manner of practical tools to cope with the conditions. These pressures have driven some clear themes—including a drive for environmental mastery, practical innovation, as well as an instinct for planning within European cultural DNA.

The next significant strand concerns the impact of the agricultural revolution. Intensive, organized agriculture arose in various parts of the world, but probably first some 14,000 years ago in the Fertile Crescent and spread to India and Egypt. It hit Europe some 7,000 years ago. Again, there is clear evidence of a diffusion of agriculture from the Middle East, up through Anatolia and into the Balkans, and then the rest of Europe. There is evidence of the spread of agriculture in the genetic signature of certain European populations. The male haplogroup *J*, which finds extremely high levels of prevalence in the Middle East and Anatolia, is also present in significant proportions in the Balkans, Italy, and southern parts of Europe. However, *J* decreases dramatically as one moves north. This is widely considered to be associated with the spread of pastoralism in the case of one of its subtypes (*J1*), and settled agriculture in the case of another (*J2*). On the mitochondrial side there is, confusingly, also a female haplogroup *J*, which is associated with the spread of agriculture from the Middle East as well. This has moderate representation, in particular, in the Balkans and Southern Europe.

The relatively moderate frequencies of the haplogroups outlined above and other evidence suggest that, while there was some impact, the advent of agriculture was a process of cultural diffusion rather than a population replacement event in Europe. Compared to the Middle East, India, and China, however, agriculture was a relatively late intrusion into Europe—especially in the north and west. I will argue later that European values around individualism and equality have in part been driven by this fact. Alcohol, which is closely associated with the rise of agriculture in most cultures, was also a late entrant into Europe. As the experience of the Native Americans and Australians illustrate, communities need time to develop both biological and cultural resistance to alcohol. This, I believe, is the underlying reason for why rates of alcohol abuse increase dramatically as one moves northward in Europe.

Research by David Reich and his colleagues—investigating the DNA structure of ancient skeletons—indicates that, as well as the original hunter-gatherer populations and the intrusion of groups associated with agriculture, European population structures also derive from an ancestral, ancient north Eurasian population, which occurred probably after the advent of agriculture.[6]

More recent impacts on European population structures and culture have come from periodic, mainly violent, intrusions of nomadic tribes and armies from central Asia. Like China, but with less severity because of distance, Europe has been vulnerable to intrusion from the Asian Steppe lands. The Huns, Mongols, and Tartars have all left their mark on populations, especially in Russia and central Asia. Ghengis Khan and his sons appear to have been particularly prolific in this regard, as over 16 million people in the regions that he conquered—over 8 percent of the population—share a clustering of genes believed to be associated with his family. Russia appears to have borne the brunt of these raids and, as with China, the inclination toward more authoritarian values on the eastern edges of Europe is likely related to populations that are used to trading freedom for security. Tolerance of individualism also increases strongly as one moves westward in Europe—again because it is a flower that flourishes best in environments where people feel secure.

Another observation about Europe is that the continent's geography—punctuated in various parts by mountain ranges and with a number of out-jutting peninsulas—inevitably created barriers to the establishment of a single unified state, as occurred in China. Some of Europe's dynamism, as well as propensity to quarrelsome fragmentation, undoubtedly arise from the particularities of this geography. Individualism and a propensity for challenging authority were also able to flourish more in an environment where a monolithic state was not able to exert control across a wide expanse of territory, as occurred on the plains of China and India.

A final and more recent point about Europe's population structure is that over the past 500 years or so, many societies on the continent have experienced significant migration to various parts of the world occupied or colonized by Europeans. Although the tendency is to think about migration predominantly as people moving from developing to more developed countries, Europe has sent more people beyond its shores than any other culture. Those who left were not a random selection of people—and the reasons for their leaving affected both the culture created in the new environments and the societies that they left behind. Britain, Spain, Ireland, and Portugal were particularly influenced by these migrations. European psychological attitudes toward class, status, and levels of achievement appear to be significantly affected by this fact.

Equality and Elitism

Iceland has a huge amount to offer tourists. Beyond its vibrant bars and nightlife, it possesses unusually evocative scenery. The island straddles the North American and the Eurasian tectonic plates and there are places where you can stand with one foot on each plate, nervously hoping that any movements will not be too extreme that day. The constant geological activity this instability creates means that the country has legions of geysers, waterfalls, hot water lagoons, and volcanic formations. Some 40 miles west of Reykjavik, there is a vast lunar like plain known as Thingvellir. On this icy plain one can see—in the midst of volcanic outcrops and canyons—an area that has been cleared and where platforms have been created using the surrounding rocks. This is the Althing, the site of the world's oldest parliament, founded in 930 AD.

The Althing was chosen early on in the settlement of Iceland as a place where all prominent Icelandic individuals could meet, democratically debate, and lay down the laws of the land. When the parliament was in session for a certain period of the year, large sections of the Icelandic population came to stay in order to participate in cultural and political events. Being Icelandic, they also knew how to party hard. One might have expected the world's first parliament to be in an urban and wealthy part of the world, where democratic rights were the outcome of a long process of social and cultural evolution. To be sure, Ancient Greeks and Romans had their versions of parliament; but these were restricted to tiny elites. The gatherings at Althing in Iceland, however, were open to all. Here, in a bitterly cold, windswept, and sparsely populated land, a group of relatively unsophisticated individuals created a form of decision making that was to become the norm for many European countries, as well as their cultural offshoots in the New World. Although surprising at first, there are good reasons for why this significant step in human political affairs occurred in a place like Iceland. These reasons are also why Scandinavian countries are some of the most equal societies in the world today.

The democratic instincts of the early Icelandic founders appear to be an expression of a strong underlying element of European DNA: a lower tolerance of inequality compared with all other major cultures in the world. On a variety of dimensions, such as sexual equality, distribution of wealth, societal support for the needy, and individual rights, one sees European nations—and other countries whose cultures have strong European roots—being more equal and less segregated. To be sure, there have been and still are today massive inequalities in Europe. However, equality is a relative concept and some societies are more equal than others. Or more accurately, since inequality is everywhere, *less unequal* than others.

There is, however, a paradox to this equality theme. European cultures are also more formal, status oriented, and in some ways more hierarchical than sister cultures in the United States, Australia, or Canada. A sense of elitism runs deep in many European countries, with class or educational background being a more important determinant of how people are seen and the chances they get than in many non-European, Western nations. In addition, whether around living standards or with respect to social elitism and hierarchy, equality varies tremendously across European societies. Understanding the factors that drive each element of this equality paradox helps explain these differences.

The United Nations regularly publishes statistics on income inequality across the world. One measure is the ratio of income that the top 10 percent of the population earn relative to the bottom 10 percent. In Scandinavian countries this ratio is about 6, in France and Germany about 9, and in Spain about 10. In the United States the figure is 16, in China 22, while surprisingly in India and the Middle East it is only around 10. Latin American and African countries have the highest ratios of all: Argentina is 30, Brazil 40, and Colombia 60. Many African countries are also extremely high, with Namibia having an eye-watering ratio of 106.[7]

The Gini coefficient, which looks at income and expenditure across all people, is another way of looking at this area. It is a rating system where 0 is perfect equality and 100 is absolute inequality. The World Bank assessment of countries across the world illustrates that European countries lead the world in terms of equality, with Gini coefficients in the 25 to 35 range, compared to the United States at 45. On this measure, Scandinavian societies are the most equal in the world.[8]

It is tempting to conclude that this is simply a function of the greater economic development of European countries—and this may be a contributory factor. However, the alternative also merits examination: Is the wealth of European countries due to their greater openness and equality? Certainly, one sees that greater levels of equality have persistently been a feature of European culture in historical records. While many cultures in Africa and India developed tribal or village forms of democracy, it was the Europeans in ancient Greece and Rome who created partial forms of it in wider civic societies. When one reads Greek treaties on their wars with the Persians, one is struck by how quarrelsome, vociferous, and independent-minded the Greek states were—but also how much more equal they were than the monolithic, regimented, and more stratified culture of the Persians. In their early, democratic phases, the Greek and Roman states were no wealthier than their Persian, Indian, or Chinese counterparts, but they did seem to have, albeit imperfectly, a greater sense of equality running through their DNA. Similarly, during the Renaissance and before the Industrial Revolution, India and China were fabulously wealthy by European standards, and respectively had something like 25 percent each of world GDP.[9] European explorers marveled at the East's wealth and treasures, but these economic advantages did not translate into greater equality in their societies. Rather, it was the Europeans who appeared to have the more open, equal, and dynamic societies.

The point is perhaps sharply illustrated when one considers polygamy as a cultural practice. Polygamy inherently has two forms of social inequality built into it. The first and most obvious is inequality between the sexes. The man gets to have a number of wives, but the wives themselves have to share the man. The women in this arrangement at least end up being looked after, having offspring, and, perhaps, the double-edged benefit of sisterly company. The more pernicious inequality built into polygamy is that between men themselves. In a polygamous society, the fact that one man has multiple wives means that many others must go without. There is no possibility of siring offspring or of finding a companion to help one through life for these men. Ultimately, it is pressure from other men that pulls down polygamy—and it is on the wane in many societies, including in the Middle East where it is still culturally and legally acceptable.

While there are plenty of historical accounts of Chinese, Indian, Turkish, and African rulers having literally hundreds, sometimes thousands, of wives, this kind of situation is largely absent from European records. Ancient European rulers and Emperors sometimes did have multiple wives, but they did not run into the numbers seen in other cultures. For example—despite presiding over and ruthlessly creating one of the largest empires in ancient history, Alexander the Great had only three wives. Had he been a Persian ruler or a Chinese emperor, it is unlikely he would have settled for such a paltry number. This is not to say that polygamy did not happen in ancient Europe, but rather that its presence was controlled and extreme expressions of it were lacking. While polygamy was historically allowed in Jewish culture, Ashkenazi Jews banned it in 10,000 AD. Sephardi Jews, however, continued to practice it for much longer. It is likely that the Ashkenazi were incorporating elements from the European culture that surrounded them, whereas the Sephardi were influenced by their own Middle Eastern sister cultures.

There appear to be three fundamental factors that have come together in the early history of European settlement to drive a greater sense of equality within European culture. Other global cultures typically possess none, or at the most one or two, of these attributes. The first point is that, as outlined earlier, Europe has much less genetic variability than many other global cultures, especially Sub-Saharan Africa and India. As we saw earlier, the much greater sense of genetic variability in India finds at least partial expression in the Indian caste system, which represents a rigid and highly regimented approach to layering in society. Europe lies at the opposite end of variability to India, which drives a fundamentally different orientation toward the creation of hierarchical barriers between others. However, this sense does not extend to European attitudes of other peoples. As will be outlined later, the other side of the coin of in-group equality is out-group domination and aggression.

The second and perhaps more important reason is that, as outlined earlier, Europe posed significant environmental challenges for modern humans, whether in the form of aggressive competitor human species, or the task of surviving in a less-than-kind environment. As discussed in prior chapters, people who live in a relatively benign environment are more easily able to put their attention to matters of how social relationships need to be organized in order to distribute rewards. Modern humans entering Europe faced no such luxuries; their biggest challenge was to metaphorically bake the cake or, more accurately, scramble hard to create anything that resembled a cake rather than arguing about who got the bigger slice. The challenges they faced fostered cooperation and drove modern humans in Europe to focus on external challenges, whether in the form of Neanderthals or the weather Gods. This fundamentally drove a greater sense of we're all in this together equality.

A third factor is that the environment, at least in northern Europe, was less conducive to settled agriculture or dense concentrations of human settlement. Europe, as we saw earlier, was relatively late in moving into such patterns of settlement. It is generally agreed that the move to agriculture and settled civilization created much greater opportunities for individuals to diverge in terms of their land ownership, control of food resources, and access to power—which quickly led to the development of a much more hierarchical society. In their analysis of cultural differences, Geert Hofstede and his colleagues argue that the advent of agriculture not only drove greater power distance in cultures, but also a higher level of collectivism as opposed to individuality.

All three of the above factors become accentuated the further north and west one moves into Europe. It is therefore not surprising that greater levels of equality are evident as one moves in this direction across the continent. If the arguments above are correct, the parliament at Althing represents an extreme version of a trend that was occurring throughout Europe: a self-selected, relatively homogeneous group of people, facing intense environmental challenges, living in a low density, predominantly nonagricultural society, coming together more or less as equals to make decisions and set rules for governing their relationships. When one stands on the icy plains of Thingvellir, it is difficult to envisage any other arrangement making sense.

However, there is also another side to equality in Europe that is worth considering. While on many measures of income and wealth distribution European countries have stronger institutional mechanisms for driving equality than other cultures, many societies on the continent are also socially more formal, hierarchical, and status driven than, for example, the United States. Here, I believe, the offshoots from European culture—the United States, Canada, and Australia—have an edge on Europe with respect to equality. The reason for this is another theme that has influenced European cultural DNA more recently: the selective migration from the Old to the New World. Those who were dissatisfied with hierarchy, or their own social exclusion from the elites, were more likely to chance their luck elsewhere than those who were more comfortably entrenched in the social order of their society. Hierarchical barriers created over time and through continuity of living were also disrupted by movement to a new environment. Pressures to break down privilege were released through the escape valve of migration—thus preserving social formality, elitism, and class or education-based barriers in European society.

This effect is particularly relevant to the UK, as Britain has sent more of people beyond its shores than virtually any other major country in the world. That is why English is, to use a paradoxical phrasing, almost the lingua franca for the world. While there are only 65 million or so people in the UK for whom English is the mother tongue, there are close to 400 million outside the country for whom this is the case. As we saw earlier with the story of who went to America, the migrants were not just a random cross section of the population. They went for particular reasons—one of which was to escape their position in the hierarchy of British society and to try their luck in a new environment. It is interesting to note the British reputation for social hierarchy and class consciousness became much more accentuated over the period that large swaths of the population were leaving. Other features of British society such as intellectualism, bureaucracy, slowness, and even the loss of the country's great engineering tradition might reflect this selective loss of certain dynamic layers of society through migration. In a lesser way, I believe this process affected other European countries also.

This sense of equality and social elitism resonates in a number of ways in business life. In many cultures, including the United States, CEOs are frequently treated in highly reverential ways, with their utterances or commands carrying the weight of religious edicts. This just happens less or rarely in Europe. Having been a CEO a long time myself, I know that my status landed very differently in different parts of the world—and reverential is not the word that springs to mind for how people responded to the title in the UK. In some parts of Europe, such as Scandinavia or Holland, the very term leadership evokes considerable discomfort, as it is seen to erode a sense of team. Leaders in Europe have to tread gently and exercise power carefully.

Decision making can also be slowed down by the need to create buy-in and let multiple people have their say. Outsiders need to learn to "go slow to go fast" in Europe, as inappropriate efforts to force things through simply backfire. The chances of decisions being smoothly implemented—always an issue in European corporate cultures—are especially low if people have not been consulted or treated as equals in the decision-making process. Organizational expressions of democracy, such as town hall meetings, open disagreement, and vociferous debate, as occurred on the icy plains of Iceland, are a regular feature of corporate life on the continent. While this can create a sense of untidiness, it can also lead to a high level of intellectual liveliness and a Darwinian process by which ideas are tested and the best ones taken up. Involvement is a more significant motivator for European leaders. By contrast, while things are changing, European leaders operating in other cultures can underestimate the barriers to the open expression of opinion or indeed people's desire for it. At times, efforts to solicit people's views can create the impression that the leader does not know or is out of their depth.

Leaders in Europe also have to work at alignment more so than in any other culture. This is not the same as investing in relationships, which actually is less necessary in Europe than, say, Indian, Chinese, or Middle Eastern business cultures. Rather, this relates to the extensive efforts required to get people on the same intellectual page. You have to convince people with data, argument, and a willingness to adjust your perspective in the light of their views. In my experience, European leaders are attuned to this early on in their role but over time, as they get used to their positions, they can slip into a less inclusive and more directive style of operating. Nevertheless, European leaders scored most strongly out of all the regions on inclusive two-way leadership, although scores generally were low on this dimension globally.

However, paradoxically, the sense of social elitism and separation alluded to earlier can also exist in European corporate culture. A while back, I was working with the senior team of the French subsidiary of a major U.S. multinational. It so happened that the U.S. CEO was visiting on the day I had individual meetings with the French leaders. When I asked them how the CEO's visit was going, it was clear that each of the French leaders had been completely taken aback by his informality—and, critically for the French, by the fact that this iconic global leader was going around wearing a sweater and jeans. The French leaders all described with varying degrees of intensity a sense of having been personally insulted by his attire. One particularly well turned-out member of the team even said the CEO had chosen to dress as a tramp to show to the French that they were not that important in his mind. The CEO made matters worse by cutting short a lunch that had been carefully prepared for him. I myself made this mistake once when working with a team in France, and was later told that the chef responsible for preparing the meal had thrown pots and pans around the kitchen in rage. When I relayed the story of the CEO to the European president of the company, he said that the French leaders had in the past been aghast at how much the American CEO was paid and, given this, had perhaps expected he would cut a more impressive figure or at least turn up dressed appropriately for the part of a big leader. Both sides of the equality paradox are neatly illustrated by these reactions.

As a consequence of the above pattern, while European leaders treat people in some ways with respect and as equals, they can also preserve a certain formality and distance in their downward relationships. As such, leaders can feel a degree detached from their organizations: neither very willing to drive a decision through the sheer exercise of power nor inclined to engage or informally interact with staff at lower levels. This can create a sense that many European corporate cultures are loose, with semi-detached leadership and multiple elements going their own way. This can create a significant problem around executional effectiveness and follow-through in European corporate cultures. In fact, European companies are perhaps the weakest in this area compared to other global organizations, where either power is exercised more overtly or leaders are closer to the action in terms of follow-through. Initiatives can take a huge amount of time to be approved and frequently are only ever implemented in parts of the company where the change seed has fortuitously landed on fertile ground. The culture's surface formality also means that people are reluctant to express disagreement and leaders can assume that their plans are being faithfully executed, when in fact a permafrost layer below the senior levels has led to the original intention being morphed out of all recognition.

European companies with cultures that combine reluctance around the overt expression of power with a sense of detachment can engage the global world with greater flexibility, but also with less internal coherence and consistency than, for example, American organizations. On the positive side, other nationalities can experience European business cultures as much more tolerant and flexible than many others. However, as companies become more global, the issue of coherence at scale becomes more problematic. There is also a big issue around driving the right ethics and corporate values when operating in other cultures. Many European companies can be much less effective in this area compared to American organizations operating on the global scale. In spite of their best intentions, leaders at the top can be taken by surprise when it emerges that very different values have been at play at ground levels. The problems that BP experienced in the United States around safety and GSK in China and Poland around sales practices with doctors did not arise because of a lapse of values in their corporate cultures. Rather they reflected a positive, if somewhat overoptimistic, desire to respect people, give them space and treat them as adults.

More generally, equality is one of the great gifts that European culture has to offer the world. No other global culture has traveled further in this direction or for so long. However, the well-documented rise in inequality since the 1980s, as popularized by the European writer Thomas Piketty, means that this area is always a challenge for societies. Equality is also a relative concept—and while Europe may be stronger on this than many other cultures—the human predilection for pecking orders and hierarchy exerts a gravitational pull everywhere. No mainstream political party in Europe would argue that the continent is a paragon of equality. However, the recognition that in the past this aspect of European DNA has imbued its society with a greater sense of openness, vitality, and innovation, as well as natural rather than artificially imposed cohesiveness, could be helpful as Europe starts to experience progressively greater economic challenges from other cultures. At one level, the instincts within the continent might be to pull up the drawbridge, preserve existing practices, and for the rich to protect themselves in their fiefdoms. However, a deeper understanding of European DNA suggests an alternative response to this challenge may be to even further deepen the sense of openness and equality in European society, because it's precisely these values that have given the continent competitive edge over other cultures in the past.

Bounded Individualism

A few years back, I came across a group of Chinese tourists exploring Soho—a bohemian, trendy, but also slightly scurrilous area of central London. The Chinese tourists had stumbled upon a large group of English teenagers dressed up as Mohicans. Their heads were completely shaved except for an aggressive outcrop of garishly colored hair running down the center of their heads. Most seemed to be wearing Doc Marten boots, brightly colored trousers and ragged tops. Much of their clothing was torn and there were plenty of chains, buckles, and outlandishly sized safety pins hanging off various parts of their bodies. To say they stood out would be an understatement. They projected a curious mixture of sullen defiance, boredom, lack of purpose, and simmering hostility—an existential ennui, tinged with aggression.

The Chinese tourists nearest to the group were looking on some-what nervously, fearing perhaps that they might be spat at or worse. The tourists who were a bit further behind were surreptitiously try-ing to take photographs, clearly regarding what they had seen as an iconic piece of imagery about London. However, I also noticed that the tourists who were furthest away from the Mohicans were laugh-ing uncontrollably, whilst trying to be somehow discreet about it, in case they caught the attention of the unpredictable Mohicans. The Chinese tourists had stumbled across a representation of English indi-viduality and, in particular, a tradition of teenage rebellion stretching back through modern British history, encompassing groups such as the Skinheads, Punks, Mods, and Rockers. I wondered as I looked on if the British tourist ministry had not paid the Mohicans to act out this distinctive slice of English culture.

The fear, fascination, and amusement this scene caused was essentially due to the collision of the Eastern collectivist mindset with Western individualism. The individualism on show in Soho varies a lot across the continent and is more marked in the north and west of Europe. These parts of Europe have also been where the continent's rock bands and musical icons have come from, although not the more mainstream Eurovision song-contest winners. Unlikely as it may seem, getting underneath the reason for this cultural theme—and understanding why it expresses itself so differently in various parts of the continent—helps explain many aspects of organizational culture, as well as more broadly the Eurozone crisis and the issues facing European integration.

The idea that Western (and, in its original form, European) culture is strong on individuality compared to other cultures is, of course, a well researched and commented upon aspect of intercul-tural research. On the dimension of individualism versus collectivism that Geert Hofstede and his associates identified, Western societies top the scale for individualism.[10] A key finding in attribution theory, a branch of social psychology that looks at how people explain events, is that Western subjects will often explain their behavior and the outcomes that they experience with reference to their own personal agency. People from the Far East, for example, will tend to attribute their actions to the desire to follow social norms or the expectations of others. Linguistic analysis also suggests that the word *I* is used much more regularly by Western subjects when creating stories or in simple conversation.

However, there is more subtlety to the picture of individualism in Europe than meets the eye, as well as a huge amount of variation across countries. When one looks deeper, on certain dimensions, European societies are quite collectivist. For example, while Europeans are low on Globe's in-group collectivism, on institutional collectivism—defined as the extent to which a society has clear rules and social obligations that all people follow—European scores are among the highest in the world. Only the Confucian cultures of the Far East begin to parallel the European scores. Institutional collectivism is highest in Scandinavian countries with most scoring higher than, for example, China. The United States is lower than most European countries and globally sits in the bottom half of the countries surveyed by the Globe project on this dimension.[11] This is not surprising from the earlier analysis of U.S. cultural DNA. A significant number of the early groups who migrated to the United States were escaping various forms of institutional control. Rejection of such intrusion is therefore hardwired into American cultural DNA. American culture has often been described as the most individualistic in the world. However, it is so only with regard to rejection of government control over people's lives. On a number of other dimensions such as patriotism, sexual freedom, or bucking the system in companies, it is far less individualistic than most European countries.

What are the roots of low in-group collectivism in Europe? Some clues appear to lie in how individualism varies in Europe—and specifically, how it increases significantly as one goes north and west to the Netherlands, and then into Britain, as well as the strong sense of individualism in Scandinavian societies. Anthropological research suggests that individualism is relatively high in pastoral societies, but declines significantly in cultures that have a strong tradition of settled agriculture. In particular, the onset of settled agriculture leads to people congregating into small, village-type communities bound by stronger and more widespread collective relationships than occurs, for example, in more dispersed pastoral contexts. However, individualism starts to increase again as societies move through the agricultural stage and become more industrialized and urbanized.

A second feature that drives individualism is the level of external threat that a society has faced. Eastern Europe has had much less security than the countries lying on the western extremities of the continent in this sense. I spoke earlier about how persistent external threat leads to an acceptance of authoritarian control in China with an associated loss of individual freedoms. Both institutional and in-group collectivism tends to be high in such countries and this is exactly the pattern we see for Russia and other East European societies, which mirror, in a paler way, patterns found in China. The geographical barriers to the creation of unified political entities in Western Europe have also probably helped to exacerbate such differences.

England was spared this sense of threat by virtue of its island status on the far west of the continent. It was also inevitably a place where agriculture was late in arriving, as well as being the earliest society to industrialize in the world. The Mohicans the Chinese visitors saw were an expression of these forces that have led to a long ingrained tradition of individualism. However, this individualism also leads to clear social rules being set for governing relationships and ensuring some form of civic society. In his work on the origins of English individualism, Alan Macfarlane describes how, even in the fourteenth and fifteenth centuries, English society was much more legalistic and rule-governed than other European societies.[12] The English may be individualistic but there are few countries in the world where people queue in such a patient way or observe all manner of rules and regulations assiduously. One senses if the rebellious Mohicans had wanted to buy a cup of tea, they would have formed an orderly and patient line at a stall.

Proof of the above arguments comes from the fact that there is a strong negative correlation between the two forms of Globe collectivism measures within Europe. Greece, for example—which is the highest in Europe on in-group collectivism—scores the lowest on institutional collectivism. Greeks feel huge loyalty and obligation to their social and familial groups, but very little to wider organizational, national, or cross-national institutions. Michael Minkov's dimension of exclusionism versus universalism expresses this inverse relationship between the two forms of collectivism. Needless to say, European societies' scores on universalism are some of the highest in the world, with Scandinavian countries being at the top globally. Greece is the lowest on universalism out of European countries.

The above themes mean that while many European organizational cultures can be highly tolerant of initiative and creativity, they can also be highly rule-governed and bureaucratic. With respect to the first area, many European business cultures can be strong on innovation at the ideas level. Our analysis found that 30 percent of European executives were seen as strong in their improvement and change orientation and only 2 percent had a development need in this area. American and Indian executives were also high on this dimension, but other cultures were weaker. Leaders managing in a European context have to give people more latitude and opportunity for self-expression than is the case even in the United States. This can lead to a pervasive sense that in European businesses people like to just talk. European organizations are also much more prone to the creation of endless-meetings cultures. Everyone wants to have a say and no one wants to just follow.

However, this creativity also exists in the context of a high level of rule following. A full 37 percent of European executives were strong with respect to responsibility and rule following. This figure was marginally higher than in many other cultures where conformity is considered the norm, such as China and the Middle East. However, the comparable figure for American executives was only 20 percent. So while European cultures can feel innovative and creative at an ideas level, they can also feel a little rigid and bureaucratic. Rule following is subtly different, however, from orienting yourself to a powerful leader—something to which there is typically resistance in European cultures.

When it comes to the actual execution of change, individualism and bureaucracy can combine to make what is always difficult *especially* problematic in a European context. People do not want to be told how to be; however, they paradoxically also want to follow clear procedures that have been laid down in the past. Change occurs through a patient process of discussion and consultations, following which new rules are laid down. Execution of change has become progressively more difficult as individual self-expression has become more important in European business life. As one executive said to me, "In the past, things happened when you pulled a lever; now the lever just comes off in your hand." This can lead to an ordered sense of chaos in an organization, which can be beneficial for intellectual innovation but less effective for actually implementing change. Execution at pace is a challenge in many European businesses and means that particular attention needs to be paid to developing this muscle in leaders. In our analysis this is graphically illustrated by the fact that only 24 percent of European leaders had a strength in action orientation compared to 40 percent of American leaders.

Another point about individualism is the extent to which it is an important precondition for effective self-reflection. One of the most consistent findings that we have established from working across the globe is that business cultures vary tremendously in terms of people's insight into themselves, as well as openness to feedback. In Chinese business cultures, for example, people are much less used to talking about themselves, their motives or drivers—or in developing a differentiated understanding of themselves as distinct from others. It is all too easy for Westerners to view this lack of interest in self-understanding as emanating from defensiveness or a lack of confidence. While this is true in some cases, a more fundamental reason is that people in less individualistic cultures are much less used to thinking about themselves as distinct entities with identities separate from the whole.

Sure enough, we find in our research that self-insight is less of an issue with European leaders than it is globally. Ten percent of leaders in Europe were considered to be strong in this area, compared to figures in the region of 3 to 7 percent for leaders in other parts of the world. The comparable figure for American leaders was 3 percent. Only 14 percent of European leaders were considered to have a development need in this area compared to figures in the 19 to 35 percent range for other regions, including 19 percent for the United States.

More broadly, individualism is something that is likely to deepen everywhere as societies industrialize, feel safer from external threats, and the cultural impact of settled agriculture recedes. Other world cultures therefore have much to learn from European and American culture in this area. Organizational cultures the world over will need to come to terms with more fluid, flexible, and person-centric ways of organizing as individualism becomes more and more pronounced. Even businesses in Western societies will need to reinvent their appeal as individualism deepens. One senses that not many of the Mohicans would be attracted by the prospects of a corporate career. The risk for many corporations in the West is that unless they radically rethink how they engage with people, they will become progressively unattractive to more and more people.

Analyisis and Structured Planning

As we saw earlier, Chinese culture was responsible for an extraordinary number of advances in practical technology across a swath of areas. Yet despite all this inventiveness, the Chinese never laid down a theory of science or outlined the principles for building a coherent view of the natural world. One sees almost the opposite problem across the Himalayas. Minds in India turned more naturally to delving into the inner mysteries of the universe and the human soul. However, Indian thinking on such matters was often highly intuitive and there was limited interest in empirical or logical proof of these insights. Even when thinking was more coherent—as with Baudhayna's "Pythagoras" theorem—the ideas were casually thrown into religious texts, almost as an afterthought.

European thought, however, combined the best of the Indian and Chinese traditions to create a wholly new and ordered way of looking at nature. There was, like the Indians, a search for the fundamental rules and truths that govern the world. However, thinking about these principles was subjected to the rigor of analysis and rational examination. Theories were proved or disproved using evidence, rather than accepted on the basis of intuitive plausibility. This was necessary because the Europeans, like the Chinese, needed ideas that worked in the practical world. In Europe's much more challenging and hostile environment, people could not afford the Indian luxury of intuitive speculation that might or might not be right. Scientific understanding was therefore, tested logically and then put to use in the service of practical goals. Cultures like the Indian and Chinese, that might have thought that they were in many ways more advanced than the barbaric Europeans, were left trailing behind by this motor of intellectual innovation in which the theoretical and the practical were always two sides of the same coin.

The reason for the West's distinctive and powerful intellectual approach lies in the fact, I believe, that Europe was uniquely influenced by two different types of cultural traditions—through the two routes that humans took in populating the continent. From their Middle Eastern origins, the Europeans inherited a search for the fundamental truths of life. The religious instinct and, in particular, the monotheistic drive to find fundamental answers and ultimate truths, are deeply rooted in the particularities of the Middle Eastern environment. It is the lack of this powerful religious instinct in Chinese culture that explains its inherent pragmatism and lack of interest in theoretical exploration. The other thrust into Europe brought a significant focus on using intellectual inquiry to master and control the environment. Planning in a structured manner was also imperative for survival—if you did not do this, you, had no chance of making it through the northern winters. These twin drivers meant that theoretical insights, empirical testing, and practical application constituted a seamless, intertwined cycle in Western culture. In addition, if one overlays on this other building blocks of European cultural DNA—such as equality and individualism—the basis for ideas being questioned and debated actively was further deepened.

Various pieces of evidence support the above thesis. First, the Western intellectual tradition was nurtured and taken to a new level by the Greek city-states. This is exactly where one would expect the fundamental truths and more mastery-oriented elements of European cultural DNA to have become most intertwined. A Goldilocks mixture of the preceding three elements seems to have been historically necessary for intellectual dynamism in the West. More practical and interested in economic and political power, the Roman Empire was also much more centralized. Unsurprisingly, its intellectual contributions were miserly compared to those of the Greeks. When the religious impulse took hold too strongly, Western intellectual dynamism stalled and was not reactivated until the influence of religion abated in the Renaissance. While interested in fundamental truths, and to a degree practical innovation, Middle Eastern societies too suffered from the fact that the religious impulse grew too dominant, as well as from being more stratified societies where the open debate of ideas was less acceptable.

The substantial contribution made by Ashkenazi Jews to European thought may also, in part, stem from the mixing of the above forces in that community, as well as reflecting the strong concentration for centuries of Ashkenazi Jews in intellectual and commercial activities. With a strong history of argumentation and debate, the Ashkenazi Jews were living examples of a Middle Eastern culture embedded in a European context. When Einstein refused to accept quantum mechanics, he did so because, although the theory worked in practice, it did not make sense at a deeper level. "God does not play dice with the Universe," was his constant rebuke to the quantum physicists.

Fast-forwarding to the present, the above feature of European culture still gives Western societies great intellectual dynamism in business and more broadly. A highly data-driven approach to business is deeply embedded in European and also Western businesses more generally. In essence, anything that moves is measured—and decisions are rarely made without detailed presentations dripping with analytical justification and data. When a question arises, the near ubiquitous response is to study the subject more deeply by getting data. Legions of consultants are employed to mine internal and market data. Performance is measured in concrete terms rather than more qualitatively. Anything that smacks of intuition in any walk of life is treated with suspicion.

European executives in our database scored strongly with respect to analytical thinking, with 38 percent displaying a strength in this area and only 4 percent a development need. The only other global culture whose leaders matched European levels was China. In addition, European executives were more reflective than executives from any other global region. Scores for this were generally low, but 11 percent of European executives had a strength in this area compared to global scores in the 2 to 4 percent range for other regions. In addition, only 10 percent had a development need in this area, the lowest score globally. Furthermore, 29 percent of European leaders were strong in strategic thinking, the highest figure globally. This compared with 24 percent for American and Indian leaders and figures in the 3-16 percent for all other cultures.

However, the question arises of the domains of business where the European analytical, structured, and long-term orientation works well and where it does not. Global business is now fast moving, unpredictably, and dynamically—a very different environment to that in which the Europeans developed their intellectual orientation toward the world. There is a pervasive and complacent feeling in many European companies that their systematic and structured approach is both professional and sophisticated. Indian intuitive thinking and the Chinese focus on practicalities, as well as the African instincts around flexibility, are all intellectual styles that make for faster decision making and movement in business. One of the most common complaints heard from Indian or Chinese leaders is that European companies can often seem overly slow, ponderous, analytical, and structured in their approach. The need to justify strategies analytically or to debate and test ideas openly before moving into action can be experienced as stultifying. This is not to say that executives from India and China are not also highly commercial or numerate. They often are, but in a quick fire rather than analytically ponderous manner. To cut through the slowness that the overly analytical approach can lead to, we often introduce European teams to the notion of "What do you know that you don't know?" The idea behind this is that often you know the answer but you don't know that you know it.

The inherently structured and long-term approach that European companies and institutions favor does, however, confer some obvious advantages. European companies can be strong in areas requiring patient and detailed analytical research, such as pharmaceuticals, chemicals, or technical engineering. One can also build institutions for success at scale patiently over time, a necessary requirement in our global world. Many of the companies from emerging economies have yet to face this challenge of scaling up beyond their borders. Decisions can also be made in a strategic manner for long-term gain.

Many of the actions of the European Union mirror the strengths and weaknesses of this approach. EU institutions have a long history of driving rules in many areas of life designed to make things better and more uniform over time. Compared to all other cultures, Europe is also more prepared to make the sacrifices needed to tackle climate change. This is an issue taken seriously across the continent and there is broad acceptance of the analytical case for global warming, as well as the strategic solutions needed to address the problem.

Yet there is also an inherent inflexibility and sense of ponderous bureaucracy around the way the EU operates. The European response to the financial crisis has been slow and deliberate, relegating many economies on the continent potentially to years of anemic growth. One senses that even if the single currency proved to be a complete disaster for many of its economies, Europe would inflexibly grind down the road, refusing to flex or alter course for many decades.

A second and different point relates to Europe's traditional intellectual strengths. The Western canon of scientific thinking now constitutes a vast and intricate body of knowledge. Creation of such a body of knowledge systematically over several centuries is one thing; absorption of it in one's own lifetime and then building on it is another. The latter requires discipline, diligence, and a parking of one's desire to make an individual contribution. This explains why, in spite of the West's historical dominance in this area, many Western universities' science departments are full of people from other cultures. The Indian intellectual tradition of faithfully memorizing and preserving for posterity voluminous amounts of information is well-suited to the requirements of absorbing current scientific knowledge. Likewise, the Chinese tradition of disciplining oneself to master the knowledge acquired by others makes this a relatively natural task for people from that culture. Western students, particularly from cultures where individualism is high, are more naturally drawn to the social sciences, literature, or other creative arts. It is easier in such subject areas to make one's mark, and the discipline of absorbing a vast body of knowledge is less burdensome. Looking forward, the West cannot assume that because it was responsible for producing and evolving significant aspects of current scientific and analytical thinking that it will be similarly successful in exploiting it or taking it to the next level.

Reserved Sociability

A recurring theme we encounter with executives who have moved to work in Europe is the sense of aloofness and coldness they experience in their interactions—particularly if they come from emotionally expressive cultures. One African executive described how he thought that he must have done something terribly wrong as he simply could not understand why people wouldn't smile at him or engage him personally as he went about his duties in a firm. He eventually realized that this was the norm, but admitted that he never truly felt comfortable in Europe. Another Brazilian executive described to me how she experienced her stay in London initially as a shock to her emotional system because of the measured way people dealt with her. Both ended up slowly but surely retreating into themselves, with their initial naturalness giving way to a more reserved and controlled external front.

Yet paradoxically, when one looks at cross-cultural personality research, European and other Western nations typically score far higher on sociability and extraversion than do people from other cultures.[13] This finding comes as something of a surprise to overseas executives who have had the kind of experiences described earlier. To be sure, one has to be careful in that people's responses to self-report personality measures are driven by the norms within their culture—making it difficult to form conclusions about cross-cultural differences. However, behavioral observations around sociability also support the notion that Western nations are higher on this dimension.

The answer to this paradox partially lies in the earlier quoted Chinese observation: "Westerners treat their family like strangers and strangers like their family." There is a tendency in European culture for relationships to be more diffuse and extensive but also less intense and personal than is the case with other cultures—particularly those that are high on in-group collectivism. While one might expect people who live in such cultures to also be social, this is only partially true. They are social with family and those who are part of their close networks; but they treat others with a degree of suspicion. In more individualist cultures, the social net is thrown wider but in a less intense or deep way.

In terms of differences in naturalness and emotional expressiveness, it is relatively easy to see why European culture might be stronger on suppressing emotions than some other cultures in the world. Various studies have shown that emotional expression in southern European countries is higher than in, say, Scandinavia or the north of Europe.[14] Interestingly, studies also indicate this to be the case in the extreme west of the continent, extending through to Ireland. For example, a U.S. study of emotional expressiveness in people with Irish or Scandinavian heritage found the Irish to be much more emotionally expressive.[15]

It is relatively clear that those European cultures predominantly influenced by the northernmost entry into Europe, from the west of Russia, show high levels of emotional suppression and regulation. The reason for this is the exact opposite of why Sub-Saharan Africans show high levels of naturalness—survival in an unfamiliar environment requires a suppression of one's natural emotional instincts, which were originally formed in our ancient African context, and the substitution of these by a more controlled and planned approach to engaging one's environment.

This reserved sociability has an important impact on the culture of most Western multinationals. Typically, the culture of such firms emphasize not just individual rights and professional relationships between people, but also the development of relatively extensive, but not necessarily particularly deep, networks of relationships. In my experience, executives from the West regard this as pretty normative and are relatively unaware of the fact that many others may find the social world that these values create somewhat alien or difficult to navigate. In particular, those from more emotionally expressive cultures can feel disoriented and experience such a culture as something of a cold shower.

A second issue relates to the ease with which people from other cultures are able to navigate the complex pattern of relationships that exist typically in multinational companies. For example, one often sees that executives from cultures where the social net is tighter genuinely struggle to establish the necessary influencing channels and globally networks, regardless of their networking or social skills in their domestic environment. In part, this relates to a natural difficulty that anybody from a nondominant culture might have in penetrating an environment driven by different cultural norms. However, it likely also reflects an inherently more cautious approach to wider relationships. People from such cultures are just not used to throwing the social net out so widely and so quickly—and this can lead to a genuine barrier for career progression for people from cultures where relationship networks are more tightly circumscribed.

For their part, Westerners can also be caught by surprise when their efforts to engage people they do not know are treated with a degree of apprehension or suspicion. Even more frustrating for Europeans is the notion that they have to build relationships with connector individuals who have networks of relationships in the culture they are seeking to engage before anything can happen. Chinese culture specifically emphasizes this, but it is also evident in other parts of the world. The Western sense of professional propriety naturally rebels against investing time and money in people who have no tangible value other than that they are connected to the networks that they need to access. However, such connectors are needed and provide comfort to those one needs to engage. In my experience, the open, direct, and move-quickly approach to building relationships that Western executives prefer can all too often hit a brick wall of "Slow down, I don't really know you." Understanding that they are the ones who are different and something of an outlier when it comes to global norms on this dimension, is likely to be helpful in smoothing out some of these difficulties.

The Diminishing Drive for Mastery

On May 20, 1498, the Indians experienced their first formal contact with European explorers in the form of Vasco da Gama. The Zamorin (King) of Calicut received the Portuguese navigator with polite attention. However, the cloaks of scarlet cloth, hats, assorted corals, and foods that the fair-skinned visitor had brought distinctly underwhelmed him; he had expected something more substantial like gold or silver. He did not have to think too hard before refusing Vasco da Gama's request for a formal commercial treaty and the creation of a small outpost. Since the Portuguese navigator had only arrived with four ships, he was forced to accept this rejection and reluctantly return home, his mission a failure.

However, the navigator was not going to give up so easily. He had shown great ingenuity in mastering the seas, circumventing the African continent, and coping with immense hardship and loss as he sought to find a route through to India. He returned in 1502, this time with a fleet of heavily armed ships, intending not to take "no" for an answer. During this voyage, he inflicted considerable acts of cruelty on a string of rulers and states. In one notorious incident, he raided a ship with 400 pilgrims traveling from Calicut to Mecca, looted its cargo, and then locked the pilgrims into the hold and set fire to the ship, ignoring pleas from the women and children for salvation.

Da Gama himself apparently watched with pleasure through a porthole as the pilgrims burned. This brutal and unprovoked attack both terrified and perplexed the local population.

When he arrived in Calicut, Vasco da Gama demanded the expulsion of all Muslim merchants who had been trading peacefully there for centuries. When his demand was rejected, he bombarded Calicut for a number of days. He captured several rice vessels and cut off the crew's hands and noses, sending them as macabre gifts to the Zamorin. When the Zamorin sent a high priest as an ambassador to try to smooth things over, Da Gama had the high priest's lips and ears cut off and sowed a pair of dog's ears to his head, before sending him back. Subsequently, after a series of battles and the use of extreme violence, the Portuguese managed to gain a foothold in India. The arrival of these Europeans on the west coast of India was particularly bad news for the Jews of India, some of whom had lived peacefully in the region from the time of King Solomon. The Portuguese initiated a virulent campaign against them. Over time, this religious intolerance also extended to Muslims and Hindus, and eventually significant proportions of the population in the area were forced to convert to Christianity.

The above story illustrates two related aspects of European psychology. The first concerns a relentless and restless drive for environmental mastery. The Portuguese had spent centuries improving their ships, navigational aids, and knowledge of the seas to help them explore and travel far beyond their shores. They were not content to simply stay where they were and live off yesterday's technologies. The Chinese, who had developed even greater sophistication in ship construction and navigation, lacked one thing the Europeans possessed: the desire to explore and master the world. Admiral Cheng Ho's famous voyages in the fifteenth century were brought to a halt by the Royal court in China that deemed such exploration frivolous and unfruitful. To boot, the authorities destroyed all the maps and records of the Admiral's voyages so others would not be seduced by his exploits.

The second aspect relates to a drive to master other peoples, including a propensity to violence against other races. The first substantial Indian contact with Europeans on the Malabar Coast foretold the experiences that many other cultures were to have the world over as Europeans spread their wings. Native American Indians, Bantus, Aboriginal Australians, Aztecs, Incas, and the Chinese all experienced largely unprovoked European aggression. When the Chinese sent out fleets in the fifteenth century to explore the world, the ships were filled with gifts and recordings of Chinese history and knowledge in order to show the power of their civilization to others. When Christopher Columbus arrived in America, his first instinct was to kidnap a number of the natives and forcibly take them back to Europe. This set the pattern pretty much for all European contact with people in the New World and more generally, as European powers built their empires and a system of slavery.

Out-group aggression was also not purely a matter of European attitudes toward the cultures they met on their travels. The history of the Jews in Europe illustrates that it also applied to minorities within the continent, with Hitler's attempt at the extermination of Jews being just one recent, obvious, and grotesque episode in a history of persecution. There was a feeling in Europe that something like that could never happen again. However, in the 1990s, much of the continent looked blithely on as the Muslim population of the former Yugoslavia was hounded and persecuted. Mass extermination and the use of concentration camps happened again. They were fortunately nipped in the bud, not by the European powers that were blithely complicit—but by U.S. President Bill Clinton deciding that enough was enough. Within Europe, a never-ending dance of armed conflict has also characterized relationships between the various subgroups and nations on the continent from time immemorial. In fact, the global empires the Europeans built were brought to an end principally as these aggressive instincts turned inward and the continent was convulsed by two epic conflicts.

I believe that two factors primarily explain the hardwiring of a greater drive for mastery in European culture than in others. The first is that the settling of Europe required an intense and prolonged period of competition both against a forbidding and challenging environment, as well as against a well-established and strong competitor human species. The process of the colonization of Europe by modern humans appears to have taken several thousand years or so before evidence of Neanderthals vanished from the European landscape.

Cultural DNA

There was powerful selective pressure during this period toward both the predilection and skill for armed conflict against other humans.

The second, and possibly more important, factor concerns the ecological niche that humans were forced to occupy in Europe. For many, particularly those settling in the north of the continent, the hunter component of the hunter-gatherer strategy was initially a far more viable option than the gathering part of the equation. In fact, the rewards for mastering big-game hunting were huge, as Europe was teeming with such species. Again it is easy to see how, over tens of thousands of years, this mix of opportunities and pressures would lead to an aptitude and skill with respect to hunting and warfare. An inclination for warfare does on the whole seem to be greater in parts of the world where settled agriculture penetrated less easily, such as in the tropical parts of Africa, the Mongolian Steppe, and with the nomadic desert tribes of Arabia. The idea of powerful, selective pressures for proficiency with respect to both hunting and warfare in Europe also finds support in the simple fact that on average, Europeans and Americans are physically bigger than people from most other cultures, with the possible exception of parts of Africa. It would be surprising if the same selective pressures that drove skills with respect to hunting and warfare did not also drive an increase in physical size. In fact, there is evidence that the onset of farming everywhere led to a reduction in the size of humans.

The mastery aspect of European DNA has driven huge levels of curiosity, creativity, and technical innovation in the past and the same is true today. Western firms still lead the way with respect to innovation, with many businesses from other cultures copying such innovations, or finding ways to more efficiently make Western products. European firms are still highly exploratory and lead the way with respect to engaging global opportunities. Like Vasco da Gama, European leaders think internationally more naturally compared to even American executives, for example—who can seem more parochial and inward looking.

However, there is evidence that this dimension of European success is fast diminishing. One of the dimensions that Shalom Schwartz has framed in his cross-cultural research is labeled mastery–harmony. This essentially refers to the extent to which people in a society are interested in dominating their social or physical environment or living in harmony with it. Today, the Anglo-Saxon countries score highly on mastery, with the United States scoring especially high. Other Latin European or Central European countries now tend toward the harmony dimension.[16] The sense of comfort and complacency, as well as interest in the good life, is a pervasive feeling in many European corporate cultures. Wages are high, lunches long, and holidays extensive. If you visit continental Europe in August, you do not see much evidence of the mastery drive propelling the continent ahead to ever-higher levels of achievement. It has been pushed to the far western corner of the continent and is pretty much on the way to being shipped across the Atlantic.

In part, this is no bad thing. Relaxing and enjoying life more will not threaten survival in the way it might have done long ago when the continent was being populated. Yet people in many parts of the world find it hard to live in the moment, just *be*, and enjoy the journey. The more relaxed orientation and focus on the quality of life gives Europe certain business strengths in aesthetics, design, and with respect to leisure and cultural activities more broadly. It is not a coincidence that the world's two premier spirits companies—Diageo and Pernod Ricard—are European. Europe's edge in these areas is likely to become even more important as other global cultures start to value these dimensions more.

A second point is that the European mastery drive was originally oriented toward physical domination of the environment as well as out-groups. This propelled technological innovation and a sense of restlessness in European culture that was perhaps unmatched by other cultures. However, as environmental mastery is achieved, motivation in more settled societies inevitably pivots toward competitive success against others and hierarchical advancement. Success here may require qualities that are not necessarily deeply embedded in European cultural DNA. The level of drive one sees today in executives from other cultures is often higher. In our analysis only 20 percent of European leaders showed a strength in achievement drive whereas figures for other global cultures were in the 40 percent range. The rates for leaders from the emerging economies of India and China were especially high. In part, this may reflect the compensatory drive of people trying to catch up. However, there may be a deeper issue here; people in such societies may be more oriented toward societal competitive success.

In their book *The Triple Package*, authors Amy Chua and Jed Rubenfeld identify a series of groups that have achieved extremely high levels of success in America. These include Indians, various Far Eastern nationalities, Lebanese, Greeks, and Jews.[17] All these communities come from cultures where settled civilization has been around longer than in most Western countries. Do people from these cultures simply have a more profoundly ingrained set of instincts for succeeding in settled societies? Self-discipline, propensity for academic learning, and commerciality may all be more deeply embedded in cultures that have had a settled civilization for longer. Indeed it would be surprising if thousands of years of having to compete in such contexts had *not* developed such psychological instincts.

A third point is that the out-group mastery element of European cultural DNA discussed above appears at one level to contradict some of the themes discussed earlier. How can strong values for respecting individual rights and for treating people with equality be reconciled with aggressive instincts toward out-groups? The answer to this question lies in the psychology of intergroup empathy. As recent research has demonstrated, we have powerful, evolved mechanisms—some at the level of mirror-neuron suppression—for reduced out-group empathy. While all groups unfortunately exhibit this effect, the European tendency for greater in-group equality on the one hand and for a degree of aggression on the other means that the process of empathy suppression potentially has more far-reaching consequences in European culture than in many others.

The capacity to commit atrocious acts of violence against others, while believing one's group to be highly principled, is a consequence of this bifurcation of emotional responses. It leads to significant psychological themes around hypocrisy and rationalization to which Europeans are potentially more prone than others. Historical examples are too plentiful to go through here. European colonialism, for example, was always wrapped up in various rationalizations around promoting religious values, ending slavery, or protecting the colonized from their local enemies. Even iconic symbols of positive Western values can display breathtaking levels of double standards. Winston Churchill, who could wax lyrical about tyranny falling across Europe, had no compunction in vehemently opposing Indian independence and encouraging severe repression of any movement opposed to British rule. Across the Atlantic, America's founding fathers did not appear to have had much difficulty in reconciling their fine sentiments around individual rights with vicious wars of extermination against the Native Americans or the existence of mass slavery in their "country of the free."

This channeling of the mastery drive toward domination of others was probably one of the most important factors in giving Europe a competitive edge over cultures like Indian or Chinese civilization. However, this route to competitive advantage has run out of road. Today's international community simply will not accept the invasion, domination, or wholesale displacement of other peoples. In some respects, Western instincts still run in a more expansive direction than do those of other global cultures. Other than as part of UN missions, there are very few Arab, Indian, African, or Chinese troops operating outside of their own natural territories. However, American and European troops are active in a swath of countries. But the energy for this kind of adventurism is muted, and there is considerable ambivalence around many of these involvements.

Now that they can no longer obtain a shortcut to competitive advantage just by being more aggressive and expansive, the West and Europe, in particular, may find themselves challenged to maintain their edge against other cultures. The temptation to resort to traditional ways of triumphing may still arise at some point if Western standards of living continue to come under pressure. In addition, it is quite possible that, particularly in Europe, as has happened countless times before, this frustration may be turned on the continent's own ethnic minorities. Understanding and appreciating this aspect of their underlying DNA may be helpful to Europeans as they negotiate these pressures. The push-and-pull tension of resorting to strategies that have worked before, while accepting the reality of what is possible in the modern world, will be a process that plays out in a complex way psychologically within Europe.

The Opportunities and Challenges for European Culture

The deep sense of equality, tolerance of individuality, and a rigorous and systematic approach to thinking have allowed Europe to provide many intellectual, material, and cultural gifts to the world. These gifts are likely to be even more relevant as many of the forces that drive equality and individualism gain momentum across other cultures. In many senses, Europe still feels like the future that other cultures are reaching toward. The original drive for environmental mastery and the resulting dynamic creativity in Europe will also continue to be sources of strength.

However, Europeans need to recognize the uncomfortable truth that at least part of the reason they surged ahead of the likes of India and China was due to the continent's external aggression and colonization of new lands. This has now run out of road and can no longer be a legitimate form of competitive advantage in the modern world. Europe has to learn to live and thrive by relying on other cultural strengths. Europeans recognize this, and the mindset of the continent is toward engaging the wider world in a more constructive and collaborative manner. This natural sense of exploration, when coupled with a tolerance of difference, will allow many European companies to engage global opportunities with flexibility and open-mindedness. However, such companies will need to recognize the limitations that their structured and, at times, overly analytical and ponderous approach may expose in the context of a fast moving, changeable global context.

Another challenge arises from the fact that the psychological characteristics required to thrive in stable and peaceful civil society are more deeply embedded in some other cultures than in Europe. In particular, European cultural DNA is strongly oriented toward environmental mastery, as opposed to competitive success within more-settled contexts. We recently conducted a survey about how graduates from different national cultures perceive each other. An overwhelming finding was the extent to which people from India, China, the Middle East, and even Africa saw their European peers as being lazy, self-indulgent, as well as semi-addicted to alcohol. More broadly, one feels a sense nowadays of a continent that is comfortable with itself and psychologically focused on maintaining the status quo, as opposed to driving hard to make itself even more competitive. Comfort with their lives and a lack of urgency around change could lead to Europeans sleepwalking their way into relative decline.

How will Europeans react to the fact that other powers, or minorities within their midst, may start to close the competitive gap and eventually surpass the continent? There are two potential dangers here based on Europe's underlying psychological DNA. First, European's tendency to engage in out-group aggression when their backs are against the wall could easily come to the fore if the continent's economic problems persist. There are already significant signs of this in the rise of far-right groups across the continent. The relatively high levels of racism that exist within parts of the European continent—such as Eastern Europe and Russia, which have done less well economically—is potentially a harbinger of what may happen more widely across the continent. The ability to suppress empathy for other groups and to rationalize actions could easily lead to a rise of virulent nationalism across the continent.

The other danger centers on Europe losing one of its traditional strengths: its capacity to be an open society. Facing the challenges of the global economy, the siren call of putting up the shutters, withdrawing from the world, and retreating into a little England, France, or Italy could be all too tempting. Such a path, however, would only provide a temporary respite, and would ultimately lead to Europe losing the exploratory, outward-reaching features of the continent's cultural DNA that have been responsible for its past, and likely future, success.

Chapter 7

The Far Continents

The final regions to be covered are the two continents furthest removed from our homes in Africa: Latin America and Australia. Latin America was the last continent to be colonized by the out-of-Africa movement, about 20,000 years ago. Australia, surprisingly, was populated about 65,000 years ago—a good 25,000 years or so before either Europe or the Far East were peopled by modern humans. Sadly, because of the near extinction of the indigenous Australian population, the cultural DNA of the continent is derived from migrations that started no more than 250 years ago. Both continents therefore represent new worlds in different ways.

Latin America—The Ever-Changing Melting Pot

Evidence suggests that modern humans made it to South America between 15,000 and 20,000 years ago. Findings in Montverde, Chile, support the presence of people on the continent some 15,000 years ago or so. Both mitochondrial and *Y*-chromosome analysis indicates that humans took the hard way into Latin America, crossing the Bering Strait into Alaska, then gradually working their way down the North American continent into Central and South America. Interestingly, there is greater genetic diversity in South America than in pre-colonial North American native populations. The most plausible explanation for this is that the ice age that occurred some 20,000 years ago pushed people south, but smaller groups survived in isolated warmer enclaves such as Beringia, an area covering parts of

Asia and Alaska, that for a variety of reasons escaped extreme conditions. As these ice sheets retreated some 12,000 years ago, North America was then slowly and substantially repopulated from this area of refuge.[1]

Although relatively isolated from developments in other parts of the world, the humans who settled Central and South America independently followed paths that humans had traveled elsewhere. By 2000 BCE they had learned to farm corn, beans, squash, and many other items. The Olmec culture is considered to be one of the earliest civilizations to have arisen in the region, in 1600 BC in the tropical lowlands of South and Central Mexico. Contemporaneously, in the tropical lowlands of Guatemala, one sees the rise of the Mayan civilization. However, it is not until 250 BCE that one sees the start of the classic period of Mayan civilization, which lasted until 900 AD. During this golden age, the Mayans built over 40 cities, each holding between 5,000 and 50,000 people, as well as a range of palaces, temples, and pyramids. For reasons that are not entirely clear, however, many of the cities of the Mayan civilization were abandoned and left to decay by 900 AD. One possibility is that constant fighting between rival city-states led to this collapse or that some catastrophic environmental shift was responsible.

However, it was not long until other civilizations emerged on the continent. In 1200 AD, we see the rise of the Inca civilization in the mountain areas of Peru. Its writ extended for nearly 4,000 kilometers and included 16 million people at its peak. It was also an advanced civilization that built tunnels, bridges, and roads, as well as complicated irrigation systems. A parallel civilization was the Aztec, which came to prominence around 1300. In 1325, the Aztecs built Tenochtitlan, their capital, on an island in a Mexican lake. Both these flourishing civilizations were brought to their knees by the arrival of the Spanish in the 1500s.

Although these civilizations were quite separate and distinctive, they did share many features believed to stem from Olmec culture. They farmed intensively and built roads, palaces, and pyramids. The societies seem to have been very hierarchical and it appears that the rulers accumulated vast amounts of silver and gold—something that attracted the Europeans, with their predatory instincts, to the continent. Another common feature appears to have been human sacrifice or bloodletting. Although the Europeans undoubtedly exaggerated the extent of this to justify their own appalling actions, there is no denying it existed. The Mayan belief was that the gods needed human blood because they had to use parts of themselves to create earth and its creatures. Humans had to repay this by offering the most important element in their body. Daily sacrifices of the unfortunate were a consequence of this move, as were frequent wars aimed at capturing people for sacrifice.

While the native populations of Latin and Central America reflect a depleted version of the genetic diversity seen in Far East Asia, there are certain differences. One of the most significant arises from the fact that this part of the world was the furthest along the long trail out of Africa. The migration gene, *DRD4-7* allele, which we have referred to before, is therefore strongly represented in Latin American populations, with rates approaching close to 70 to 80 percent in some indigenous communities. You'll recall that this version of the gene is associated with exploratory sensation seeking, and, to some extent, independent-minded behaviors. Even today, something like 50 percent of Latin Americans have this version, a figure far greater than any other region of the world—which has likely had some impact on the cultural DNA of the region.[2]

Another feature of many of these South American empires is that, despite their power, wealth, and impressive achievements, many were organized like broad confederations, comprising smaller city or regional states. Perhaps because some people were not too enthusiastic about being sacrificed to the gods, there seems to have been plenty of internal rebellion and conflict. So while they were hierarchical civilizations, it would appear that authority was constantly and persistently being challenged.

This was the world into which the Europeans, in the form predominantly of the Spanish and then the Portuguese, stumbled. Christopher Columbus' original expeditions made the Spanish crown aware of the existence of these rich lands and fabulous tales of the wealth of the empires that existed began to circulate in Spain. In the wars against the Moors, the Spanish crown had developed a system of strong military leaders, *caudillos*, who were given free rein to wage war in return for ownership of the towns and lands that they were able to take. The warfare that resulted was essentially an exercise in free enterprise, smash-and-grab warfare that attracted avaricious but entrepreneurial strongmen. When Latin America came to the attention of the Spanish crown, it was not a difficult decision to extend this policy to this new and tempting opportunity. Mesmerized by tales of fabulous wealth, the less well-to-do nobles from the west and south of Spain took up the challenge and set sail for Latin America.

The arrival of the Europeans was an unmitigated disaster for the native populations of Latin and Central America. A military expedition by Hernan Cortes led to the demise of the Aztec empire. Cortes arrived in 1519 with only 600 or so men, but was able to exploit the fact that the Aztec empire was a loose confederation of warring city-states. He enlisted a number of allies and boldly went for the jugular, capturing the capital, Tenochtitlan. Similarly, Francisco Pizarro took advantage of a war of succession between two brothers, as well as the decimation of the population due to diseases the Europeans brought over, to bring the Inca Empire to its knees.

Following the conquests, a legion of chancers and opportunists arrived from Spain and Portugal to grab a share of the booty. The legend of El Dorado, a mythical city deep in the jungle full of treasure and gold, also helped to whet people's appetite. Much as happened with the Moorish lands, following conquest the new rulers divided the land into *encomiendas*—extremely large parcels of territory whose assigned ruler owned all produce, minerals, and people. This early pattern of extractive exploitation set a cultural template for economic plunder by elites that has been a consistent feature of Latin American cultural DNA. Darren Ace moglu and James Robinson attribute many of the economic problems that the continent has suffered historically to this legacy.[3]

The Spanish and Portuguese rulers needed the native population for labor. However, a combination of disease, warfare, and their own myopic and exploitative attitudes fairly quickly reduced the population to a fraction of the size that it had been before the Europeans' arrival. Although estimates vary widely, it is believed that almost 50 million people lived in Central and Latin America prior to European influx—and as many as 90 percent of these may have been wiped out over a period of 100 years or so.

Desperate for labor, the Europeans turned their attention to Africa and began the importation of slaves from the continent. While the transatlantic slave trade is popularly associated with North America, only 600,000 out of the 12 million or so who were brought across went to North America. The remainder went to the Caribbean, predominantly to Central and South America. Brazil was one of the largest recipients. Importing slaves allowed the Europeans to carry on with their extractive exploitation of the wealth of the continent, despite the decimation of the local population.

However, while the above account paints a dramatically harrowing picture of European activities in Central and Latin America, there is another part of the story. The professed aim of capturing the continent for Christianity had always been a blatantly fraudulent fig leaf of an excuse used by the conquistadors. The only people who took it seriously were the priests who also migrated to the continent. To everyone's irritation they started to make vehement demands about the treatment of the indigenous people and slaves, particularly of those who had converted to Christianity. Goaded, the Spanish crown made efforts to rein in the adventurers and plunder-seekers' activities. In addition, there were various campaigns to improve the conditions of people, prompted, in part, by constant rebellions and challenges to authority. The Spanish crown eventually forbade slavery in 1820, and while this led many of the elites to promptly declare their countries' independence, the institution did die over time.

The second point concerns the mixing of the different populations. Unlike the Europeans who went to America and Australia, the Spanish and the Portuguese started to mix and have children with members of both the indigenous and slave communities. In part, this was driven by the fact that early on the Spanish Crown forbade single women from traveling to the new world. This might also have reflected, despite the horrendous exploitation, the warmer approach to human relations more typical of southern Europeans. Over time this mixing created a veritable melting pot of peoples in Central and Latin America, especially in the north. The initial instincts around hierarchy led people to try and stratify this emerging population into different categories, chiefly depending upon the amount of pure Spanish or Portuguese blood that people had. The sheer level of intermixing led to a proliferation of categories. Eventually, over 100 *castas*, the root for the English term caste, were created in some countries, which delineated the precise nature of mixing that had occurred in people's background. Over time it became a relatively exhausting social process to observe these gradations, and many of the terms lapsed into disuse.

The precise nature of the constituent populations varies markedly across Latin America. In some—Bolivia, Guatemala, and Peru—the Native American population is significant or even dominant. In others, like Mexico, Nicaragua, and Colombia, it is people of mixed European and Native-American ancestry. In Brazil, Europeans and those with mixed European-African heritage dominate. In Argentina, the majority of the population has European roots. This leads to a kaleidoscope of subcultures and traditions, not to mention tensions and rivalries, across the continent.

There are a number of psychological themes that spring from the above account. Firstly, it is clear that even in pre-Columbus times, but certainly following the European early settlements, a culture of elite domination has held sway. Historically, Latin American societies have been some of the most unequal in the world. Until recently, many countries on the continent had a Gini coefficient in the range of 0.52—making the region more unequal than Sub-Saharan Africa.[4]

The theme of elite superiority finds expression in a relatively hierarchical exercise of power within organizations as well. Patriarchal styles of leadership are evident in many Latin American companies, with decision making and power concentrated at the top. Power-distance scores, using the Hofstede measures, have traditionally been very high in Latin America but not as high as some Asian countries. The GLOBE survey also shows power-distance scores to be high in some Latin American countries but intermediate in others, suggesting a degree of complexity to the picture.

There are two aspects to this situation. While elites dominate, power is typically exercised in patriarchal fashion. There is an expectation that leaders get involved and consult with people as opposed to being interpersonally more distant. A paternalistic concern for the workforce and a focus on how to keep people personally engaged seems to be evident. More distant leadership styles or leaders who exercise power in a less clear-cut manner, both create uncertainty. In our analysis, only 2 percent of Latin American leaders had a strength in stepping back and leading through others, the lowest score globally. However, a full 44 percent were strong in teamwork and collaboration, the highest score by far across the regions.

A second theme is almost the opposite of the above. There is strong evidence of a history of challenging power and rebellion that goes back a long way on the continent. So while elites have power, an underlying high level of independent mindedness is likely hardwired into the mindset of people. Migrants always have tendencies in this direction, and whether one is talking about the continent's original population or the Europeans who arrived there later, there is likely to have been a self-selection for an independent view of life. The very high *DRD7-7* allele rate in this population, which approaches 50 percent, is consistent with this view, even when it comes to the Spanish, Portuguese, or other European migrants.

It is therefore not surprising that while power has historically been exercised ruthlessly, Latin America also has had an almost uninterrupted tradition of insurrection, rebellion, and revolution. This refusal to accept the status quo and to not simply live life along tramlines is also evident in the region's high crime rates. According to the United Nations, 41 of the top 50 most dangerous cities in the world are located in Latin America, which has 9 percent of the world's population but 28 percent of the world's murders. The extreme levels of violence and casual disregard for human life that is implied by these statistics is unfortunately something that is well embedded in the cultural fabric of the continent—starting with the the sacrifice ceremonies of the original civilizations and accentuated by the horrors committed during the European invasions and slavery. Drug cartels, which involve a combination of the ruthless exercise of patriarchal power but also rebellion against wider societal norms, capture both of the polarities outlined above. Ironically, drug barons can become esteemed figures and have *narcocorridos*—musical dedications—composed for them by those who seek to celebrate their disregard for conventional authority.

In organizations, despite the patriarchal exercise of power, there is a desire on the part of people to have their say and not to be simple executors without ideas of their own. The tell style of paternalistic leadership is far less likely to produce results than a warmer, more engaging, and inclusive type of paternalism. Passive resistance to the inappropriate exercise of power is also not uncommon and can lead to a wide gap between intent and what is actually executed on the ground.

A third theme that reflects the positive side of the above theme is the sheer level of dynamic creativity one sees in Latin American society. Resourcefulness, flexibility, and creativity have been the order of the day for some time. Thirty-three percent of Latin American executives in our database had strengths around intellectual flexibility and creativity—the second-highest level in the world after Africa. Latin American cities exude a sense of energy, vitality, and creativity. However, both at an organizational level and, perhaps, widely in society, the hierarchical approach to the exercise of power prevents people from always channeling this creativity in an open or constructive way.

A fourth theme, which stems naturally from the three major constituent groups that make up the Latin American population, is a strong emphasis on relationships. More than just about any other part of the world, Latin Americans define themselves as a people's people. Latin American societies achieve some of the highest scores in the world on the Hofstede measure of collectivism and the Globe measure of in-group collectivism. This is reflected in the day-to-day experience of relationships as well as the rhythm of life on the continent. Whether during social activities, standing up to employers through trade unions, or facing the government, there is an ethos of collaboration in much of Latin America. Bosses are expected to develop intense and personal connections with their employees. Work relationships also expand easily and naturally into the personal sphere. In our data, a massive 61 percent of Latin American executives had strength in being engaging, likeable, and building relationships easily, while the global average for this quality was 20 percent.

However, there is a widespread feeling across the continent that Latin Americans are difficult to get really close to on the interpersonal level. In Brazil, they have a saying: "Latin Americans are like a peach whereas people from the United States are like a coconut." A peach is easy to connect to but it has a relatively tough and harder to penetrate internal core. By contrast, people from the United States are harder to engage with initially, except on a superficial level—like coconuts—but when you get inside you are able to connect in a more meaningful way with a greater range of people. Only just over 1 percent of Latin American executives were rated as strong on forming close personal bonds. The drive for positive relationships in Latin American also means people can hold back from tough or honest feedback around performance to each other, due to a genuine desire not to hurt the other person. This means that self-insight is not always high. In our analysis, close to 50 percent of Latin American leaders had a development need with respect to self-insight, the highest score globally. Indian and Middle-Eastern executives were also challenged in this area with scores of 34 and 31 percent, respectively.

Another theme that emerges from this relational approach is people's general emotional expressiveness. The naturalness discussed with respect to Sub-Saharan Africa and the emotional expressiveness of the Southern Europeans have combined to create a culture with a high level of emotional intensity. Over 40 percent of Latin American executives in our database had strength in positivity and emotional resilience, the highest score in the world. There is a sense of passion, and feelings are expressed in a relatively exaggerated manner on the continent. As a result, Latin Americans can find organizations that demand a more restrained approach frustrating and just plain cold. This also means that Latin American people have a strong need to be emotionally inspired by their leaders—more so than many other regions. This comes from a desire for personal connection and for their leaders to energize through a positive and compelling vision. The expressiveness of Latin American music, dance, and drama also mirrors this natural and open display of emotions. While Brazil was broadly passionate about the 2014 World Cup, reflecting the rebellious and independent-mindedness mindset, a sizeable majority also actively and vociferously campaigned against the event on the basis of its cost. The vibrancy of the passion on both sides of the divide was noticeable.

Looking ahead, Latin America has much to offer the world. In particular, it is the most diverse melting pot of global cultures to be seen anywhere on the planet, especially so in its north and center. The inherent creativity, dynamism, and opportunity this presents has been constrained in the past by the highly authoritarian and extractive nature of the continent's political and economic institutions. These powerful elites are being challenged everywhere as countries move toward more open, balanced, and transparent ways of conducting their affairs. As this process unfolds, the underlying strengths of Latin American cultural DNA are coming to the fore. However, change in the continent has always been a two steps forward and one step back process, with many false starts and turning points. There is growing confidence that this time things will be different. For much of the twentieth century, Latin Americans have lived under the shadow of their northern neighbors. That feeling is slowly but surely being eroded.

Australia: Mateship in a Far-Off Land

The first point to note about Australia is that modern humans settled it a relatively long time ago, way before Europeans arrived. In fact, recent finds suggest that modern humans positively raced around the southern coast of Arabia and the Indian coast to arrive in Australia 50,000 to 60,000 years ago—a good 10,000 to 20,000 years before Europe was settled. The first European settlers arrived on January 26, 1788; a day honored as Australia Day by today's descendants of the early settlers, but what some members of the Indigenous population refer to as Invasion Day.

The reason for the first settlement was that a newly independent America unsurprisingly decided that it did not want to continue being at the wrong end of Britain's policy of transporting convicts abroad. The prevalence of extremely draconian penalties for even petty crimes, when coupled with an increasingly restive population and the reluctance of the authorities to invest in institutions for the feckless, meant that Britain's convict population was overflowing its penal facilities. When the American South disappeared as an option for dealing with this overflow, there was a desperate race to find an alternative. British leaders decided the best way of sweeping the problem away was to create a penal colony and European outpost on a continent that people were only dimly aware of, and which required eight weeks of hard sailing to reach. Between 1788 and 1861, when the formal transportation of convicts ended, over 150,000 convicts were transported. Although free settlers outnumbered them, this represents a significant founder effect. It is estimated that a quarter of the population currently has roots that include at least one convict relative.[5]

The transportation of convicts was slowed down in 1840, and by 1851 Australia had 400,000 mostly British and Irish settlers—half convicts and the rest free citizens. A significant event with regard to migration was the gold rush that started in 1851, causing the population to rise to 1.1 million in the space of 10 years. This was a period of famine, particularly in Ireland, but also in parts of the UK. Therefore, the prospect of hitting a jackpot, when combined with assistance from the UK government for the passage, proved too much of a lure, particularly for those who were struggling to survive in their host society. The gold rush ended in 1861. However, it had a significant impact on Australian society.

At one level, dropping everything you have and racing to the other side of the world represents a huge gamble. You may strike it rich beyond your wildest dreams; but you could just as easily lose everything you have and end up stranded in a part of the world that you would not otherwise have chosen. Individuals who get caught up in a gold rush are, therefore, likely to be risk takers. They're people inclined to go for the main chance and who are more attracted than the average person by the prospect of finding shortcuts in life. These are not all bad qualities. In many situations some of these traits can inject a sense of freshness to living life, as well as confidence in rejecting tried and tested routes for pursuing one's life path.

I've found all of these qualities to exist in Australian culture. During my stays there, I have been particularly struck by the popularity of get-rich schemes and, in particular, various exotic types of pyramid-selling scams. Conventional forms of gambling in all manifestations are also very popular. While Australia's population is only 22 million, it had over 20 percent of the world's gaming machines in 2007. It's as if the whole country is a diluted but vast version of Las Vegas. Over 80 percent of the population gamble in some way, whether this is on what Australians call the *pokies* (button/handle machines that are to be found in countless bars), lottery or scratch cards, the horses, or the giant casino complexes that exist in the major urban centers. An average of 12 percent of state and territory revenue comes from gambling; the government seems as addicted to gambling as the people.

It is probable that the gold rush migration had a significant impact on Australian culture, and not just with respect to gambling, as the ability and inclination to mine and excavate stems in part from these roots as well. When the British army brought Australian soldiers over during World War I, they were so impressed by their ability to dig trenches that they somewhat patronizingly and self-servingly put them at the forefront of the dangerous digging effort. The perception stuck and all Australian soldiers since have been called Diggers. It is easy to see the mining boom that Australia is now experiencing as purely due to the natural resources the country has, without recognizing the effort, skill, ingenuity, and resilience that are needed to find and extract this wealth. However this aspect of Australia's cultural DNA is also possibly one reason that its economy is dominated by primary as opposed to more tertiary industries.

It is estimated that up to 100,000 Chinese people came to Australia during the gold rush period. They proved to be both astute and hardworking when it came to prospecting for gold. Stories abounded of mines abandoned by white settlers where the Chinese returned to unearth gold. Chinese success bred great resentment in the white community, and this group experienced vicious and desperate racism. In the end, a large number were forced to leave. Within years, Australia had enacted a White Australia policy, forbidding the entry of all but European people to its shores. Following this period, a steady stream of migrants, again mostly from England, Ireland, and Scotland, made their way to Australia, lured by the prospect of escaping poverty back home. After the Second World War, Australia became anxious about its relatively small population, and populate or perish became the mantra. As the Immigration Minister of the time said, "We have 25 years to populate this country or we will be overrun by other races." Australia opened its doors to refugees from Italy, Greece, Yugoslavia, and a number of other European states. The famous Ten Pound Pom scheme was also enacted to persuade people from Britain and Ireland to migrate.

The White Australia policy wasn't officially abandoned until 1973. From this point onward there has been a steady trickle of immigrants from various Asian nations, including a significant population from Vietnam. The formal demise of the White Australia policy also resulted in opening the doors to some communities from the Middle East. The arrival of nonwhite people in Australia has been a source of considerable debate and is still something around which some members of Australian society have not found a point of equilibrium or comfort.

There are a number of facets to understanding Australia's cultural DNA. The first point concerns the mindset, social status, and reasons for leaving associated with the types of individuals who initially migrated to Australia. Clearly, many of the convict population did not make the active choice to be there. However, a number of the free settlers, and particularly the spurt of migration that occurred during the gold rush, was partly driven by push factors around famine in Ireland and the UK. For a long time, both the British and Australian governments provided the incentive for people who might not otherwise have been able to afford to make the journey to Australia. Push migrants tend, for the most part, to come from echelons of society that are on the back foot in some way. They therefore carry the instincts, inclinations, and preferences of people who are not in command or on top in their societies.

The other key factor to note is the conditions that the migrants to Australia found upon landing on the continent. For the most part, these were arduous and difficult, requiring huge levels of energy, resilience, and perseverance. The environment was physically challenging, and the huge distance from home meant they had to face these challenges on their own with little support from outside. This sense of isolation was reinforced by a pervasive fear of being outnumbered by alien peoples, whether indigenous or from the surrounding Asian land mass.

Individuals in any society can be put on a scale according to the extent to which they identify with the existing social order versus having a more insurgent or challenging mindset. It seems that Australia's convict roots, plus other aspects of its migration history, have biased it strongly toward the insurgency mindset. That is to say, there is a natural suspicion of authority, a high level of independent mindedness, and a capacity to question those in power. The famous example of the Australian Diggers refusing to salute their British officers in World War II is a case in point. In my view, there is always a healthy spirit of rebellious independent mindedness under the surface of Australian culture. This is associated with a strong sense of egalitarianism and powerful values around being down to earth and straightforward in dealing with people. Anyone who is suspected of putting on airs and graces is quickly and humorously cut down. Australians talk of the *tall poppy syndrome*—their tendency to bring down to earth anybody who feels that they're a cut above the rest. Politicians the world over endeavor to be men and women of the people, but Australian leaders seem to go to extraordinary lengths to cultivate the right unaffected accents and mannerisms.

However, the insurgency–egalitarianism mindset also coexists with a strong sense of mateship and a collective ethos around meeting challenges. Visitors to Australia are immediately struck by how friendly and welcoming the people are and how much effort they make to pull you into a shared sense of community. Australia's big centers are generously endowed with public amenities, parks, museums, walkways, and sporting facilities, and unionism is much stronger than in the United States. We can understand all of this in terms of a population with strong egalitarian instincts to help each other and pull together in the face of the adversity they encountered, both on the journey and on landing on the shores. So curiously, while Australians have a strong insurgency mindset, they also have quite a strong collectivist ethos. Compared to the United States, Australians still cling to their coasts, and the gung ho, individualistic frontier mentality that one senses in the United States is much less prevalent. The resilience and tenacity is there, but so also is the desire and willingness to help your fellow battlers.

Another, unexpected feature of Australian culture is the extent to which the lives of people are regulated by a vast array of generally practical and sensible rules. Australia is the only country in the world where I have been breathalyzed for alcohol when driving—not just once but several times. Where I live in Britain, police are not able to stop you unless you are swerving around recklessly. A plethora of health and safety rules that you do not see in other places exist and are rigorously enforced in Australia. For example, Australians visiting Europe or the United States on holiday are often horrified by the lack of fencing around swimming pools, which is a legal requirement in Australia. Since swimming pools are one of the most common causes of accidental death for children in the West, this is a sensible policy on the part of Australians.

Many Australians, however, do complain of a nanny state that seeks to regulate everything and everyone. The state government of Victoria, for example, has instituted fines on the spot for obscene language—a kind of official government swear box. When you arrive in Australia, you are quickly made aware of the paranoia around the importation of food, plants, or anything else that might jeopardize Australian agriculture or livestock. You are made to feel like a drug smuggler if you have so much as eaten a foreign apple on your journey. All these tendencies make sense if you think about the other side of the convict migration DNA—the law enforcers whose job it was to keep a potentially unruly population under control and on the right side of the law and, paternalistically, safe in a hostile environment. There are a lot of government officials in Australia who feel similar responsibilities and whose work is driven by an underlying assumption that given half a chance the population will run amok or succumb to some sinister threat.

Many aspects of Australian culture can also be seen as a reflection of British and Irish working-class values. A fundamentally practical and pragmatic approach to life, suspicion of intellectualism, love of sport, and the ability to get on with things rather than reflect, are all examples. Even the language, where there is the tendency to keep communication as direct as possible, fits the British sociologist Basil Bernstein's view of the restricted versus elaborate verbal codes that one sees in different strata of society and which essentially follow class patterns.[6] In this respect Australian values and styles of speech reflect the dominant subcultures from which the early inhabitants came, and which they dutifully replicated. Apart from the names which have native Australian heritage, the early settlers chose down to earth and simple names that had resonance with their past. Australians also love to shorten any word that seems overly complicated. Bernstein argues that one of the drivers of a restricted speech code is the sense of group uniformity and solidarity that exists in a population. When you have a strong sense of in-group, and subtly or otherwise want to exclude outsiders, you develop your own verbal shorthand. In this way Australian speech patterns can be seen as an extension of the mateship culture.

There is another aspect of Australian culture that also reflects its roots. As discussed previously, those who actively chose to come were prepared to make a disjunctive and radical decision to change the circumstances of their lives—which is not something that all people are prepared to do. This preparedness to try new ways of doing things lies at the roots of Australian inventiveness and creativity, and often leads to practical-minded innovation. Of the many global companies that we work for, we find that the Australian part of their business is often seen as being quite innovative and groundbreaking. In part, this reflects the fact that one can test out new ideas more readily in a circumscribed market such as Australia than in a larger, more variegated market. Australian architecture is often innovative and fresh, and its cuisine is similarly inventive and experimental.

When it comes to scientific research, Australia publishes more articles per capita than any other developed country, bucking the stereotypes that might exist that Australians would rather be on the beach than conducting research or writing articles. In fact, Australia has a strong history of pioneering, particularly around biotechnology and pharmaceuticals. Per capita, Australia has one of the highest rates of winning Nobel prizes, the overwhelming majority of them in the sciences.

However, there are some less positive aspects of Australia's cultural DNA. One deeply ingrained feature of Australian culture could be termed fear of the other. There seems to be, in some cases, deep-seated antipathy, watchfulness, and fear with respect to people of non-European backgrounds, especially with respect to them living and settling in Australia. The roots of this lie deep in the history of Australia, as well as its positioning as a European outpost on the edge of Asia Pacific. Although there is a kind of collective amnesia around it, the stark reality is that the native Australian population was effectively wiped out when the Europeans settled Australia. There is naturally some dispute as to how much this occurred as a result of disease, alcoholism, or actual extermination. In many Australian towns you find a Boundary Road, which in many cases reflects the boundary erected by settlers to separate themselves from the native Australian population, much like with apartheid in South Africa.

While Australians are generally open and welcoming on a day-to-day level, this deep fear of the other still resonates powerfully within the culture. Gratuitous references to other races are commonplace in Australia, perhaps because political correctness is seen as insincere. Whole elections can be swung by narrow debates around how an astonishingly small number of refugees from boats should be treated. Given the country's enormous size and the fact that it has a population of a mere 20 million or so, the lack of generosity entailed in these debates is breathtaking. Politicians also routinely engage in dog whistle politics—that is, covert and coded messages about threats to Australian culture from the presence of other races.

This fear of the other may stem from a broader issue in Australian cultural DNA that many people may not recognize. Underneath the down to earth, no nonsense, bullish bravado, there lurks perhaps a fundamental lack of self-confidence. Australians call their nation the lucky country, a phrase that reflects an external attribution for success, rather than necessarily a robust internal belief in their own qualities. A dominant instinct in the culture is to see this block of luck as something that needs to be desperately conserved for the ordinary white people of Australia. This contrasts sharply with the expansive and more confident instincts Americans tend to show.

Much of this lack of deep confidence may arise from the strata of British and Irish society from which Australia's founder population predominantly originated. Business leaders from global companies will commonly talk about the defensiveness of those that they have to deal with in Australia. Underneath the surface bravado lurks a sense that "I might not be quite good enough," which leads to, in part, a degree of internal posturing that masks an inner insecurity. Aspects of this national lack of confidence expresses itself in Australian's attitude to the UK, which many still regard as the mother country. There is a surface "Don't you dare patronize us" attitude that exists alongside a reluctance to cut themselves off from their roots by, for example, declaring Australia to be a republic rather than have the Queen as Head of State.

Another quality that is related to the above concerns is that Australians occasionally lack self-awareness. In my experience, how Australians view themselves does not always match the views that others might form. Part of this lack of self-insight stems from, and is expressed by, a strong desire to airbrush away the uncomfortable facts about their history or their society. Even when it comes to sporting achievements, I know that Australia will have done badly at something if it is not widely reported in the daily news that night. Coming from the UK where the reverse is the case, and large parts of the population take a morbid delight in picking over the entrails of any defeat, this was initially a surprise to me. When Australian sportsmen are caught cheating or engage in unsportsmanlike conduct, there tends to be a collective amnesia about it, which is quite distinct from the reportage one gets when other countries are accused of such crimes.

Of course, outer directedness and lack of open self-reflection do have advantages. It allows you to get on with things in an unquestioning manner and not to tie yourself up in knots. However, it creates issues when problems arise or change needs to be negotiated. I have seen this when Australian males encounter psychological difficulties. The need to preserve a casual "I am okay" image, when coupled with difficulty in genuinely accessing and verbalizing feelings, means that problems can build inside. It has always struck me how much the sunny, affluent, lucky country just does not seem happy when one pauses to reflect on the emotions that lie underneath people's surface conviviality.

Another point also needs to be made about Australia's cultural DNA—it is changing fast. In part, this is because the natural wealth of the country is sucking in many 'pull' migrants from much wider parts of the world. Sydney is like a lot of Australian cities—cosmopolitan and multifaceted. The country's confidence is also changing, which is bringing about a more honest discussion of history. Australian schoolchildren are now inundated with material on Indigenous Australian culture. Many businesses and successful people also seek ways to give back through charities, in particular, aimed at helping the small Indigenous population. Increasing economic prosperity has also enabled large numbers of Australians to travel abroad, and those returning have come back with fresh perspectives and a desire to question aspects of their culture. Australian culture, like many others in the world, is in a state of flux and just like anywhere, these changes create excitement as well as anxiety.

The psychological qualities of insurgency, egalitarianism, innovation, practical-mindedness, mateship, pulling together, and incredible resilience in difficult conditions are all traits that will help sustain Australia in the future. However, despite recent changes, there are other aspects of its psychological DNA that have inhibited the country and will continue to do so until they are addressed. In a globalizing world of which the Asia-Pacific region is fast becoming the economic center, Australian attitudes to other races will need to shift at a deep rather than superficial level if they are truly to embrace the possibilities inherent in the circumstances they face. More generally, Australians would benefit from dialing down the strong instincts to protect, conserve, and jealously guard what they have, and embrace a mindset of abundance and possibility. This requires more big-picture thinking from its leaders than one typically sees in Australia, where the dominant instinct is to pander to the prejudices and insecurities of people. Australians could also usefully attend to the dangers of becoming an over-regulated nanny state, which also stems from this urge to protect. Crucial to beginning to do this is recognizing where some of these less positive instincts come from, and why attitudes that might have been appropriate once are no longer so, as the country faces the opportunity of finding a more significant and confident place in the modern, global world. Being more reflective as a culture and more inner directed at a psychological level would also allow Australians to make more informed and better choices about their future.

Conclusions

Having completed our psychological tour of the world, it is helpful to reflect upon some broad themes.

First, I hope the material covered has helped readers develop deep and genuine empathy for the cultures covered. Each culture's instincts are finely attuned to the environmental challenges people face in various parts of the world. These challenges were not greater or less in particular regions; they were just different. These challenges were not trivial either, and our ancestors showed great ingenuity and resilience in moving into and developing ways of surviving in different contexts. Acknowledging this reality is necessary to genuinely respect each of the world's cultures.

The above point notwithstanding, it is also undoubtedly true that the ecology of our new global world creates a novel context that each culture is now required to engage. Businesses and societies throughout the world would do well to reflect upon elements of their cultural DNA that can serve them well in this new ecology, as well as those dimensions they need to question or adapt. Indeed, every culture has elements that will be increasingly relevant, but also some that will act as handbrakes in the new context. An honest appreciation of both sides of the coin is necessary for businesses as they engage the new multipolar world.

Another point centers on the importance of looking at one's own culture from the outside in rather than inside out. The ways of thinking and behaving in any particular culture can often seem like the only way of being, simply because the patterns are so pervasive. The only way of getting genuine perspective is to step out and look at one's own culture from an external perspective. In global business, this means executives need to make a particular effort to listen to and process feedback from people outside of their home location to get a sense of perspective. It's helpful to constantly ask the questions "How would others look at this?" and "How might they do things differently?"

Almost the opposite point applies when you're engaging other cultures; this is where you need to look at issues from the inside out, rather than from the outside in. Try and understand why people might come at things differently and, even more, why it might be helpful sometimes. If you're trying to change a company's culture in a different environment, figure out how you can build on that culture's dominant instincts to achieve the change rather than try to push water uphill. Businesses that fail to do this always feel frustrated by the talent and cultural challenges in different parts of the world. Yet the other side of the coin is that companies also have to be clear about their core values and what is non-negotiable. It's necessary to take a loose-tight mentality that gives clear latitude in many areas while specifying what is *not* up for grabs.

Another point relates to the paradox of the similarities and differences that are created as the global world pushes people together more and more. In many senses, people across the world share the same instincts, hopes, fears, and foibles. Many elements of our global world are helping to pull people together into more common and uniform ways of looking at things. Additionally, a great many global businesses tiptoe around imagined sensitivities and fail to recognize that in most scenarios, *people are just people*. Simply ignoring differences can be helpful in some instances. However, on other occasions, it is important to understand the nuance and subtlety associated with each culture. Navigating this polarity of both greater similarity and greater difference requires that we constantly judge and refine our attitudes. It is also important not to judge individuals lazily, with reference to the themes that are relevant to their culture. Each person is different, and understanding broad cultural patterns can never be a shortcut for understanding particular people from that culture.

A final and broad point is that without being trite or platitudinous, it is undoubtedly the case that each of the cultures covered has some fundamental gifts to offer the global world that is emerging in the twenty-first century. For example, as the sheer rate of change gathers pace, the world has much to learn from a theme that is deeply embedded in the United States cultural DNA: the bold and positive capacity to embrace disjunctive change. This orientation has in the recent past allowed America to renew itself and deliver innovation to the world in a host of areas and other cultures could internalize this strength.

Similarly, as our human destructive capacities increase exponentially, the world has much to learn from India's instincts around *ahimsa* and nonviolence. The Indian focus on the inner self—including tangible gifts such as meditation and yoga—is also increasingly relevant to a world that is rapidly moving up the Maslow hierarchy. Now that we have gained good control of our environment, we also have much to learn from the Sub-Saharan African cultural capacity for creative flexibility and for living and finding joy in the moment.

These are just some examples. Our emerging global culture can take deep and valuable lessons from each society. This is beginning to happen organically as the flow of information and general connectivity increases across the world. The world's great global cities are often the most dynamic places on the planet, both economically and culturally, in no small measure because they really are a fusion of nationalities. All too often, people can get frustrated when they engage other societies and find they are only a pale or poor reflection of their own cultures. Similarly, it is natural to feel somewhat threatened when people from other cultures migrate to your own society. Appreciating what we can learn and take home from each culture is a much more constructive way of engaging differences in our modern world.

Notes

Introduction

1. See review by James K. Jackson, "U.S. Direct Investment Abroad: Trends and Current Issues," Congressional Research Service, December 11, 2013, http://fas.org/sgp/crs/misc/RS21118.pdf.
2. Stephen Oppenheimer, *Out of Eden: The Peopling of the World* (London: Robinson Publishing, 2004).
3. Stephen Oppenheimer, *The Origins of the British: A Genetic Detective Story* (London: Robinson Publishing, 2007).
4. Favell Lee Mortimer, *The Countries of Europe Described* (New York: G. S. Appleton, 1850).
5. Favell Lee Mortimer, *Far Off, or, Asia and Australia Described* (New York: R. Carter & Brothers, 1856).
6. S. L. Gaertner and J. P. McLaughlin, "Racial Stereotypes: Associations and Ascriptions of Positive and Negative Characteristics," *Social Psychology Quarterly* 46 (1983): 23–30.
7. M. Lyubansky, "Studies of Unconscious Bias: Racism Not Always by Racists," *Psychology Today*, April 25, 2012.
8. E. T. Protho and L. H. Melikian, "Studies in Stereotypes: V. Familiarity and the Kernel of Truth Hypothesis," *Journal of Social Psychology* 41 (1955): 3–10.
9. C. F. Bond Jr., D. S. Berry, and A. Omar, "The Kernel of Truth in Judgments of Deceptiveness," *Basic and Applied Social Psychology* 15 (1994): 523–534.
10. M. Rothbart, S. Fulero, C. Jensen, J. Howard, and P. Birell, "From Individual to Group Impressions: Availability Heuristics in Stereotype Formation," *Journal of Experimental Social Psychology* 14 (1978): 237–255.
11. R. Inglehart and C. Weizel, *The WVS Cultural Map of the World*, World Value Survey, 2013, www.worldvaluessurvey.org/wvs/articles/folder_published/article_base_54.

12. Robert J. House, Paul J. Hanges, Mansour Javidan, Peter W. Dorfman, and Vipin Gupta, *Culture, Leadership and Organization: The GLOBE Study of 62 Societies* (Thousand Oaks, CA: SAGE Publications, 2004).

13. G. Hofstede, G. J. Hofstede, and M. Minkov, *Cultures and Organizations: Software of the Mind,* 3rd ed. (New York: McGraw-Hill, 2010).

14. Michael Minkov, *Cultural Differences in a Globalizing World* (Bingley, UK: Emerald Group Publishing Limited, 2011).

15. S. H. Schwartz, and W. Bilsky, "Toward a Theory of the Universal Content and Structure of Values," *Journal of Personality and Social Psychology* 58, no. 5 (May 1990): 878–889.

16. K. P. Lesch et al., "Association of Anxiety-Related Traits with a Polymorphism in the Serotonin Transporter Gene Regulatory Region," *Science* 274 (1996): 1527–1531.

17. C. Chen, M. Burton, E. Greenberg, and J. Dmitrieva, "Population Migration and the Variation of Dopamine D4 Receptor (DRD4) Allele Frequencies around the Globe," *Evolution and Human Behaviour* 20 (1999): 309–324.

18. See Henri Tajfel, *Human Groups and Social Categories: Studies in Social Psychology* (New York: Cambridge University Press, 1981).

19. Richard Hernstein and Charles Murray, *The Bell Curve* (New York: Free Press, 1994).

20. Nicholas Wade, *A Troublesome Inheritance* (New York: Penguin Books, 2014).

21. James R. Flynn, *Are We Getting Smarter? Rising IQ in the Twenty First Century* (Cambridge: Cambridge University Press, 2012).

22. T.W. Teasdale and D.R.Owen, "Secular Declines in Cognitive Test Performance: A Reversal of the Flynn Effect," *Intelligence* 36 (2008): 121-126.

23. G. Rizzolatti and L. Craighero, "The Mirror Neuron System Review," *Neuroscience* 27 (2004): 169–192.

24. V. Ramachandran, *The Neurons that Shaped Civilization,* TED Talks Online, 2009, www.ted.com/talks/vs_ramachandran_the _neurons_that_shaped_civilization?language=en.

25. A. Avenanti, A. Sirigu, and S.M. Aglioti, "Racial Bias Reduces Empathic Sensorimotor Resonance with Other-Race Pain," *Current Biology* 20 (2010): 1018–1022.

Chapter 1

1. Francis Fukuyama, *The End of History and the Last Man* (London: Penguin, 2012).
2. D. W. Neklason et al., "American Founder Mutation for Attenuated Familial Adenomatous Polyposis," *Clinical Gastroenterological Hepatology* 6 (2008): 46–52.
3. D. Hackett Fischer, *Albion's Seed: Four British Folkways in America* (Oxford: Oxford University Press, 1992).
4. D. Cohen, R. Nisbett, B. Bowdle, and N. Schwartz, "Insult, Aggression, and the Southern Culture of Honour: An 'Experimental Ethnography,'" *Journal of Personality and Social Psychology* 70 (1996): 945–960.
5. AON Hewitt, Trends in Global Employee Engagement, 2013, www.aon.com/attachments/human-capital-consulting/2013_Trends_in_Global_Employee_Engagement_Highlights.pdf.
6. Tomas Chamorro-Premuzic, *Confidence: The Surprising Truth About How Much You Need and How to Get It* (London: Profile Books Ltd, 2013).
7. Richard E. Nisbett, *The Geography of Thought* (New York: The Free Press, 2003).
8. E. Fox, A. Ridgewell, and C. Ashwin, "Looking on the Bright Side: Biased Attention and the Human Serotonin Transporter Gene," *Proceedings of the Royal Society (Biological Sciences)* 276 (2009): 1747–1751.
9. S. Taylor, "Tend and Befriend: Biobehavioural Bases of Affiliation under Stress," *Current Directions in Psychological Science* 15 (2006): 273–277.
10. J. Y. Sasaki, H. S. Kim, and J. Xu, "Religion and Well Being: The Moderating Role of Culture and the Oxytocin Receptor (OXTR) Gene," *Journal of Cross-Cultural Psychology*, 2011, http://jcc.sagepub.com/content/early/2011/07/02/0022022111412526.
11. Barbara Ehrenreich, *Bright-Sided: How Positive Thinking Is Undermining America* (New York: Metropolitan Books, 2009).
12. Pew Foundation, U.S. Religious Landscape Survey Religious Affiliation: Diverse and Dynamic, 2008, *The Pew Forum on Religion and Public Life*, http://religions.pewforum.org/pdf/report-religious-landscape-study-full.pdf.

13. Alexis de Tocqueville, *Democracy in America* (Digireads.com, 2007).

14. J. Twenge and T. Kasser, "Today's Teens: More Materialistic, Less Willing to Work," *Personality and Social Psychology Bulletin* 39, no. 7 (2013): 883–897.

15. C. Gregoire, "The Psychology of Materialism and Why This Makes You Unhappy," *Huffington Post,* 2014, www.huffingtonpost.com /2013/12/15/psychology-materialism_n_4425982.html.

16. Mercer (2012), *Worldwide benefits and employment guidelines.* For access see www.imercer.com/products/wbeg.aspx

17. Fons Trompenaars and Charles Hampden-Turner, *Riding the Waves of Culture: Understanding Cultural Diversity in Business* (London: McGraw-Hill, 1997).

18. Thomas Geoghegan, *Were You Born on the Wrong Continent? How the European Model Can Help You Get a Life* (London: The New Press, 2011).

19. Kenneth Hopper and William Hopper, *The Puritan Gift: Reclaiming the American Dream Amidst Global Financial Chaos* (London: L. B. Tauris & Co Ltd., 2009).

20. Clotaire Rapaille, *The Culture Code: An Ingenious Way to Understand Why People Around the World Buy and Live as They Do* (New York: Broadway Books, 2006).

21. D. Longinecker, *America the Literal,* 2011, www.patheos.com /blogs/standingonmyhead/2011/04/america-the-literal.html.

22. Amy Chua and Jed Rubenfeld, *The Triple Package: How Three Unlikely Traits Explain the Rise and Fall of Cultural Groups in America* (New York: Penguin Press, 2014).

Chapter 2

1. M. C. Campbell and S. A. Tishkoff, "African Genetic Diversity: Implications for Human Demographic History, Modern Human Origins, and Complex Disease Mapping," *Annual Review of Genomics and Human Genetics,* 9 (2008): 403–433.

2. Jared Diamond, *Guns, Germs, and Steel: A Short History of Everybody for the Last 13,000 Years* (London: Vintage Books, 1998).

3. C. L. Fincher, R. Thornhill, D. R. Murray, and M. Schaller, "Pathogen Prevalence Predicts Human Cross-Cultural Variability

in Individualism/Collectivism," *Proceedings of The Royal Society* 275, no. 1640 (2008): 1279–1285.

4. J. Philippe Rushton, *Race, Evolution, and Behavior: A Life History Perspective*, 2nd ed. (Port Huron, MI: Charles Darwin Research Institute, 2000).

5. Michael O. Eze, *Intellectual History in Contemporary South Africa* (New York: Palgrave McMillan, 2010), 190–191.

6. Michela Wrong, *It's Our Turn to Eat Now* (London: Fourth Estate, 2010).

7. Ryszard Kapuściński and Klara Glowczewska, *The Shadow of the Sun: My African Life* (London: Penguin Books, 2002).

8. Ken Pryce, *Endless Pressure: A Study of West Indian Lifestyles in Bristol* (London: Penguin Education, 1979).

9. Geert Hofstede, Gert Jan Hofstede, and Michael Minkov, *Cultures and Organizations: Software of the Mind*, 3rd ed. (New York: McGraw-Hill, 2010).

10. W. Mischel, "Preference for Delayed Reinforcement: An Experimental Study of a Cultural Observation," *The Journal of Abnormal and Social Psychology* 56 (1958): 57–61.

11. W. Mischel, "Father Absence and Delay of Gratification: Cross-Cultural Comparisons," *Journal of Abnormal and Social Psychology* 63 (1961): 116–124.

12. Richard Dowden, *Africa: Altered States, Ordinary Miracles* (London: Portobello Books, 2009).

13. John Mbiti, *African Religions and Philosophy*, 2nd ed. (Portsmouth, NH: Heinemann, 1990).

14. Paul Theroux, *Dark Star Safari: Overland from Cairo to Cape Town* (London: Penguin, 2003).

15. B. Tortora, Witchcraft Believers in Sub-Saharan Africa Rate Lives Worse, *Gallup World,* 2010, www.gallup.com/poll/142640 /witchcraft-believers-sub-saharan-africa-rate-lives-worse.aspx.

16. Blaine Harden, *Africa: Dispatches from a Fragile Continent* (London: Flamingo, 1992).

Chapter 3

1. D. Reich, "Reconstructing Indian Population History," *Nature* 461 (2009): 489–495.

2. M. Bamshad et al., "Genetic Evidence on the Origins of Indian Caste Populations," *Genome Res.* 11, no. 6 (2001): 994–1004 and M. K. Bhasin and H. Walter, "Genetics of Castes and Tribes of India: Indian Population Milieu," *International Journal of Human Genetics*, 2001, www.krepublishers.com/02-Journals/IJHG/IJHG-06-0-000-000-2006-Web/IJHG-06-3-177-280-2006-Abst-PDF/IJHG-06-3-233-274-2006-000-Bhasin-M-K/IJHG-06-3-233-274-2006-000-Bhasin-M-K-Text.PDF.

3. The McKinsey Global Survey of Business Executives, *McKinsey Quarterly*, January 2006, http://mckinseyquarterly.com.

4. P. Capelli et al., "Leadership Lessons from India," *Harvard Business Review*, 2010, http://hbr.org/2010/03/leadership-lessons-from-india/ar/1.

5. Gurnek Bains, *Meaning, Inc.: The Blueprint for Business Success in the 21st Century* (London: Profile Books, 2007).

6. V. S. Naipaul, *India: A Million Mutinies Now* (New York: Vintage International, 2011).

7. Amartya Sen, *The Argumentative Indian* (London: Penguin Books, 2005).

8. Amaury de Riencourt, *The Soul of India* (New York: Sterling Publishers, 1986).

9. Walter Isaacson, *Steve Jobs* (New York: Simon & Schuster, 2011).

10. P. Moorjani et al., "Genetic Evidence for Recent Population Mixture in India," *The American Journal of Human Genetics* 93 (2013): 422–438.

11. S. Gurumurthy, "Communities as Open-Air Business Schools," *The Hindu Business Line*, May 2013, www.thehindubusinessline.com/opinion/communities-as-openair-business-schools/article4766385.ece.

12. Harish Damodaran, *India's New Capitalists: Caste, Business, and Industry in a Modern Nation* (London: Palgrave Macmillan, 2008).

13. The idea of Pythagoras being influenced by Indian cultures was first proposed by Ludwig von Schröder in his book *Pythagoras und die Inder* (*Pythagoras and the Indians*), published in 1884.

14. See, for example, www.ndtv.com/article/india/50-per-cent-of-indian-graduates-not-fit-to-be-hired-report-384202.

15. In 2012, Indian students came second from last in the PISA tests, covering 73 countries.
16. Leah Hyslop and AFP, "Red Tape in India Causes Problems for Expats," *The Telegraph*, June 3, 2010, www.telegraph.co.uk/expat /expatnews/7801030/Red-tape-in-India-causes-problems-for -expats.html.
17. *The Times of India*, "Courts Will Take 320 Years to Clear Backlog Cases: Justice Rao," March 6, 2010, http://timesofindia.indiatimes .com/india/Courts-will-take-320-years-to-clear-backlog-cases -Justice-Rao/articleshow/5651782.cms.
18. *Doing Business 2005: Removing Obstacles to Growth*, World Bank Group, www.doingbusiness.org/reports/global-reports/doing -business-2005.

Chapter 4

1. See research by Ofer Bar-Yosef, "Did Humans and Neanderthals Battle for Control of the Middle East?" *National Geographic News*, October 28, 2010.
2. Stephen Oppenheimer, *Out of Eden: The Peopling of the World* (London: Robinson Publishing, 2004).
3. Arthur Koestler, *The Thirteenth Tribe* (New York: Random House, 1976).
4. Janet Bennion, *Desert Patriarchy: Mormon and Mennonite Communities in the Chihuahua Valley* (Tucson: University of Arizona Press, 2004).
5. Scores for Australian aboriginal populations are quoted in the following: www.harzing.com/download/hgindices.xls.
6. Michael Minkov, "Cultural Differences in a Globalizing World," 2011, Emerald Group Publishing, www.harzing.com/download /hgindices.xls.
7. Transactional analysis is a theory ultimately originating from Freud's concepts of super ego, ego, and id processes and looks at how these dominant forms show up in interpersonal relationships.
8. William J. Bernstein, *A Splendid Exchange* (New York: Atlantic Monthly Press, 2008).

9. Christopher Schroeder, "Witnessing the Middle East's 'Entre-preneurial Revolution,'" May 30, 2014, http://knowledge.wharton.upenn.edu/region/arabic/.

10. Christopher Schroeder, *Startup Rising: The Entrepreneurial Revolution Remaking the Middle East* (New York: Palgrave Macmillan, 2013).

11. Steve Royston, (2011) Middle East Project Management: An Oxymoron?, *MidEast Posts*, October 10, 2011, http://mideastposts.com/middle-east-business/middle-east-project-management-an-oxymoron.

12. 620 government employees found using fake degrees reported by Abdullah Al-Qatani in *Okaz Saudi Gazette* (2013).

13. Steve Royston, "Culture: What Really Drives Middle East Companies?" *MidEast Posts*, January 28, 2013, http://mideastposts.com/middle-east-business/culture-what-really-drives-middle-east-companies/.

Chapter 5

1. Alice Roberts, *The Incredible Human Journey* (London: Bloomsbury Publishing, 2010).

2. Stephen Oppenheimer, *Out of Eden: The Peopling of the World* (London: Constable & Robinson Ltd., 2004).

3. Amaury de Riencourt, *The Soul of China* (New York: Harper Colophon Books, 1965).

4. J. Philippe Rushton, *Race, Evolution & Behavior: A Life History Perspective*, 3rd ed. (Port Huron, MI: Charles Darwin Research Institute, 2000).

5. Richard E. Nisbett, *The Geography of Thought* (New York: The Free Press, 2004).

6. See Introduction, note 15.

7. As before, with the Globe we are focused on the practice scores. For details of these scores see www.harzing.com/download/hgindices.xls.

8. Baldwin Way and Matthew D. Lieberman, "Is There a Genetic Contribution to Cultural Differences? Selectivism, Individualism and Genetic Markers of Social Sensitivity," *Social Cognitive and Effective Neuroscience* 5, no. 2–3 (2010): 203–211.

9. See Joan Y. Chiao and Katherine D. Blizinsky, "Culture-Gene Coevolution of Individualism—Collectivism and a Serotonin Transporter Gene," *Proceedings of the Royal Society B,* http://rspb .royalsocietypublishing.org/content/early/2009/10/27/rspb.2009 .1650.

10. T. Talhelm et al., "Large-Scale Psychological Differences Within China Explained by Rice versus Wheat Agriculture," *Cultural Science* 344, no. 6184 (2014): 603–608.

11. Fons Trompenaars and Charles Hampden-Turner, *Riding the Waves of Culture* (London: Nicholas Brierly, 1999): 12.

12. Francesco Sofo, "Thinking Styles of Modern Chinese Leaders: Independence and Exploration in an Historically Conditional China," *Australian Journal of Adult Learning* 45, no. 3 (2005), http://files.eric.ed.gov/fulltext/EJ797617.pdf.

13. Gavin Menzies, *1434: The Year a Magnificent Chinese Fleet Sailed to Italy and Ignited the Renaissance* (New York: HarperCollins, 2008).

14. Robert Levine, 'The Pace of Life in 31 countries' Journal of Cross Cultural Psychology, 30(1999), 178/205

15. See www.richardwiseman.com/quirkology/pace.

16. Romin W. Tafarodi et al., "Disregard for Outsiders: A Cultural Comparison," *Journal of Cross-Cultural Psychology* 40(2009), 567–583, http://jcc.sagepub.com/content/40/4/567.full.pdf+html.

17. Stephen Myler, "Chinese Cultural Lack of Empathy in Development—Counselling Practice," *Ezine Articles*, January 21, 2009, http://ezinearticles.com/?Chinese-Cultural-Lack-of-Empathy-in-Development—Counselling-Practice&id=1907719.

18. Sir John Barrow, *Travels in China* (London: W. F. M'Laughlin, 1805), http://books.google.co.uk/books/about/Travels_in_China .html?id=8aNFAAAAIAAJ.

19. See 'Chinese Students Struggle for Returns on Education in U.S.' The Wall Street Journal. reproduced China realt Time http://blogs.wsj.com/chinarealtime/2013/03/27/chinese-students-struggle-for-returns-on-education-in-u-s/ March 27, 2013.

20. Jonathan Bailey, "The Growing Chinese Plagiarism Problem," *iThenticate*, November 8, 2012, www.ithenticate.com/plagiarism -detection-blog/bid/88747/The-Growing-Chinese-Plagiarism -Problem#.VBLMa_ldWMI.

Chapter 6

1. Chief Economist Unit, *European Union in the World*, European Commission, 2014, http://trade.ec.europa.eu/doclib/docs/2006/september/tradoc_122532.pdf.

2. S. Shultz and R. Dunbar, "Encephalization Is Not a Universal Macroevolutionary Phenomenon in Mammals but Is Associated with Sociality." *Proceedings of the National Academy of Sciences* 107, no. 50 (2010): 21582–21586.

3. Stephen Oppenheimer, *Out of Eden: The Peopling of the World* (London: Robinson Publishing, 2004).

4. The distribution of haplogroups across Europe is documented in www.eupedia.com/europe/Haplogroup_E1b1b_Y-DNA.shtml.

5. Stephen Oppenheimer, *The Origins of the British: A Genetic Detective Story* (London: Robinson Publishing, 2007).

6. D. Reich et al., "Ancient Human Genomes Suggest Three Ancestral Populations for Present-Day Europeans," *Nature* 513 (2014): 409–413, www.nature.com/nature/journal/v513/n7518/full/nature13673.html.

7. United Nations, *Human Development Report*, United Nations Development Program, 2009, http://hdr.undp.org/en/content/human-development-report-2009.

8. World Bank, "World Developmental Indicators: Distribution of Income and Consumption the World Bank," WorldBank.com, 2014, http://wdi.worldbank.org/table/2.9.

9. Angus Maddison, *The World Economy: A Millennial Perspective* (Development Centre Studies: Organisation for Economic Co-operation and Development, 2001).

10. Geert Hofstede, *Culture's Consequences: Comparing Values, Behaviors, Institutions and Organizations Across Nations* (Sage: London, 2001).

11. The above figures refer, as before, to practice rather than value Globe scores.

12. Alan Macfarlane, *The Origins of English Individualism: Family, Property and Social Transition* (London: Basil Blackwell, 1979).

13. David P. Schmitt, J.Allik, R. McRae, and V. Benet-Martinez, "The Geographic Distribution of Big Five Personality Traits," Journal of Cross-Cultural Psychology, 38 (2007) 173-212.

14. P. Collett, *Foreign Bodies: A-Z of European Mannerisms* (New York: Simon & Schuster, 1994).
15. J. L. Tsai and Y. Chentsova-Dutton, "Variation among European Americans in Emotional Facial Expression," *Journal of Cross-Cultural Psychology* 34 (2003): 650–657.
16. S. Schwartz, "Theory of Cultural Values and Some Implications for Work," *Applied Psychology: An International Review* 1999, no. 48: 1, 23–47.
17. Amy Chua and Jed Rubenfeld, *The Triple Package* (New York: Penguin, 2014).

Chapter 7

1. Stephen Oppenheimer, *Out of Eden: The Peopling of the World* (London: Robinson Publishing, 2004).
2. C. Chen, M. Burton, E. Greenberg, and J. Dmitrieva, "Population Migration and the Variation of Dopamine D4 Receptor (DRD4) Allele Frequencies around the Globe," *Evolution and Human Behaviour* 20 (1999): 309–324.
3. Daron Acemoglu and James Robinson, *Why Nations Fail: The Origins of Power, Prosperity and Poverty* (London: Profile Books, 2013).
4. See Chapter 6, note 6.
5. Babette Smith, *Australia's Birthstain: The Startling Legacy of the Convict Era* (Crows Nest, New South Wales: Allen & Unwin, 2009).
6. Basil Berstein, "Social Class, Linguistic Codes and Grammatical Elements," *Language and Speech* 5, no. 1 (1962): 31–46.

Index

271